MURDER AT WHITE HOUSE FARM

MURDER AT WHITE HOUSE FARM

The Story of Jeremy Bamber

Claire Powell

HEADLINE

First published in 1994
by HEADLINE BOOK PUBLISHING

10 9 8 7 6 5 4 3 2 1

British Library Cataloguing in Publication Data

Powell, Claire
  Jeremy Bamber
  I. Title
  364.1

  ISBN 0-7472-0973-1

Typeset by Keyboard Services, Luton

Printed and bound in Great Britain by
Mackays of Chatham PLC, Chatham, Kent

HEADLINE BOOK PUBLISHING
A division of Hodder Headline PLC
338 Euston Road
London NW1 3BH

ACKNOWLEDGMENTS

I would like to thank the dozens of people who agreed to speak to me during the writing of this book. For many of these people it meant reliving a time they would have preferred to forget and the majority preferred to tell the stories without attribution.

The book was coaxed along by the endless patience of Celia Kent and Alan Brooke at Headline and my agent Anne McDermid at Curtis Brown. Help, support and encouragement were provided by Caroline Coon, Mark Hollingsworth, Paul Halloran and Sebastian Cody. Finally, there is always someone 'without whom this book could not have been written,' in this case, the cliché belongs fairly and squarely to Peter Grimsditch for his sheer hard work and unfailing good humour.

CONTENTS

PREFACE
The dead of night

The door opened slowly, quietly, carefully. The room was warm and silent, a smell of dinner clung to the folds of heavy summertime air.

Past the chairs, round the table with the telephone, it took only a few more steps to reach the kitchen door. Outside, the moon glowed as generously as the sun. Inside was shade and shadow. The rifle was still leaning against the wall and nearby lay the magazine. It took several minutes to load the bullets, forcing them one by one with clumsy, fumbling fingers.

The bolt squeaked loudly but there was another sound.

The door into the hall was pushed further open. 'Oh, it's you, I didn't know who could be prowling around here at this time of night. What's the matter, can't you sleep?'

Then he saw the gun and slowly, slowly he understood that it was serious. They looked at each other, neither sure of what to do. He tried to talk but he kept moving towards that long rifle. The first shots made him gasp but he jumped and grabbed for the handle. The bullets threw aside the delicate tightrope balance of nerves and they fought. One for life, the other for death.

He should have won. He was an old man, but tall and still strong. But the bullets drained him and the gun was more effective as a club, beating him to the ground, harder and harder until shards of casing flew through the air.

It took a lot of bullets to put him down. More had to be fed into the greedy rifle. Through the hall and up the stairs. There hadn't been a sound, but she was awake in the bedroom. Perhaps she had felt her husband get up and sensed that the footsteps coming towards her were not his.

The bullets peppered the pillow and the sheets and she had no time to say anything. There was a noise, however. The little dog was cowering and whimpering behind the door. The only place to put it was in the wardrobe, out of the way. The idea of an animal running over the bedroom, over the final resting place, was obscene.

The twins were sad and sweet. They were still asleep and it was exactly as it should have been. Calm and quiet and painless. It was really because of them that this had to be done.

But she couldn't live in peace and she did not die that way, either. She had struggled out of bed and as far as the bedroom door. It took two more bullets to make certain.

At long last it was almost over. The Bible was waiting on a bedside table. There were bullets in the gun.

1

White House Farm

The call came through in the early morning of Wednesday, 7 August 1985. The duty officer at Chelmsford Police Station unhurriedly reached for the receiver. The phone ringing was the ordinary station number, not the emergency line.

The caller was a young man who was so agitated that he could hardly get his words out. It took a while for the officer to understand his story.

Just after 3 a.m., said the caller, he had been woken by the phone ringing at his cottage in the village of Goldhanger. It was his father, sounding extremely frightened. 'Come quickly,' he had said, 'your sister has gone mad and she's got a gun.' The bewildered young man said he heard a noise which could have been a shot, then the line went dead. He tried to ring back but there was no answer. He told the policeman that his father had rung from the family home at White House Farm in the village of

Tolleshunt D'Arcy. The caller added one more detail. 'My name,' he said, 'is Jeremy Bamber.'

The sergeant told him to go over to the farm and wait outside for the police. It was a peculiar story but the duty officer was taking no chances. This might be a hoax – but it could be a real emergency.

Within minutes officers from the nearby station at Witham were on their way to the farmhouse. Back in Chelmsford ten marksmen were called up from the Essex tactical support unit. Reinforced by a squad of officers from police headquarters they sped towards the tiny village of Tolleshunt D'Arcy.

It took them nearly twenty minutes to reach the village and a few more vital moments to find the farm which was hidden at the end of Pages Lane, a winding, private road. On the way they passed a car travelling slowly. It followed them down the farm track, past a couple of labourers' cottages and pulled up behind the police cars at the farm gate.

A tall, slim, dark-haired young man jumped out and ran over to the police officers to whom he began to repeat the story he had given over the phone. He said the farm belonged to his parents, Nevill and June Bamber. His sister, Sheila Caffell, was staying at the farmhouse with her twin six-year-old sons, Nicholas and Daniel. Sheila had a history of mental problems, he said, in fact, she was schizophrenic. 'She suffers from paranoid schizophrenia,' Bamber explained to one of the officers. He added bluntly: 'She's a nutter. She's gone doolally.'

The young man quickly poured out an amazing tale. He

2

told the horrified detectives that Sheila suffered from fits of violence and delusions, sometimes believing she was the Virgin Mary or Joan of Arc. Her mental troubles were long standing and had been brought on by a series of miscarriages and an abortion, he claimed. It was hard for the detectives standing in the well-kept farmyard surrounded by flat fields next to the tranquil, handsome farmhouse to grasp such a bizarre story.

As the senior officers huddled together to assess the situation, Bamber began to pace up and down, anxiously talking to himself. 'Oh God,' he muttered. 'I hope she hasn't done anything stupid.'

The farmhouse was deadly quiet, but the police decided to take no chances. They had to put it under siege in case Sheila was lying in wait with a loaded shotgun. She might even be holding her family hostage. Jeremy told them about his father's collection of guns, stored inside the farmhouse in a downstairs study. There were at least half a dozen weapons, all in good condition, and ammunition was kept there too.

The grounds were quickly searched in case Sheila had left the house and hidden herself in the garden or in one of the surrounding sheds. Then the trained marksmen moved into position around the building, aiming their rifles at the windows and doors.

Detective Chief Inspector Edward Thomas 'Taff' Jones took charge of the situation. Creeping as close to the house as he dared and clutching a loud-hailer, he appealed for anyone inside the building to come out with their hands up. There was a noise from within and fingers tightened around triggers – only to relax again. The sound was the barking of the family dog. There was no other response at all.

Taff Jones went over to talk to Jeremy. He wanted to know how they could appeal to Sheila. Was there anyone she would talk to? What was the best way of getting through to her?

Bamber thought hard for a minute. 'You could try her psychiatrist. She likes him. His name is Dr Ferguson and he works in Harley Street,' he suggested. 'Oh yes, there's something else: Sheila likes to be told she's pretty,' he added.

It was already getting light. Another beautiful August sunrise was bursting over the horizon. A couple of the uniformed officers tried to chat to Jeremy, who was nervously pacing up and down and smoking one cigarette after another. As they approached, Bamber shouted to them: 'What if anything has happened in there? They are all the family I have got!'

To calm him down they began to talk about jobs and cars and Jeremy joined in, saying he wanted to get rid of his own Vauxhall Astra: 'I expect the family business will be able to stand me a Porsche some time this year,' he said with a smile.

Around seven o'clock, Taff Jones made the decision: it was time to go in. Jeremy was brought along to where the senior officers were grouped and a last-minute consultation was held. A plan of the two floors of the farmhouse was rapidly sketched out by Jeremy and studied by the marksmen. It was decided that the best way in would be through the scullery door at the back of the house. The front door was thick, solid wood and flanked by windows, making the police easy targets for anyone with a rifle.

Quickly and efficiently the armed officers moved into position with hand guns, leaving a couple of marksmen at the front of the house. Taff Jones gave the signal and two men armed with sledgehammers attacked the scullery door. Within seconds the wood had been splintered and the door was hanging off its hinges. The marksmen poured into the house, spreading out with guns at the ready.

There was no sound. There was no movement. The men ran from room to room and then cautiously climbed the stairs. But there was no one left alive in White House Farm to challenge them. After a search to make sure no gunman – or woman – was hiding in the building they pulled out and let the regular officers in to begin their investigation.

'It is just dreadful in there, bodies are sprawled everywhere,' said one of the retreating policemen. 'At least the children were still asleep and knew nothing about the horror of it all.'

It was undoubtedly an horrific sight. Nevill Bamber was in the kitchen, slumped in an armchair. His body was battered and covered in blood and he had obviously been shot many times. The room itself had been ripped apart. All the furniture was overturned, crockery and lamps had been smashed and fragments of a rifle butt lay amongst the debris on the floor. It was clear at first glance that the murdered man had put up a terrific struggle for his life.

The walls were stained with splashes of blood from the wounds of the dead man. More blood was spattered on the closed kitchen door and the air, already warm in the mild August morning, was heavy with the stench of it. One of the officers gagged as the smell hit him and turned back to gulp repeatedly at the scullery door. The team moved cautiously across the room, crunching shattered glass and pottery underfoot.

All the remaining downstairs rooms were scrupulously neat and tidy, showing no trace of any intruder. Another room, the parlour, had not been touched. The cushions were plumped up and placed squarely on the sofa and armchairs. The coffee table had neat piles of women's magazines, *Country Life* and three scribbled colouring books for children. Before going upstairs, the detectives noticed that the front door was securely locked and, despite the warm night, the windows were shut.

At the top of the stairs they turned into a large bedroom containing two single beds. In each bed lay a small boy, tiny and golden-haired. They were both curled up as if fast asleep, tucked under light blankets, their faces half-buried in the pillows. They had both been shot through the head. From their positions the officers could tell that the children had still been asleep when the murderer put the gun to their heads. One of them still had his thumb in his mouth. The back of his head had been blown off.

The killer had been merciless. One bullet would have made certain that the little boys would never wake up again, but they had been shot repeatedly. The detectives stared at each other wordlessly. It was a waking nightmare, more ghastly than any of them could ever have imagined.

There was more to come. They crossed the landing into a

large room, the master bedroom of the house. A body was slumped near the doorway, forcing the sickened detectives to step over it to get into the room. It was June Bamber, sprawled on the floor in her nightdress. She had been shot several times and trickles of blood were drying from wounds all over her body. Her high-necked gown had been ripped apart by the force of the bullets tearing through the thin material. A gaping wound showed one bullet had struck her right between her eyes. The bed sheets were thrown back and the pillows were stained with blood and punctured with bullet holes.

There was another body in the spacious bedroom. The slim figure was neatly dressed in a fresh nightgown. The dark, red-tinted hair was thick and glossy and the outstretched hands were tipped by long, blood-red nails. The face was pale and pretty but underneath the chin ran two lines of blood. It was the body of Sheila Caffell. Across her chest lay a rifle with a smashed handle and near to her side was a blue leather-bound Bible.

That was it. There was no one else in White House Farm. The detectives gathered in the master bedroom, discussing in low voices what was to be done in the house of horror. Suddenly they all froze. A soft whimpering noise came from the far side of the room. The detectives were aghast, fearing that there was another victim lying half-dead somewhere in the room.

Finally one officer snapped out of the paralysis that seemed to have gripped all the detectives. He crept quietly across the room and, gun at the ready, pulled open the door of a large wardrobe. A small, furry dog was huddled against the back wall, crying like a baby. The officer picked up the cowering animal. A tag on its collar read 'Crispy'. He carried it outside, the only living creature to come out of White House Farm that morning.

Following the detectives into the house was police surgeon Dr Iain Craig. He rapidly examined the bodies the officers left in their wake, trying to roughly assess the time of death. The cause of death was all too apparent.

By now more officers had arrived on the scene. They were shocked as their colleagues reeled out of the farmhouse, stunned by what they had seen. Inside the house an unnatural quiet reigned. Only the blood-spattered walls and the pathetic corpses bore witness to the explosion of savagery which had raged in the rooms a few hours earlier.

'I went into the farmhouse and the kitchen was a mess,' said an officer at the scene. 'There was blood all over the place and everything was smashed. It looked very violent. I'll never forget those poor little boys; they looked as if they were fast asleep, heads still on the pillow. It was one of the worst sights I have ever seen.'

Pulling themselves together on the gravel driveway outside the house, the detectives saw Jeremy Bamber pacing up and down by the farm gate. It fell to Dr Craig to tell the young man that his whole family were lying dead inside the house. The doctor suggested to Jeremy that they take a walk away from the farm: 'Jeremy said to me, "Why can't my father come?"

'I said, "Because he has been killed." He broke down and cried,' remembered Dr Craig.

The two men walked on and Jeremy began to tell the doctor about a family discussion the previous evening. His parents had been arguing with Sheila about her twin sons, Nicholas and Daniel. They were worried that Sheila was not looking after the children properly and suggested that the little boys should be fostered. It was not the first time that the idea of fostering had been raised, added Jeremy. It had been mentioned after his parents suspected that Sheila had hurt the twins.

'I asked if it had been reported to the police and social services and he said no,' recalled Dr Craig. 'He made it clear the row was about the twins.'

Detective Chief Inspector Jones called Dr Craig aside to ask if Jeremy was fit to be interviewed. He was anxious to get the young man away from the farmhouse where detectives, led by the scenes-of-crime officer, Detective Inspector Ronald Cook, were photographing the bodies and assembling evidence for forensic experts.

The doctor thought Jeremy was in shock and gave him a whisky before allowing him to be interviewed. But the alcohol did not help. Jeremy staggered away to the gate post and held on to it, retching violently. Taff Jones told him to go home to Goldhanger and wait for an officer to come and take his statement. The DCI detailed two of his officers, Detective Sergeant Stan Jones and Detective Constable Michael Clark, to call on Bamber and take his statement later in the morning. He then turned his attention to Jeremy. Several of the officers were trying to get him back on his feet.

'I was outside the farmhouse when I saw Jeremy trying to

9

vomit. I wasn't quite sure what was going on inside the house but I could tell that Jeremy was making himself vomit,' said one constable. 'I was a short distance away from him. He said something about having just had some whisky that had made him ill.'

Inside the house the scenes-of-crime officers were painstakingly combing their way through the ghastly debris of the massacre. A detective who joined in the room-by-room search of the house later recalled one of his vivid impressions of the morning. 'I went upstairs and saw Sheila. She was so clean, strikingly clean as if she had just got out of a bath. I didn't know what had happened,' he remembered.

It took Michael Clark and Stan Jones less than ten minutes to drive from Pages Lane to Jeremy's little cottage in Head Street, Goldhanger. The place, which looked a bit run-down, was the end building of a row of three small houses. Jones walked round to the side of the building and knocked on the back door. 'Jeremy opened the door and said, "I'm starving, I was just about to have some breakfast. Do you fancy some bacon and eggs?"'

The detectives declined and played with cups of tea while Jeremy got on with the cooking and then sat down to a hearty breakfast.

The detectives chatted a little before they got on with the business of taking Jeremy's statement. The young man went over the events of the previous evening, the panic-stricken phone call from his father in the early hours, and his own call to the police. He told them about his family, their ages, their jobs. Nevill and June were both sixty-one. She had lived all her life in the area and Nevill had settled there after their marriage. Nevill was tenant of White House Farm and had been a local magistrate for years.

Sheila, his sister, was a troubled woman, said Jeremy. She was twenty-eight and, like himself, had been adopted as a baby by Nevill and June. He was quick to point out that he and Sheila were not originally from the same family. She had had a nervous breakdown in her teens and another one earlier that year. After leaving home, she had worked as a fashion model in London, but her mental problems made it hard for her to follow a real career in the business.

Sheila had been married, but was recently divorced and her parents were very worried about her two sons, Nicholas and Daniel. They felt Sheila could not look after them properly and suspected that she harmed the children. Jeremy added that Sheila did not get on well with her mother and they had argued almost as soon as she arrived with the boys from London on Monday, the day before the murders.

He had last seen her and his parents the previous evening in the farmhouse. The next thing he knew was being wakened by the phone. His father sounded frantic, saying that Sheila had gone mad with a gun. The line went dead before Jeremy had a chance to reply and the line was engaged when he tried to phone back. That was when he called the police. Now, apart from a handful of relatives – the Boutflours, the Eatons and the Pargeters, all local people – Jeremy was the only remaining member of the family.

Michael Clark and Stanley Jones listened sympathetic-
ally, allowing Bamber to talk and guiding him with
questions. By now they both realised that Jeremy was not
the sort of character they could warm to. There was nothing
deliberately offensive about him; rather it was Bamber's
whole attitude. He was so calm, so straight in what he had
to say; there were no tears. The detectives knew that
people reacted to tragedy in different ways. This young
man had clearly decided that practicality was the best
antidote to grief. He talked about the problems of the farm
and even mentioned that it would probably be sensible if he
went to see the bank manager that afternoon. It was a
hard-headed attitude but obviously a very sensible one.
Asked if there was anyone who could come and stay with
him, Jeremy mentioned two people: his girlfriend, Julie
Mugford, and a friend, Brett Collins.

Julie Mugford appeared soon afterwards after being
brought at high speed from London by police car. She was
originally from Colchester and had been going out with
Jeremy for eighteen months. They had met at a local
restaurant where they were both earning extra money
waiting on tables. Julie spent most of the week in south
London, where she had just qualified as a primary school
teacher. In contrast to Jeremy's relaxed behaviour Julie
appeared suspicious and hard-edged. As soon as she
walked into the cottage, Jeremy asked if he could spend
some time alone with his girlfriend.

The officers were happy to agree as Jeremy threw his
arms around his girlfriend. The detectives walked out of
the room but as Stan Jones closed the door on the hugging

and kissing couple he heard Jeremy make a peculiar noise. It sounded almost like a chuckle. The detective sergeant shrugged – obviously he had been mistaken, it was probably just a cough, Jeremy clearing his throat before he poured out his tale to his girlfriend.

Alone with Julie, Jeremy told her the story which by now was beginning to filter through to the press: Sheila had gone berserk – perhaps it was a brainstorm, perhaps it was the threat of losing the twins. Whatever the reason, she had cracked, seized a gun and blasted her family to death before shooting herself in the head. Four murders and a suicide, Jeremy told her. Now he was the only surviving member of the Bamber family.

2
Family fortunes

Nevill Ralph Bamber and June Speakman would make perfect partners. That was the feeling of the organisers of the local tennis tournament as they drew up the lists of players. The August of 1949 was long and hot and lazy and the ladies of the Essex countryside around the seaside town of Maldon were keen to take advantage of the weather by arranging a little entertainment.

Even the least sporting of the local ladies began to look out their tennis dresses and practise their 'Little Mo' backhands in anticipation of some fun. It had been a long time since anyone could remember enjoying such carefree days and even a few sets of tennis generated excitement. The war years had seen all the available young men sent off to fight while their jobs on the land were taken over by women. Then there had been a real sense of danger and of pulling together to repulse the common enemy. Now, in those years immediately after the war, there was still rationing of food and clothes and it sometimes felt there was rationing of enjoyment, too.

The tennis tournament gave the village girls a much-needed opportunity to meet some of the young men recently drafted into the area to help with the harvest. There were just not that many eligible bachelors around for the young ladies and, stuck in the heart of the Essex countryside as they were, it was difficult to meet new people. In the past there had been plenty of farmers to choose from; now potential husbands were few and far between.

The tennis partners were culled from the handful of villages which lay in the countryside surrounding Maldon. Most of the hamlets were situated between the two major centres, nearby Chelmsford – only forty miles from London – and Colchester, a bustling town some twenty-five miles further north. Close as they were, it was still a major haul to get into one or other of the towns: mums and dads were loath to squander precious petrol on driving their daughters to a dance or the cinema.

June Speakman was pleased to hear that she would partner Nevill Bamber. She, too, felt they would make a perfect couple on the court. Their physical dissimilarity meant that they complemented each other beautifully. Nevill, at six foot four, towered over the petite June by nearly a foot. His long legs and lengthy reach allowed him to dominate the back of the court, destroying high lobs with impossible-to-reach smashes. June was quick around the court, nimbly scooping up any volley or drop-shot that trickled over the net.

16

The twenty-five-year-old June already knew Nevill Bamber by sight, since he was working on her father's farm. It was hard to miss his imposing figure and several of her friends had already noticed his curly blond hair and blue eyes. The tennis partners could not have been more unalike in colouring, either: June had thick, dark hair and dark eyes, her face was strong rather than pretty, but her smile was very charming.

The pair were the same age, but Nevill had seen a lot more of the world in his short life than June. When war was declared he had joined the RAF as soon as he was able and had become a fighter pilot. He never boasted about his wartime exploits or talked about the suffering and death he had witnessed which had forced him to mature quickly into a responsible young man. Following his successful record as a pilot, Nevill left the RAF after the war to return to his first love, the countryside. He was a clever man who realised earlier than most that the post-war farmer would have to know as much about business as about farming if he was to earn a decent living.

With that in mind, he applied for and won a place at the Royal Agricultural College in Cirencester, Gloucestershire. Before the summer term was over the college had received several calls for help from farmers in other counties. Able-bodied men were at a premium in the post-war days and crops threatened to spoil if they were not gathered in time. The college sent students to help gather the harvest on these farms, enabling them to gain some practical experience of farming at the same time.

Nevill was assigned to one of the farms belonging to

17

Leslie Speakman, an Essex landowner. He enjoyed the work and his polite manners and good looks made him a favourite with the local families. After the grim war years when death was always close by, Nevill was delighted to be able to relax and join in all the little entertainments devised by the girls of the nearby villages. But the tennis party was to prove special. By the end of it Nevill and his partner June Speakman were aware that they were attracted to each other. Within a matter of months they were married in the church of the local village, Goldhanger.

They settled down to farm nearly 300 acres of land in the stretch of countryside which edged towards the estuary of the River Blackwater and the English Channel. The young couple moved into White House Farm, an attractive Georgian building set at the end of a narrow private road just outside the little village of Tolleshunt D'Arcy. It was a tenant farm which had belonged to June's father, Leslie Speakman. The trustees who owned the land were only too happy to let it continue 'in the family' under the responsible care of Nevill Bamber.

Their early married life was very quiet and Nevill worked hard to build up a secure base for the family which both he and June were keen to start as soon as possible. June's sister, Pamela, was married to Robert Boutflour, who farmed some twenty-five miles away. The couple had a son, David, and a daughter, Christine-Anne. There were also numerous cousins scattered around the Essex countryside and gatherings of the clan were frequent. The couple did not look for any kind of amusement outside the family circle – Tolleshunt D'Arcy had a population of less than a

18

thousand and as neither Nevill nor June were drinkers, there was nothing to tempt them into the village which offered little apart from two pubs.

Goldhanger, about four miles away from White House Farm along a twisting country road, was even less inviting. A burst of building after the war saw the emergence of several rows of ugly council houses and the erection of a village hall which had the appearance of a heavily fortified bus shelter. The village was larger and not as pleasant as its neighbour, Tolleshunt D'Arcy. The haphazard streets and turnings of Goldhanger sprawled untidily over the country-side. Surrounded as it was by fields and farms, it was easy to forget just how near the village was to the coast. A sea wall ran to one side of the main street and a stretch of water named The Stumble was a short walk away over the fields.

Tolleshunt D'Arcy and Goldhanger are just two of half a dozen small villages strung by the side of a minor road, the B1026. The road is not wide but busy enough to disrupt what was once very quiet countryside. The local landscape is not picture-postcard pretty. It is predominantly flat, largely treeless and intensively farmed. The only change in scenery is afforded by the acres of fruit trees around the nearby town of Tiptree, home of the local jam manu-facturing company.

In those early days Nevill could neither find nor afford much help on the farm. He was lucky enough to build up a core of loyal farmhands, some of whom, like Len Foakes, were devoted to Nevill and worked for him for many years. Len lived with his wife Dorothy and their children in the little group of tied cottages halfway down Pages Lane, the private track that led to White House Farm. They were the nearest neighbours; otherwise the farm was solitary, standing on its own in the middle of flat fields.

June Bamber had all the time in the world to lavish on the farmhouse. Her neatness bordered on the obsessive and the house was kept in immaculate condition; nothing was allowed to disturb the order of the rooms. June took a pride in the several pieces of good furniture which had been handed down through her family from generation to generation. She also managed to gather together a small collection of antiques, mainly silverware and ornaments. Like Nevill, she longed for a family, but as the years passed and there were still no children June made an effort to direct her energies elsewhere. Like most country folk, June had been brought up to attend church regularly. But her beliefs were not simply a matter of duty, they were deeply felt and had strengthened over the years. As the young wife of one of the local farmers, June was conscious of her position in the nearby village and keen to play a prominent part in its religious life.

Tolleshunt D'Arcy was proud of the handsome fourteenth-century church of St Nicholas, which stood in the middle of the village. June became good friends with each of the vicars assigned to the tiny church over the years. They, in turn, relied on her ever-ready willingness to help out at the major festivals or even at the weekly services, when she would take turns decorating the church with flowers. Nevill was concerned that June should fill her time to prevent her brooding over their inability to start a family and encouraged her to become actively involved with the church. Both Nevill and June became churchwardens and June was still a warden at the time of her murder. In later years the current vicar of Tolleshunt D'Arcy was lavish in his praise of the farmer's wife: 'She was always visiting the sick and elderly in the village,' he remembered. 'Mrs Bamber's great strength was in dealing with people. She made newcomers very welcome at the church.'

The couple were very happy. The farm was thriving and the irksome years of rationing did not hit quite so hard in the countryside, where there was a good supply of fresh fruit, vegetables and meat. Nevill and June were content with each other's company and although they were young, they had no wish for any kind of nightlife. The only cloud in their lives was their failure to have a child. Obviously the future of the estate was at stake, but more important than that consideration was the longing of both Nevill and June to enjoy the pleasures of children. The more established and secure they became, the more they felt the need for a family of their own. After eight childless years, they decided to try to adopt a child.

Their credentials could not have been better: they were the right age, sufficiently affluent and had an ideal home to offer a child. June suggested that they try to find a child through the Church of England Children's Society, and the Bambers were accepted at once as potential parents by the organisation. In September 1957 the Bambers were told of an eight-week-old baby girl who needed a home. The child had been born to the daughter of a chaplain to the Archbishop of Canterbury, the result of an illicit affair.

Nevill and June were overjoyed with the little girl, whom

they christened Sheila Jean, and the adoption papers were approved at Essex County Court in Maldon on 6 February 1958. Local people remember Sheila as a pretty and quiet youngster who was rather timid and sensitive at an age when most children are boisterous. She liked animals but, perhaps understandably, was frightened by some of the rituals of farming, crying whenever a chicken had its neck wrung or any of the livestock were slaughtered. She never ventured far from the farmhouse and refused to walk with her parents when Nevill took one of his collection of guns on a rabbit hunt.

Less than four years after Sheila's adoption, the Children's Society contacted the Bambers again. Nevill and June had made it clear that they wished to adopt at least two children, if not more, and they were delighted to hear that there was the possibility of another child for them. This time the baby was a boy, born in January 1961 to the daughter of a company director, a schoolgirl who had been involved with an officer in the Army Medical Corps. The Bambers now had the family they had longed for. Their new son, whom they named Jeremy, was brought to White House Farm at the age of three months and the adoption process was completed four months later.

June now had more than enough to occupy her time caring for the two dark-haired, blue-eyed children. She was determined that they should be brought up carefully and in the long days before Sheila and Jeremy came to the farm she had laid her plans carefully for the future of the children she hoped to bring up. Jeremy, of course, would help his father with the farm and gradually resume responsibility for it. Like Nevill, he needed to cultivate a good business brain as well as an understanding of the countryside. Sheila would grow into a perfect country girl and her wedding could be held in the village at St Nicholas's.

Although she loved the children, June was reserved by nature and her care expressed itself in practical actions rather than hugs and cuddles. The children were well clothed, well fed and great care was taken with their basic education, but brother and sister both felt a lack of tangible affection. Jeremy's girlfriends were to remember him as a little boy lost who craved hugs and snuggles. When a mother herself, Sheila was to heap love on her sons in an effort to compensate for what she saw as her own affection-starved childhood. As an adult, she still felt the lack of affection keenly and confided in several friends about her stern upbringing.

'She told me that there had never been any warmth in her family, even when she was a child,' recalled a girlfriend. '"You know," she would say, "My mother has never hugged me or cuddled me or kissed me. They just didn't do things like that. I was never, ever made to feel loved. They did give me a lot of things – you know, they made sure I had everything I needed – but my mother just wasn't going to give me any closeness."

'I said to her, "But surely it must have been better sometimes, what about Christmas? They must have been more relaxed and loving at Christmas?"

'"No," she said. "That was just the same: presents, but no affection. They just didn't know how to do things like that."'

June had no hesitation in making the children aware of the fact that they were adopted as soon as they were old enough to understand. Her decision was obviously a fair one – it prevented any great shocks later in life for the little boy and girl. Unfortunately, both children found the news disturbing, all the more so as June did not wish them to discuss it at any length. There was no contact with any of the natural parents, and, inevitably, the news only increased the children's growing feeling that they were unlovable and unloved.

June Bamber regarded the issue as one of mere information. She was unaware that her news might have a deeply emotional and disturbing effect on the children. Too young to appreciate logic, both children were at an age where they were able to respond only to affection, which was not forthcoming. Nevill was a kind and indulgent father, but farm life meant that he saw little of the youngsters. He was at work in the fields by the time they got up and often had not finished by the early evening when they were bathed and put to bed.

To June and, to a lesser extent, Nevill, the world outside Tolleshunt D'Arcy and its neighbouring villages was largely unknown. Sheila and Jeremy were brought up in the decade that saw the explosion of youth culture, when public morality shifted its attitude on issues such as drugs, sex before marriage, contraception and abortion. Music and fashion were the overriding preoccupations of young people and the generation that fought a war was shocked by the generation that marched in order to halt another one.

Most of this upheaval played little part in the daily life of the Bambers. June's temperament was conservative and restrictive. She was a good, conscientious mother to her children but lacked the breadth of vision to realise that the society she once knew had disappeared. Nevill had a more tolerant, genial frame of mind. He may have regretted many of the changes taking place, but appreciated that every generation was different. Soon after Jeremy's adoption, Nevill was appointed a Justice of the Peace and sat on the bench at Witham Magistrates' Court. His work as a magistrate enabled Nevill to keep more in touch with the changing society around him. Witham, like many surrounding villages, was developing into a small town with a purpose-built shopping precinct and pubs where adults over a certain age did not dare to venture for fear of the juke-box. The petty criminals before him were as likely to be joyriders as poachers and the old way of life was rapidly being replaced by a brash new urban lifestyle.

The farm was doing well and Nevill had decided to expand his business interests. In partnership with June's sister, Pamela, and her husband Robert Boutflour, the Bambers bought a 400-berth caravan site in Osea Bay, near Maldon. The holiday-home venture proved successful and became a regular summer pilgrimage for east-enders on holiday. It was rumoured that, in between jobs, several very successful villains frequently made the trip to Osea, where they could rent berths next to the handful of Metropolitan police officers who also relaxed on the site. The management of the park gradually came to rest with the Boutflours' daughter Anne, after her marriage to gun-dealer and farmer Peter Eaton, and she proved to be a power-house in supervising the running of the site.

The years when the children were youngsters were particularly happy times for the Bambers. The couple were frequently praised for their willingness to get involved in village affairs and for their upright natures. Nevill, considered more approachable than his rather reserved wife, was especially liked by those who knew him. He treated his farm helpers well, never failing to take everyone for a drink in The Red Lion every Christmas, and even local poachers felt they were dealing with a gentleman when caught red-handed.

Nevill had his sporting hobbies – shooting and salmon fishing – and June kept up her church work. They had few close friends but it was obvious to outsiders that the couple enjoyed each other's company. 'Mr and Mrs Bamber were inseparable,' commented one villager. 'You would often see them hand-in-hand at fêtes and gardening shows. They looked like a couple still very much in love.'

Unknown to her acquaintances, June was finding it increasingly hard to cope with her own nervous moods. She had always been highly strung and much more introverted than her expansive husband. Now the demands of the children and her concern over their upbringing aggravated her tensions. The children were growing up quickly and June made sure that the toddlers were brought up as true Christians, teaching them their prayers and sending them to local Sunday School classes.

She reinforced their lessons with her own teachings, reading to the children from the Bible and stressing the importance of always being on their guard against the wiles of the Devil. The wide-eyed youngsters drank in her words. Sheila, a few years older than Jeremy, fervently believed in her mother's stories of God and the Devil fighting with good and bad angels. She became terrified that the Devil might sneak up on her unawares and take her over in her sleep, and she began to have nightmares.

June's worn nerves were given some respite when first Sheila and then Jeremy were bought their new uniforms and satchels and sent off to school.

Schooldays were not happy times for either of the children. Both Sheila and Jeremy were taught the three 'R's at local primary schools. As they had been brought up on the isolated farm, it was the first opportunity for them to spend any length of time with children of their own age and they were ill equipped to cope.

June was a doting mother, but the combination of her undemonstrative love and her strict discipline proved unfortunate for the little boy and girl. They were both aware that they were different from most of the village children; they had a different way of life, they even spoke differently from everyone else. Both children showed a profound awareness of their distinctiveness. To Sheila, it was a sign that she was somehow abnormal, out of place, and it worried her deeply. Jeremy, however, took refuge in a sense of superiority and a developing arrogance. Jeremy and Sheila went to primary school in the nearby town of Maldon. They travelled to the seaside school by special bus every morning, and even at this early age, Jeremy found it hard to mix with boys of his own age. One of his friends from that time remembers that Jeremy was handicapped by his well-bred accent, something that June had taken great pains to cultivate in her children.

'He was so snooty and spoke so posh on the school bus that the local lads used to tease him mercilessly,' recalled Bob Cross, a primary school friend. 'He was a real wimp and would just burst into tears instead of fighting back. His sister stuck up for him a lot and he hated that.'

Nevill and June wanted their son and daughter to have the best education they could afford to give them. Jeremy had to be groomed as a gentleman farmer like his father, and the Bambers felt it would be difficult to achieve this in a village school. Instead, they wanted him to mix with boys from a similar class and with similar prospects to his own. Their first move was to place him at Maldon Court, a private prep school in the town, instead of the local state school. Nevill Bamber was certainly not a snob, but he was a traditionalist and felt it would be counter-productive for Jeremy to be educated alongside the village kids, whom he might even employ some day. Better to send him to a school with a good academic record and a less free-and-easy atmosphere than the local establishments.

The Bambers could not aspire to Eton or Harrow, but when the time came for Jeremy to leave prep school they found a boarding school which seemed to have everything they wanted for their eleven-year-old son. Gresham Boys' Public School, situated in the small Norfolk town of Holt, was home to Jeremy for the next five years of his life. Parents paid more than £5,000 per year for the privilege of sending their sons to board at the strictly run school, which still boasts a fine academic reputation. Gresham is famous

28

for its Army Cadet Force and many sons of military families are sent to the school as the traditional first step to a career in the forces. Nevill, the former RAF pilot, felt that the values of discipline, loyalty and self-sufficiency taught at the school were ideal principles for his son to develop.

The demands for Sheila's education were less specific. June wanted her daughter, already a pretty, dainty little girl, to learn the traditional feminine skills of sewing, cooking and dressmaking. There were no hard and fast plans for her future, but the Bambers wanted to ensure she acquired a certain refinement which they felt would be beyond the range of a village school. Like most country people, the women in the Bamber family did not pursue independent careers. Life within a farming community kept them sufficiently occupied.

June Bamber was a typical farmer's wife, and as well as keeping her home scrupulously neat, she cooked huge meals for her husband and occasionally for his labourers, and helped organise the efficient running of the estate. This was the sort of life she understood and enjoyed, and she hoped that Sheila would grow up to be part of it, too. With this in mind, Sheila was sent to a private boarding school for girls in Norwich.

Unfortunately, both Sheila and Jeremy found it impossible to settle down in the schools their parents had chosen for them. Once away from home, both children began to rebel against the strict moral principles which had ruled their days at White House Farm. The expensive education proved to be largely a waste of money as Jeremy and Sheila revelled in their first taste of the outside world. Even

29

worse, the two children who arrived at the farm each holiday were rapidly becoming strangers to their doting parents. Their language and behaviour, their aspirations and pursuits were out of place in the countryside. By the time Nevill and June realised that something was terribly wrong it was already too late. The damage had been done.

3
Growing up

Sensitive little Sheila took her time to adapt to the regime of school life. By the age of eleven she was already a dreamy, impractical girl, likeable but very shy and easily led. For the first time in her life she was constantly in the company of girls her own age and quickly developed a taste for the pastimes her friends enjoyed: dancing, make-up, clothes and records. While her friends chafed at the restrictions of boarding school Sheila, by contrast, found a freedom she had not experienced at White House Farm. It was a new world of giggles and magazines and incessant gossip about boys.

Sheila was not a studious pupil and found no satisfaction in her lessons. Her poor academic progress and the inevitable reprimands greatly upset her. She tried hard, but she found sustained periods of concentration almost impossible and dreaded exams and the end-of-term report cards which she soon gave up hope of trying to improve on.

Even the most optimistic of her teachers realised that Sheila did not have the capacity to advance her education further, and it was agreed that the reluctant pupil should leave school as soon as she was old enough. Nevill and June were disappointed but they were forced to concede that college was out of the question. Instead Sheila was enrolled in an establishment in Swiss Cottage, half finishing school, half secretarial college, where she took courses in typing and shorthand, grooming and deportment.

But Sheila's immediate future was to take a much more turbulent course than that mapped out for her by Nevill and June. The little girl had emerged from boarding school a very attractive young woman. By the time she was sixteen Sheila had grown to her full height of five foot seven. She had a very slim, well-proportioned figure and pale, clear skin. Her thick, dark hair fell to her shoulders and she had already begun to add dark red highlights to make it even more striking. Her greatest asset was her big, blue eyes, which turned down slightly at the corners giving her a wistful, slightly mournful expression. She was not merely pretty, she possessed stunning good looks. At school she had been nicknamed 'Bambi', and her family and close friends all knew her as 'Bambs'.

June's expectations of her daughter were fulfilled in one respect: Sheila had matured into a graceful and very feminine young woman. She was also attractive to and attracted to men. There was nothing unusual in that, but June found it difficult to cope with what a modern teenager considered to be normal fun. The years spent in boarding school with infrequent visits to White House Farm had

32

turned Sheila into a stranger in Tolleshunt D'Arcy. She could not adapt to a rural way of life, and likewise her own habits were totally alien to her parents. June, born and bred in the country, expected her daughter to accede to the strict regime which she had established both for the farm and for her personal conduct. June could be a hard task-master and the time spent at home, between boarding school and finishing school, became increasingly fraught.

There was tension on both sides, and June and Sheila no longer understood each other. Her daughter's day-dreaming exasperated June, and for her part Sheila chafed at her mother's restrictions on how and with whom she spent her time. Shortly after her seventeenth birthday, in July 1974, Sheila and June clashed head-on in an incident which was to scar both women for the rest of their lives.

During her solitary walks about the farm, Sheila met a good-looking young man helping out in the fields. They began to see a lot of each other but Sheila was careful to keep the relationship secret, aware that her mother would never permit a liaison with a farm labourer. Instead she would creep out of the farmhouse and slip unseen through the fields to a remote spot for a clandestine meeting. Sheila was inexperienced with men of her own age and her physical development far outstripped her emotional under-standing. The pair became lovers quickly and recklessly. For Sheila, completely swept off her feet by passion, this was the first outpouring of love and tenderness she had ever received. Her guard was down and the pair became more audacious. It was only a matter of time before June noticed a change in Sheila's usually docile manner. She began to watch the young woman closely.

Late one afternoon June set off in pursuit of Sheila, who once again had seized a quiet moment to steal away from the house to find her lover. After a long, fruitless search, June decided to give up and take a short cut through the fields back to the house. Two minutes later she almost stumbled over the pair as they lay – her daughter and a young farmhand making love in a ditch.

Even a sophisticated young woman would have found it difficult to talk her way out of that situation, and Sheila did not even try. June was hysterical: the incident was a catastrophe almost beyond her comprehension. She hauled Sheila back to the farm, screaming all the way. She was completely devastated by her daughter's behaviour, nothing she had ever known could have prepared her for such a crippling blow. Then, quite suddenly, she realised she knew the truth. Turning to her terrified daughter, June calmly explained it over and over again: Sheila was the child of the Devil, she was the Devil's child on earth, spreading evil around her. The words sank deep into Sheila, who was almost out of her mind with fear and confusion.

It was a phrase that Sheila would never forget and which would become the root of her latent paranoia. She did not have the ability to defend herself against her mother's frenzied outburst. Neither woman had any real idea about normal human desires and expectations: June thought Sheila's sexual development was ungodly, the work of the

Devil; Sheila, disturbed by the power of her newly awakened sexuality, guiltily acknowledged that her behaviour was the result of an evil mind. Nevill was informed of the episode and reprimanded Sheila but could do little to alleviate the incredible ferocity of his wife's reaction. The incident was kept within the family, and so there was no confidant to reassure Sheila that her actions were not evil but merely ill advised.

June Bamber had already suffered one nervous breakdown and would within a few years succumb to another. Unlike most parents who catch their teenage children petting on sofas or in bus shelters, June was not able to take the incident in her stride and content herself with a stern reprimand. She unwittingly planted a seed of foreboding in her daughter that in time would grow too great for Sheila to conquer. The teenager was dangerously impressionable and did not possess the ability to vanquish superstition with logic. Her self-esteem was tenuous and had been so ever since her childhood, when she had been coldly informed of her adoption. The sense of alienation had inevitably increased when she was dispatched to boarding school and now she was more than ever an outcast in her surrogate home.

Sheila would never shake off the repercussions of that brief affair, but there was yet another, more immediate consequence to be dealt with. Sheila was pregnant, and in June's eyes her disgrace was complete. Marriage was completely out of the question, and Sheila was clearly ill equipped to be a mother even with the support of her parents. After much heart-searching Nevill and June decided there could be only one solution. Sheila did not object – she simply wanted to please her parents after causing them so much pain. The pregnancy was terminated.

Sheila went to London as planned, but quickly became bored with her courses. She loathed the grinding monotony of shorthand and typing and did not have the willpower to endure the nightly hours of practice. Gradually, she recovered from the trauma of the previous few months and began to make new friends.

One night she joined a group of fellow students in a north London pub and quickly found her attention monopolised by a handsome, dark-haired young artist, Colin Caffell.

'It was love at first sight,' recalled Caffell. 'If there had been a coffee table there I would have fallen over it. There was a heavenly apparition sitting in the corner.'

Sheila was equally impressed and responded enthusiastically to Colin's calm, easy-going temperament. He was the steady rock she needed, and before very long the couple had set up home together. Nevill and June disapproved, but Colin's affection now held more sway in Sheila's heart than her parents' censure. She abandoned the Swiss Cottage academy and began to train as a hairdresser with the Robert Fielding chain of salons in London. Her striking good looks drew a lot of attention from customers and several people advised Sheila to seriously consider a career in modelling. Colin was enthusiastic, and with his support, Sheila made the rounds of modelling agencies and eventually found her way on to the books of the Lucie

Clayton agency. With Colin by her side and the prospect of a new career, Sheila appeared to have shaken off the trauma of White House Farm.

This reversal of fortune came as a tremendous relief to her parents. Nevill and June had devoted much time and energy to their daughter's troubles, and June had begun to show signs of acute stress. Nevill hoped a period of calm and rest would help and with Sheila happily settled in London it seemed that life at the farm could return to normal.

Sheila's problems undoubtedly took precedence during that traumatic period and it was some time before Nevill and June realised their son was also in difficulties. Jeremy deeply resented his incarceration in boarding school. He saw the decision to send him away in the worst possible light, interpreting the move as his mother's desire to get rid of him. 'He resented his mother because she sent him away to boarding school and he never forgave her for that,' said one of his friends. 'He always said he couldn't see the point of adopting a child and sending it away to boarding school.'

Jeremy was not an easy child. His moods swung between fits of sullenness and bursts of high spirits. His relatives became used to his attempts to gain attention at family gatherings. While Sheila stood quietly in the background, Jeremy performed his party trick of dancing with a full glass of wine on his forehead, a routine which never failed to bring him the applause he craved.

Boarding school had brought him back to earth with a terrible jolt. He was just the same as any of the boarders at Gresham, and Jeremy did not possess the requisite charm or precocity that might have singled him out from the crowd. At home he competed with Sheila for his parents' attention but at school he gave up the struggle and became a sulky, troublesome individual. 'He was a rather quiet, prickly sort of boy,' recalled Mr Logie Bruce-Lockhart, the headmaster of Gresham, 'I believe some of the boys found him irritating in that he could be a relentless tease. I think he showed a touch of arrogance at a very early age.'

There may have been more disturbing reasons for Jeremy's hatred of boarding-school life. His New Zealand friend, Brett Collins, later claimed that Jeremy had been sexually molested when he was eleven years old – the age he started as a boarder at Gresham. Collins offered his own psychological interpretation of the alleged incident, claiming that Bamber was deeply affected by the incident and developed a deep aversion to homosexuals. Pressed further, Collins admitted that Jeremy was, in fact, bisexual and that most of Bamber's acquaintances were under the impression that he had had at least one homosexual affair. As he matured, Jeremy could seemingly switch sexual attitudes at will, jumping from aggressive philandering to possessive tenderness towards women. His friendship with Brett Collins, however, was not subject to such vicissitudes: the two young men were devoted to each other and shared a mutual understanding. Whatever the extent of Jeremy's homosexual experiences at school, his later escapades showed complete acceptance of a bisexual nature.

With the onset of puberty and its accompanying erratic moods, Jeremy's behaviour became increasingly wayward.

38

One of his contemporaries remembers him as unpopular with other pupils, a loner who seemed to derive pleasure from the petty bullying of younger boys. Jeremy revelled in deliberate disorderly behaviour, which he believed gave him a certain cachet in the classroom. His colleagues were not impressed: they simply wrote him off as an oddball, a braggart whose pranks were no longer amusing.

Inevitably, Jeremy's school work suffered. Although basically intelligent, he showed as little interest in academic achievement as his sister. He appealed to Nevill and June to transfer him to another school closer to home, but his parents were adamant: Jeremy was going to get the best education they could afford. Jeremy retaliated by pouring all his energies into flouting the rules and encouraging others to join him. He resented the lack of freedom and what he believed to be an excessively strict regime imposed on pupils by the school authorities.

'Jeremy and I got beaten when we used to sneak out for concerts,' recollected John Fielding, a schoolfriend. 'We went to see Suzi Quatro and got caught by the house-master, Mr Thomas. He reported us to the headmaster and the next day me and Jeremy got beaten. I remember him suggesting we wore umpteen pairs of underpants.

'We had the choice: you could either be rusticated – stopped from leaving the grounds for half a term – or you could get beaten. Jeremy said he would take the beating.'

Nevill and June were mortified when Jeremy left Gresham without passing any exams. His natural intelligence had atrophied during his school days, but Jeremy felt he had proved his point to his parents, albeit at great cost to himself. Later it emerged that he suffered from a form of dyslexia which made it impossible for him to write with any real fluency. This handicap had gone undiscovered at Gresham and must have heightened Jeremy's reluctance to tackle his lessons and increased his sense of isolation from his schoolmates.

Jeremy returned to White House Farm, but this was no return of the prodigal son. Nevill made no secret of his annoyance at Jeremy's laziness and the rows were lengthy and unpleasant, but at least they eventually finished. Much more infuriating was the disapproval shown by June, who could not let the matter drop. After a while, Jeremy stopped answering back; he simply refused to speak to June and their silences began to stretch for days.

The Bambers' agreement that Jeremy could leave Gresham was reached only on the understanding that he enrolled at the nearby sixth-form college in Colchester. Jeremy responded well to the relaxed atmosphere of the establishment. Students were treated like adults rather than pupils, and in this atmosphere Jeremy blossomed. He worked hard and passed seven 'O' levels, much to the delight of his parents.

Jeremy's journey through adolescence now took a smoother course. For the first time in his life, Jeremy had no difficulty in making and keeping friends. His social life took off, helped by the fact that he passed his driving test with ease as soon as he was seventeen. Years of driving the farm tractor at harvest time had paid off and he enjoyed piling his gang into an old van and touring local pubs after college was over for the day. Another, very welcome, development was the change in the teenager's appearance. The pale, pudding-faced schoolboy of Gresham was rapidly maturing into a very handsome young man. Jeremy's looks attracted a lot of attention from the sixth-form girls. He was the classic 'tall, dark and handsome' man with large, intensely blue eyes and a very sensual mouth. He bore a striking resemblance to the American 'brat pack' film star Rob Lowe, and wasted no time in capitalising on his outstanding good looks.

Nevill Bamber took heart from his son's belated academic success, but he was still concerned about what to do with the boy. Nevill wanted Jeremy to learn the entire business of farming, but the young man made it clear that he had no intention of spending years labouring in the fields at White House Farm. Jeremy wanted to start at the top, helping Nevill make decisions and supervising the labourers. Nevill insisted that his adopted son could not shirk the dirty work; he was as yet far too immature and irresponsible to play a greater role in the running of the 300 acres.

The issue appeared to be deadlocked when Jeremy took matters into his own hands, declaring that he wanted to train as a deep-sea diver in New Zealand. It was a madcap scheme, born out of Jeremy's desire for adventure and fun, but the Bambers reluctantly agreed to finance the trip. They had already paid for Sheila's 'finishing' course and Jeremy successfully argued that he was entitled to a similar venture. Nevill and June were sceptical of Jeremy's new-found enthusiasm for diving, but they rationalised the expenditure as a means of allowing Jeremy to get some of the restlessness out of his system. He would have to be responsible for himself and although they felt there was not the slightest chance of their son actually qualifying as a diver, they did hope that he might finally reconcile himself to becoming a hard-working farmer.

The vicissitudes of Sheila and Jeremy laid a heavy burden on their parents. It seemed to Nevill and June that no sooner had they rescued one of their children from a set of difficulties, than the other one fell into the mire. A traumatic year coping with Sheila's abortion and then her decision to live with her boyfriend was immediately followed by Jeremy's crisis at school. Once Jeremy had settled down at college they hoped their children were over their respective problems. But it was not to be.

Sheila was yet again giving her parents cause for concern. The Bambers were not overly excited about Sheila's decision to model but had dutifully agreed to help, paying for Sheila's portfolio of professional photographs. Just as she was beginning to make some headway in the fashion world, the young woman became pregnant. Sheila was glad to be pregnant, but neither she nor Colin were concerned about marriage. June Bamber was outraged, and once again the arguments between mother and daughter reached epic proportions.

Sheila lost the baby after a couple of months and shortly afterwards she miscarried again. She was physically unharmed, apart from having to have a stitch in her cervix, but the loss of the babies upset her greatly and sparked off a preoccupation with the state of her health and the care of her body which her modelling career only exacerbated.

Although Sheila was undoubtedly lovely, her temperament was not suited to the tough, competitive world of fashion modelling. The constant appraisals and rejections of modelling auditions can undermine the confidence of the most self-assured aspirants. Sheila, with her shaky equilibrium, had to fight hard against allowing herself to be completely demoralised by the process.

Sheila persevered and Colin never flagged in his encouragement. After two years together, the couple decided they would after all get married. Sheila was just twenty and Colin nearly twenty-seven. The future was still precarious: their joint income varied from subsistence level to comparative affluence when Sheila had a photographic shoot or Colin sold some artwork or pottery. Nevertheless, they had a great feeling of optimism for the future and Sheila was happier than she had ever been before.

Nevill and June had once hoped for a prosperous farmer as a son-in-law, but they now managed to put their dreams behind them. They had both been impressed by Colin's obvious devotion to Sheila and he seemed to bring the best out in her; he understood her fragile psyche better than they could themselves. The wedding was a traditional affair, with Sheila demure in a high-necked white dress with Juliet cap and veil. Colin was unexpectedly dapper in a smart dark suit and tie, complete with a flower in his buttonhole.

As Jeremy made his way across the world, Colin and Sheila settled down to their life together. In 1979, after less than two years of marriage, Sheila was pregnant again and this time gave birth to twin sons, Nicholas and Daniel. The two little boys were all that was needed to finally reconcile Nevill and June to Sheila's way of life. The couple doted on their grandchildren and encouraged Sheila and Colin to visit White House Farm as often as they could. Sheila, at twenty-two, said she was still determined to carry on with her modelling career and made a real effort to get back into shape after the twins' birth.

Yet just as everything appeared to be going well for Sheila, the old demons crawled out of her past to haunt her again. She found it impossible to cope with the pressure of marriage, two babies and a struggling career all at the same time. Like many other over-burdened young mothers, she fell prey to a form of post-natal depression. Unfortunately, this led to a revival of the turmoil she had suffered as an adolescent. Once again her thoughts dwelled obsessively on the accusations hurled at her during her teenage days by June.

Sheila's relationship with her husband disintegrated swiftly. At times she became convinced that she was an emissary of the Devil himself or that good and evil were fighting for possession of her soul. There was nothing Colin could do or say to help. The young man's calm manner, once so attractive to Sheila, now infuriated her beyond reason. Colin's attempts to defuse her tantrums ended more and more frequently with pots and pans whistling through the air and clattering to the floor. Sheila rarely aimed at Colin, just hurling the objects at nothing in particular made her feel better. On one occasion, however, she tried to provoke a response from the unflappable Colin by slapping his face. When he turned away, Sheila plunged her hands through a window, cutting them on the glass. It was the final straw. They both knew that their life together had become unbearable and, only four months after the birth of the twins, the couple decided to part.

On the other side of the world, Jeremy was raising hell out of sight and sound of his parents. The sunny, outdoor life of New Zealand lost its appeal for him after a couple of weeks, and as his parents had predicted, decided he was not cut out to be a diver. He had no intention of sitting around in the diving school classroom when he could be out having a good time. Jeremy was now nineteen and this was the first time in his life he had been away from the watchful eyes of teachers or parents and able to do exactly what he wanted.

Jeremy then met the Kiwi who was to become his closest friend. Brett Collins was nearly five years older than Jeremy but the two young men were kindred spirits. Collins was a restless rolling stone who moved from job to job as the fancy took him. Like Jeremy, he could be charming when the occasion demanded and had an abundance of self-confidence. Collins was also handsome, with butterscotch-coloured hair and small, twinkling blue eyes deeply set in a permanently tanned face spoiled only by a petulant mouth. Slightly shorter than Jeremy, Collins was vain about his looks and infected his new friend with a passion for expensive clothes. Jeremy became fast friends with him.

Soon after their first meeting in New Zealand, the two made their way over the water to Sydney, Australia. The cosmopolitan bustle of the big city was much more to Jeremy's taste than the quiet of New Zealand. He and Brett began to enjoy life, spending their days at the beaches surrounding Sydney and their evenings in the bars and clubs of the city. At first his jaunts were financed by the money Jeremy had been given by his parents. When that ran out, he joined Brett as a cocktail waiter. But he also got involved in more dangerous escapades. Jeremy always refused to specify exactly what happened in Australia, but would occasionally refer to forays into smuggling and drug-dealing. They moved up the coast to Queensland, where Collins had a share in a Brisbane restaurant, but instead of working he spent most of his time teaching Jeremy how to body-surf.

Jeremy and Brett were coy about their relationship with each other. Collins had on one occasion said that he was bisexual but Bamber would not publicly admit to affairs with men. However, he later confided in his girlfriend, Julie Mugford, that he had had a homosexual affair and she was in no doubt that his partner was Brett Collins. 'We just enjoyed each other's company,' claimed Collins. 'He has everything most women like. He's handsome, smart and intelligent. But that also attracts men sometimes. He had to tell one man to cool it because he was becoming too intense.'

Jeremy was very impressed by the cool, swaggering Collins. Brett refused to take anything or anyone seriously; life was a lark and they should make the most of it, he told his young friend.

In New Zealand, Bamber burgled a jewellery shop and stole a handful of items, including two expensive watches. On his return to England he presented one of them to a girlfriend. He also liked to boast that he had been involved in heroin smuggling during his time abroad. Bamber's cousin, David Boutflour, later said that Jeremy had been forced to get out of New Zealand quickly after a police investigation into a more serious crime. 'Jeremy became involved in a homosexual club over there which was implicated in an armed robbery and killing,' he said. 'Although he was not directly involved with the crime, he obviously felt he had to leave in a hurry.'

After nearly a year away, Jeremy was completely out of funds and could barely scrape together enough money to afford his air fare home. Rumours of his activities had already begun to reach his parents, who reluctantly concluded that far from encouraging Jeremy to settle down, the trip had probably made him even less willing to work at a steady job.

Jeremy's return confirmed their worst fears. Any deference he had once held towards his parents had completely disappeared. He declared that he had no intention of working on the farm and refused to consider training for an alternative career. Instead he sought the low-paid manual jobs he had done in Australia, working as a waiter or barman. However, the compensations of menial work in Australia – the wonderful climate, cheap standard of living and a life spent mainly on the beach – were non-existent in Essex.

From body-surfing on Bondi Beach, Jeremy was reduced to working as a waiter at a Little Chef on the A12. To make life more bearable, he took a job in a Colchester nightclub and agreed to return to White House Farm. He simply wanted the comforts of home life, but June made it quite clear that once back at home he would have to abide by her rules. Although he was now twenty, Jeremy was still in thrall to his mother. He resented her domination but knew he had no choice but to obey. He could not afford to do anything else.

Soon after his return from Australia, Jeremy began the first long-term relationship of his life. Suzette Ford was an attractive barmaid thirteen years his senior and married with three children when she and Jeremy met in a Colchester wine bar. Jeremy was flattered to be dating an experienced woman who was so much more sophisticated than his previous high-school girlfriends. Suzette was also deeply maternal and spoiled her young lover with the affection and undivided attention that he craved. She had recently separated from her husband, who remained behind at their home on the island of Jersey, and she appreciated the attentions of a handsome young man. 'Right from the start I was very attracted to him – he seemed so sensitive, but was a bit of a clown as well,' she recalled. 'After being married for thirteen years and having three children I found it marvellously refreshing to be with someone who didn't seem to have a care in the world.'

Their affair progressed rapidly and soon Bamber was spending nearly all his evenings with dark-haired, green-eyed Suzette. She was aware of the tensions in his family life but was bemused by the way Jeremy guiltily hurried back to White House Farm every evening to avoid incurring the wrath of his parents. 'They were still very strict with him and he had to be home by a certain time or there would be trouble,' remembered Suzette. 'I found it quite funny. He was making love to an older woman every night and then going home because his parents didn't like him staying out late.'

Although Suzette was impressed by Jeremy's skill in bed – she described him as 'a thoughtful and beautiful lover' – their affair had strong overtones of a mother-and-son relationship. He enjoyed cuddles and baby-talk. He gave her his old teddy bear, which led Suzette to nickname him Jeremy Bear while he called her Wulie Woo. Although the two soon started living together in Suzette's Colchester flat, Bamber was afraid of his parents' reaction to their relationship and spun a web of lies to stop Nevill and June discovering his secret.

'I think he said he was staying with friends at first. But a couple of months later we went out with his mum and dad for a meal on his twenty-first birthday and if they didn't know he was living with me they must have guessed what was going on,' recalled Suzette. 'Jeremy seemed fond of them both, although I knew things were a bit strained with his mother. She was very religious and strait-laced and was obviously against him being with me, although she was too polite to say so. But he always got on well with his father.'

Like his sister, Jeremy appeared keen to start a family as soon as possible. His favourite expression for love-making was 'Let's go to bed and make babies', and Suzette Ford claimed that she miscarried three times during her affair with the young man. She felt the loss of the babies was a bitter blow to Jeremy and a major factor in the break-up of their relationship.

49

After nearly two years the affair was running out of steam. Nevill and June made another costly attempt to persuade Jeremy to settle down by buying him a terraced cottage in the little village of Goldhanger, nearly four miles from White House Farm. Jeremy moved in but still continued his life of serving food and drinks in the nightclubs and restaurants of Chelmsford and Colchester. He was not yet ready to give up the small-town nightlife, but he looked after the cottage, sharing it with his pet dog, a frisky little mongrel he named Brambles.

'I actually think that Brambles was the one thing that Jeremy ever loved,' said one of his friends. 'He cared about the dog a lot more than his family or girlfriends and when it was run over he was really and truly devastated.'

The Bambers bought the Goldhanger cottage for Jeremy in their usual spirit of even-handedness. They had already begun to look at flats in London with the intention of providing a home for their daughter and grandsons.

By 1982 Sheila was in the final throes of her break-up with Colin. Several reconciliations had failed and, a couple of years after their marriage, both Sheila and Colin knew that they would never again be able to live together, so quietly and amicably they decided to divorce. There was no question of custody battles or squabbles over alimony: Colin would gladly have given Sheila everything he owned and Sheila never stopped regarding him as a support she could lean on. But as neither of them was able to earn much money, Nevill and June decided to step in and buy a London home for the little family.

The break-up of her marriage was a terrible blow to

50

Sheila and she was acutely conscious of disappointing her parents yet again. Nevill was able to take this new disaster in his stride, but although June struggled to be understanding, she felt the blow very keenly. Divorce had hitherto been unheard of in the family and she couldn't help but think that Sheila had once more let the side down. And what sort of home would the twins have? It was deeply worrying for all the family.

Sheila was well aware of her mother's feelings and her own sense of alienation returned in full force. She knew she could never be part of June's world, with its high moral tone and strict principles.

As divorce proceedings began, Sheila pondered on her apparent inability to sustain the love of those close to her. She wondered whether first her mother and then her husband had sensed an innate evil in her. Or was it simply that neither her adoptive mother nor her soon-to-be ex-husband had the requisite understanding to form a real affinity with her? After several months, Sheila believed she had found the answer. She was convinced that the only person who could understand her was her real mother, and she began the search to find her.

By the time the divorce was finalised, Sheila had managed to achieve her objective. After more than a year she had eventually traced her natural mother to Canada and contacted her with the help of British and Canadian social services. The two women arranged to meet at Heathrow Airport – their first sight of each other since Sheila had been an eight-week-old baby. According to one of the social workers involved, this initial meeting was full of tension and very stressful. Sheila, however, was delighted. There was a further meeting and Sheila confided to a girlfriend that her long-lost mother was all she had hoped for.

'You know, it was marvellous,' Sheila told her friend Sonja. 'My mother was just like me. I mean she was very affectionate and she liked me straight away. I knew immediately she was my real mother and I felt much more at home with her than with my other mother. We were crying and hugging and I'm going to see a lot of her, I'm going to make sure I see her regularly. She lives in Canada, but now I've found her I'm going to make sure that we keep together. Now I've found her I want to see her.'

'She told me that her mother had been a student when she got pregnant,' Sonja remembered. 'She couldn't manage to keep on studying and bring up a baby and had been forced to have her adopted. I think her father was a student as well. Sheila was delighted they had met up and that her mother was so pleased to see her,' said Sonja.

The joyful effects of the reunion did not last very long, however. Soon Sheila's natural mother returned to Canada and those close to Sheila realised with concern that her behaviour was becoming increasingly erratic. Nevill Bamber was especially sensitive to Sheila's condition. Only a few months earlier he had had to cope with June's nervous breakdown. No one was quite sure what had provoked this new crisis but June had been skilfully treated by a Harley Street psychiatrist. Nevill felt he had now no option but to send his daughter to the same doctor in the hope that something could be done for Sheila.

After an initial consultation Dr Hugh Ferguson concluded that Sheila was in a very agitated and psychotic state and recommended that she be treated as a patient at St Andrew's Hospital, Northampton. She was admitted on 4 August 1983 and stayed for five weeks while doctors tried to help her resolve her fear that good and evil were fighting for possession of her soul. 'She was particularly caught up with the idea that the Devil had taken her over and given her the power to direct his evil not only on to other people but particularly her twin sons,' stated Dr Ferguson later in court.

The blond-haired, blue-eyed twins stayed with their father in his Kilburn flat until Mummy got better. Despite the turmoil of her life, Sheila was devoted to her sons and her modelling career was almost forgotten as she plunged all her energies into caring for the boys. 'She was a nice, pretty girl, quiet, a little withdrawn and totally committed to looking after her children. But sometimes she could be a little strange,' remembered one of her former modelling agents.

With the attention of his parents firmly fixed on his sister, Jeremy had more freedom to enjoy himself without incurring censure. For some months he had been working as a barman in a Colchester restaurant where he was friendly with the owners, Malcolm Waters and Michael Deckers. Sloppy Joe's was an American-style pizzeria with a genuine fifties juke-box and a salad bar housed in the back end of a Chevrolet. The atmosphere was boisterous and Jeremy made the most of it. His employers remember Jeremy as a young man who, in their words, could have any girl he wanted. His friends thought that behind the fun-loving image Jeremy was an elusive person, something of an enigma.

'He is a very complex character. He is a loner, very self-sufficient, but despite his moods, he could still be great fun on a night out. I wouldn't describe him as a man's man. He was always very attractive to the ladies. He had a lot of girlfriends, one-night stands. He liked to impress the ladies, particularly by driving fast,' said one of his friends.

Jeremy certainly enjoyed sowing his wild oats, but his womanising slowed down a little when he met Julie Mugford at Christmas 1983. Julie was an attractive, vivacious dark-haired girl training to become a primary school teacher. During her student holidays, she worked as a waitress at Sloppy Joe's and soon she and Jeremy progressed from casual dating to some form of commitment. Julie, a couple of years younger than her new boyfriend, was dazzled by Bamber's recklessness and apparent sophistication. He, in turn, seemed to revel in the courtship, planning an elaborate first-night seduction worthy of a romantic novel.

'There were flowers, a candlelit dinner and then the honeymoon suite in a posh hotel. He smiled and said "We'll have our honeymoon before the wedding,"' said the infatuated young girl. 'When I got home the next day there were a dozen red roses waiting for me with a card which said "Nothing like a four-poster bed."'

Jeremy made such flamboyant gestures with an insouciance that his cronies could not hope to emulate. He had enough self-assurance to carry off his sentimental

54

wooing without any awkwardness. Jeremy's confidence derived from the thought that one day he would have a lot of things all to himself – the farm, money, a business, land, antiques, a new car. It was all going to be his without any sharing or any interference. Despite his menial job, Jeremy had a certain aplomb that set him apart from his contemporaries – he knew that one day he would be a man of substance and that certainty gave him assurance in his dealings with the world.

It was not long before Julie was totally besotted with her handsome lover. His previous affairs, especially those with experienced women like Suzette Ford, had given him a sophistication in the bedroom that was unknown to Julie and totally captivated her: 'Jeremy completely swept me off my feet. He was a skilful lover. He taught me how to enjoy sex in a way I never had before,' she admitted.

He could also be aggressive and domineering. Julie told her girlfriends that Jeremy enjoyed pinning her to the bed and taking her by force. He liked to feel in control and on one occasion he covered her arms with bruises and bites so they would be clearly visible to their friends. The message was unmistakable: Julie was his property, and she acquiesced without a murmur.

But he could also be charming and proved very perceptive about women. Julie remembered that Jeremy was the only boyfriend she had ever had who did not make fun of the dark hairs that sometimes grew on her upper lip. Instead of teasing her, he would simply remind her, 'Time for the electrolysis,' and say no more about it. It was no wonder that Julie openly admitted to being besotted with

Jeremy. She likened herself to a faithful old dog who would do anything for him and Jeremy had no reason to doubt her.

Julie spent all her free time at Jeremy's Goldhanger cottage, cleaning, washing, ironing and cooking for him. She was there when he came home from work and fussed around him, trying to anticipate his every wish.

Jeremy's enthusiasm for earning his own living in the clubs and bars of nearby towns began to dwindle. He decided to bow to his parents' wishes and go back to work on the farm alongside Nevill. Jeremy and his father maintained a reasonably good relationship but there was still tension between him and his mother. June disapproved strongly of Julie staying at the Goldhanger cottage and several times complained to her son about his relationship with 'that harlot'. Jeremy kept the peace by simply refusing to speak to his mother. Instead he spent a lot of time in Colchester at the home of Julie's mother, and soon began to call her 'Mummy'.

As a farm worker, Jeremy earned less than £100 per week – spending money which did not go far for a young man with his tastes in gourmet food and champagne. But his parents had paid for his cottage, bought him a car, given him a third share in a forty-eight-acre field and also allowed him an eight per cent stake in the family caravan site at Osea Bay. In return for his position as a director of the company, Jeremy was expected to learn the business and help run the site. Yet the young man was still dissatisfied, as one of his friends remembered: 'He wanted a flat in London, he wanted to go out drinking, take people out to dinner, go abroad. He hated having to run to his parents every time he wanted some extra cash.'

Jeremy's only consolation was to plunge into a hectic nightlife, worlds removed from the hard-working regime of White House Farm. He was part of a group of thrill-seekers whose exploits were regarded as outrageous in the quiet towns of Chelmsford and Colchester.

'Anything went with that crowd,' claimed one of his girlfriends, Anji Greaves. 'They were into group sex. There were three-in-a-bed romps, some lesbianism and that sort of thing. Some of their parties were just orgies where they all piled in. Jeremy liked a joint and there was a lot of cocaine about.'

Jeremy liked to command the attention of his peers and began to dress in outrageous outfits – skin-tight trousers, billowing silk shirts and Chinese slippers – to excite comment. He added make-up to the ensemble, using eyeliner and mascara and the occasional touch of lipstick. The ever-patient Julie took it all in her stride. She thought his use of make-up and his occasional adventures in women's clothing were nothing out of the ordinary.

He found Essex pretty dull and mocked himself as 'a provincial labourer'. He wanted to be in London away from the muck and toil of the farmyard and lived for his forays to London nightclubs, where he tried to shock his crowd with wild antics. 'He was so pretty he used to get a lot of attention,' recalled a friend. 'One night he went down to Stringfellow's. He was messing around, mock-fighting and hugging. All Jeremy did was go round asking the cocktail waitresses where to get some cocaine, just to impress.'

Despite his protestations, Jeremy found consolation in the humdrum atmosphere of Essex where he could make a real impression on the locals. People were shocked or titillated by his camp behaviour and treated him with some regard. In London there were hundreds of young men like Jeremy trying to make an impact, but in Colchester there were very few and he quickly became notorious.

The relationship between Jeremy and Julie began to cool. Julie started her teaching course at Goldsmith's College and spent several nights a week at a south London flat she shared with friends. Jeremy took the opportunity to go back to his old ways and soon there was a steady procession of women in and out of the little cottage in Goldhanger. His philandering had some unpleasant consequences: it was not long before Jeremy was forced to seek treatment after contracting a form of the herpes virus, but this did little to halt his stream of conquests.

His only other form of amusement was tending a healthy number of cannabis plants which he grew in the back garden of the cottage. Jeremy smoked dope rather than cigarettes and occasionally made buying trips to the Continent, smuggling back small quantities of the drug. He developed a reputation in the area as someone who could be relied upon to provide cannabis for parties. Sometimes he would make the short journey to London, where he could always be certain of scoring whatever drugs he wanted. On these trips he would stay either with Julie or with his sister Sheila, now settled in a central London flat.

4

The gorgeous girls

The divorce was finalised and Sheila was on her own.

It was the very first time in her life that she had been completely responsible for herself. As a girl she had either been dominated by her mother or subject to the strict regime of a boarding school. Either way, independence had not been encouraged, and someone else had always made decisions for her. There had been a brief spell of flat-sharing with girlfriends after leaving home, but in no time at all she and Colin had been living together, and then there was the wedding and the babies. Now it was just Sheila and the boys.

Sheila may have been living alone, but her family and friends ensured she had a great deal of support, both practical and emotional. Her home had been paid for by Nevill and June. They described it as the 'family flat', but there was no question that it belonged to Sheila and the twins. Although relations with June fluctuated, depending on the moods of both mother and daughter, Nevill was still a tower of strength. He could be rung at any time, day or night. Sheila was especially fond of phoning him in the evening, after the twins had been put to bed, when they would talk for hours. For more immediate comfort there was Colin, who could still be relied on to help out in a crisis. His flat in Kilburn was only a short distance from Sheila's more spacious apartment.

Maida Vale and St John's Wood are home to many aspiring models and actresses. Street after street of well-kept nineteenth-century houses cluster around the pretty Grand Union Canal and a stretch of park, the prosaically named Paddington Recreation Ground. The large houses are almost all converted into flats – not nearly as expensive as nearby Hampstead but sufficiently pricey to give the whole area a well-cared-for appearance. Morshead Mansions is an imposing red-brick block of flats in a prime position, directly overlooking the park. Sheila and the twins settled in Flat 2, on the ground floor.

The flat was fairly large, with a dining room, kitchen and bathroom. Sheila had her own bedroom, the twins shared a room large enough to contain two single beds and the small study was converted into a brightly coloured playroom. The flat was always kept in immaculate condition. Her friends remember that Sheila never neglected the housework, no matter what chaos was ensuing in her personal life.

At twenty-four, Sheila found herself part of a circle of young women, all with a great deal in common. They were young and pretty – so pretty, in fact, that almost all of them had modelled or worked for the glamour industry in one capacity or another; some had even managed to break into the world of acting. They all had children and, almost without exception, they all had traumatic relationships.

Kirstie, a beautiful American model who had worked for New York's prestigious Ford agency, was one of the first women to befriend 'Bambi', as Sheila still liked to be known. 'I got to know Bambi several years before the murders. I met her when I was enrolling my daughter in the local primary school, Robinsfield, in St John's Wood. She used to take the little boys, the twins, over to the nearby Paddington Recreation Ground and I would go there with Lorna, my daughter. Eventually we got talking and we talked about everything,' remembered Kirstie.

The energetic, tawny-haired American girl still had lots of friends in the fashion world and Bambi gradually joined the crowd. Her own brief modelling career made her feel at ease in the group, alongside other young women who were struggling with shaky relationships and growing children and, all too often, insufficient funds.

A pattern of sorts emerged over the following weeks and months. Mornings were spent cleaning, shopping and generally drifting around – perhaps even recovering from the night before. Some time after lunch the children would be rounded up, woken from naps or collected from nursery school, and one by one, the little family troupes would collect in the park.

Sonja, a stunning Danish model whose striking blonde good looks regularly appeared on the cover of *Vogue* and other international fashion magazines at that time, remembered many of the quiet afternoons. 'I got to know Sheila, or Bambi as we all called her, through a girlfriend of mine who lived in the same area and, like me, was a model and had a young child. Bambi's twin boys were the same age as my little boy. We both used to take our children to a little park in Maida Vale which had a paddling pool where the boys could play. We would sit on a bench and watch the children and talk about what was happening in our lives and things like that.'

Several of the girls shared the role of confidante to Bambi. It became clear to all of them that the pretty young divorcee had problems with her life that she could not solve by herself. Bambi found it difficult to make the day-to-day decisions that most people take for granted. She needed constant reassurance and encouragement that she was doing the right thing.

'I met Bambi because her sons went to nursery school with my daughter, Amber. We were introduced by one of the other mums and after that she used to seek me out. She was a very insecure girl, very nervous about nearly everything in her life,' said Jilly, a vivacious young actress and model. 'She used to ask my advice about every little thing. I think she used me as a sort of role model – she wanted to know what to wear and I used to advise her on her make-up and her hairstyle. Although she had been a model herself, she needed to be reminded to make an effort with her clothes and make-up. She had shoulder-length dark hair that used to get straggly and every so often I would have to tell her, "Bambi, your hair is in rat's-tails, get it cut," and she would.'

Jilly, like several of Sheila's girlfriends, quickly realised that the attractive young woman had more trouble coping with life than the rest of the crowd. Much as she may have resented her mother's interference and sought to break free from Colin's affectionate guidance, Sheila did need someone watching over her. But her new circle of friends had their own worries to sort out and found it impossible to give Sheila the full-time attention she craved.

'I have to say that I backed away from her a bit. She was clingy, always desperate for help and desperate to talk. She really, really wanted to find the right man. It was, I think, a bit of an identity crisis. I don't think she knew who she was or what she was doing, she needed other people to tell her. She tended to latch on to you and it could be stifling,' said Jilly.

Most of the girls spent a great part of the day gossiping, spinning dreams for the future over bottomless cups of coffee and chains of cigarettes, but, to the more observant, Sheila's chatter had a desperate edge to it. 'She seemed to want to confide all the time,' said Sonja. 'It was impossible to have a straightforward conversation. I always had the impression that she wasn't simply talking to me, she was confiding, asking my advice, using me as a surrogate mother. I think she was like this quite a lot, needing people to look up to.'

Sheila made it clear to her friends that the precarious state of her personal equilibrium stemmed largely from her peculiar relationship with June. She was morbidly sensitive to any hint of disapproval from her mother. It was a theme she reverted to constantly: 'She talked a lot about her mother and her background,' said Sonja. 'She told me that she and her mother didn't get on. Sheila told me many times that she could not talk to her mother at all, that there was no form of communication between them. She said her mother was never happy with her or with what she did.'

The girls helped each other out during the day, collecting the children from nursery schools, babysitting for the lucky few who had modelling assignments, even picking up the odd bit of shopping for each other. Most weeks there would be a visit to their favourite clairvoyant, in an attempt to make some sense of their confused lives. Before long, the friendships which began in the sunny afternoons in the park grew stronger. The children enjoyed an endless round of parties – impromptu ones around a paddling pool in one of the back gardens, or grander affairs complete with fancy dress at Christmas. On the twins' birthday Sheila took her turn to open the ground-floor flat to a collection of exuberant under-tens, the mums supervising riotous games and providing sandwiches, cakes and crisps.

The adults had their parties too. But the games they played were not quite as innocent. 'There were a lot of drugs going around – heroin, coke, you name it,' said one regular partygoer. 'That was in the early eighties when there didn't seem to be the same sort of stigma attached to cocaine that there is nowadays. Everyone used it. All the models did. You'd go to a party and there would be cigarettes, booze and lines of coke on the table. I'd go for the first two, but I never touched cocaine although it didn't bother me if other people snorted it. I know Bambi tried it.'

Sheila also attended more lavish parties hosted by wealthy foreign businessmen, whom some of the girls occasionally dated. To an outsider, it must have appeared a glamorous scene – parties held in luxurious homes in an exclusive area of London, filled with models, actresses, drink and drugs. Sheila was just one of half a dozen young women for whom the parties were a high point in their otherwise humdrum lives. She would spend hours getting ready for these special occasions and took special care with her long nails, which were always well-manicured and painted red.

For Sheila, the parties provided the best chance she had of meeting new people, especially new men. It should have been easy for a woman as attractive as the former Mrs Caffell to find boyfriends. But, as one of the partygoers soon realised, a lot of unhappiness was hidden behind the glossy smiles of her companions: 'God, they were a desperately sad lot, those gorgeous girls. It dawned on me pretty quickly how awful the set-up was. At first, I admit, it was a bit intimidating. I'd go to parties that were filled with these beautiful, beautiful women, just gorgeous – and they were a mess. Bambi was perhaps about the worst of the lot,' said Caroline, a member of the group.

'They always – and I mean always – had the most disgusting men you can imagine as boyfriends. The sort of men that no normal girl would even want to be in the same room with. Pathetic, balding, short, squat, ignorant men. Men who these poor little girls relied upon.'

These were the girls whose faces beamed out from magazine pages all over the country, girls who could walk into a fashionable restaurant or bar and have the attention of every man in the place. Seeing photographs of them modelling clothes or advertising products, most women would feel envious of the exciting lives and terrific boyfriends these gorgeous girls must have. Yet in reality, few of them achieved any kind of real happiness or security with their partners. All too often the men they encountered were married or only interested in having an attractive woman draped on their arm. There were decent men around, but, as Bambi quickly discovered, parties and nightclubs did not go hand-in-hand with the kind of man who was happy to maintain a stable relationship, run a household and bring up a family. Dependable partners became harder to find. The kind of man who gambled and drank into the early hours was not the kind of man who would be helping in the morning when the children had to be given their breakfast. But a strong dependency existed between the gorgeous girls and their inferior lovers.

'It worked liked this,' said one of the circle. 'There would be a girl like Bambi who was very sweet and very pretty. All her life she had been used to people getting to know her because of her looks. Decent men would be either intimidated or dismissive. It was left to the creeps, who were practically all pushing drugs, to fasten on to these girls. They would tell the girls they were ugly, they didn't like the way they looked, they were getting too old to model, that sort of thing – absolute shit. And of course the girls would think, "Hey, he really likes me. He doesn't care about the way I look, he likes me as a person." They really did fall for that, ridiculous though it may sound.'

'And the guys bullied the girls and humiliated them, treated them like trash and more or less pimped off them. Nearly all the girls had some wastrel boyfriend, whom they paid for and who always seemed to need money for a business deal or some project or other that would never work out. And these poor girls trembled in case they did anything wrong.'

It was a vicious circle. The girls became hooked on the hurtful criticism that passed as compassionate honesty and on the bullying reassurance of their partners. It was a technique particularly successful with girls who relied on their looks for their livelihood, playing as it did on their insecurities and their desire to be liked and admired.

'The girls were convinced that they were brainless idiots with no social skills, and these guys were quite happy to reinforce that. It kept the girls – their meal-tickets – under the thumb,' said Caroline. 'I would give dinner parties and invite these couples. The men would sit and talk and the girls would just sit and say nothing. I couldn't believe that these gorgeous girls who I had seen talking intelligently and with humour earlier in the day could be so frightened. They had been told they had nothing to say for themselves and they believed it. They would follow me into the kitchen in between courses because they were too scared to sit at the table and make conversation. It was so sad, because they were not stupid by any means. They were just scared.

'Well, Bambi was part of that scene. We used to call her "Bonkers Bambi" because we were all slightly mad at the

67

time, but she was that little bit more wild-eyed than everyone else.'

Almost by chance, Sheila had stumbled into a way of life that only increased her own instability. She had found some loyal friends, but none of them were sufficiently mature or free from problems to become the tower of strength that she desperately needed. It became all too tempting for the girls to use the readily available drugs as an antidote to their depressions. Caroline vividly remembered an incident which shocked her into the realisation of just how dangerous their fun and games had become.

'One of the girls had a boyfriend who was the "Mr Big" of the drug-dealing world in central London,' she said. 'One day they threw a party for their daughter; my kids went and Sheila's boys went to it. After my kids got home, my girlfriend rang in a panic asking whether the children had brought home a bag that wasn't theirs. I looked and couldn't find anything. Then she told me that a bag of heroin had gone missing. It had been in an open drawer in the room that the children were in. I was outraged. I mean, the kids could just have licked the bag and they would have been dead. I couldn't believe that the woman didn't realise what she had done. She couldn't understand the fuss I was making. I fell out with her over that.'

The girls were nearly all dissatisfied with their lives and their men, but they could do little about it. Away from the glamorous parties they were simply isolated young mums, trapped at home by their children and their lack of professional skills. Sheila still clung to the hope that her all-too-brief modelling career might be revitalised. This blind faith, which lasted for a couple of years, made her reluctant to entertain thoughts of another serious career. There was little that Sheila or her friends could do except talk about their problems and gradually the long afternoon chats became more personal.

'Bambi and I had a fair amount in common,' said Caroline. 'Our children were round about the same age. We both had broken marriages which had hurt a lot. She and I and a couple of other girlfriends had these chats that would turn into self-supporting sessions. We desperately tried to boost each other's egos. We'd say things like, "Oh, you're so gorgeous, you're bound to meet someone great soon." Or, "You shouldn't worry about your age, you could still get great modelling jobs." You know the sort of thing, trying to get our morale back together. It was a depressing time.'

As far as most of the girls were concerned a new man was the best boost their fragile egos could receive. Bambi was as anxious as her friends to meet Mr Right – and quickly. 'Like most of us, she was on the prowl. She was looking for men, mainly as a way of restoring her self-confidence, I think,' said one of her friends. 'Bambi did need a steady man around. She liked the attention of men very much. She responded to it; in fact, she was rather vulnerable to it because I think it made her feel more confident about herself.'

There was still Colin, who had been sweet and dependable during their marriage and was certainly an exemplary father to the boys. The divorced couple would often stroll through the park together while the twins played nearby. Colin made no secret of the fact that he still adored his former wife and was devoted to his twin sons, and many of Sheila's girlfriends believed it was only a matter of time before the couple were reunited. In reality, Colin had worked hard to rebuild his life without Sheila. He had a new girlfriend, and although he was supportive of his family, he was no longer on call twenty-four hours a day.

The more she thought about it, the more Sheila was forced to admit that she was not exactly sure what she wanted from her life. To some of her friends, Sheila expressed a longing for adventure, for a passionate, exciting affair far removed from her domestic life with Colin. 'I didn't think she and her ex-husband would get together again. He was a darling, but I don't think he and Bambi were that well suited,' observed another of her friends. 'He was sensitive and sweet, but I think Bambi needed a very strong man, she certainly seemed to admire the macho-man type. There were a few boyfriends around but she could never find the right one. It was a real shame. She needed the direction a steady man could have given her but she liked the domineering type.'

Sheila found that as modelling jobs became harder to get, the opportunities to meet the right sort of man grew more distant. Instead, the loosely knit circle of friends passed on partners to each other. 'When I first met Bambi she had been going out with my second husband,' said Kirstie. 'It had already ended. I knew he liked to play around and Bambi was one of several girls he had been seeing. I didn't hold it against her – she was a nice girl and wasn't trying to run off with him. She told me she never would have gone out with him if she had known me already. She also went out with David, my first husband, an Englishman living in New York. He nicknamed her "Pickles" and they had a really friendly, joky relationship. It was good fun, but he wasn't able to come over to London very often.

'I then introduced her to another of my friends, Derek. Bambi just wanted a nice rich man to look after her and I thought Derek would be perfect. But it didn't last. We did all stay good friends, though. She actually would have made a rich man a good wife when she had straightened herself out. She was an amazing cook, really great. She would make Lancashire hotpot, all these traditional English dishes. I remember her trying to teach me how to make tuna croquettes – that was another of her specialities.'

It was apparent to many of her friends that Sheila did not have the right temperament for playing the field. She was far too vulnerable to survive the emotional rough-and-tumble of the singles scene. Although there were occasional one-night stands, it was clear that for Bambi the ultimate goal was affection rather than sex. 'She did have quite a few boyfriends and seemed susceptible to those men who took the trouble to pay her attention. However, one of my friends, who had spent the whole evening chatting her up, took her home only to be told very firmly that he wasn't coming into the flat. She obviously didn't sleep with just anyone, and he was a very well-educated, good-looking guy,' said Caroline. 'But she ended up with some awful guy who hung around in seedy clubs and restaurants. He was married and it was one of those situations where there was never any question that he would leave his wife. I remember he was pretty horrible and I don't think he treated Bambi too well. She had quite a few boyfriends, but then again, who didn't? Sure, she was looking for someone or something, but then, in a way, we all were.'

Sheila may have been vulnerable in her private life but she took her responsibilities as a mother seriously and was very wary of possible mistakes she might make in the upbringing of the twins. Colin described her as a loving and dedicated mother and her friends believed she was extremely cautious with the little boys. 'She was awfully careful who she took home,' remembered one of her friends. 'She told me once that she didn't want the twins waking up to find strange men in the flat. She was very protective of them in that way.'

She did introduce some men to her sons, but she was careful to make sure that the meetings took place during the daytime and that the men concerned were more than just casual acquaintances. A boyfriend whom she occasionally dated remembered Bambi as a quiet girl whose life centred on the twins: 'She was devoted to her two boys and I really don't think she was interested in a promiscuous lifestyle,' he said. 'We went out a couple of times, for drinks or a meal. She was very pretty and very sweet, but we just weren't on the same wavelength, so our relationship did not go any further. But she was attractive and pleasant company.'

Freddie Emami, an Iranian businessman who described himself as Sheila's 'confidant', involved himself with the family, helping Sheila take the twins on outings whenever he could. 'I respected and loved her family very much,' he declared. 'I loved the twins like they were my own children. They were beautiful boys.'

However, one of Sheila's girlfriends sensed problems in the claustrophobic attention that the young mother lavished on her sons. 'The twins were gorgeous little boys. Very thin, very frail-looking with little arms and legs like matchsticks, but bright and lively,' she remembered. 'Bambi had a funny attitude towards them, though. I remember once the boys came up to her as we were sitting on a bench in the park and they clung on to her, saying. "Oh Mummy, we want to stay with you." I think they had been frightened by some other child. Bambi was quite annoyed. She sort of shrugged them off and said to me, "They're such wimps, they're such cowards. I wish they were tougher." I replied "Come on, Bambi, they're lovely as they are."

'The boys were very artistic. Apparently they were both great at painting and drawing even when they were very young. I knew their father was involved in art so I thought they probably got it from him. But Bambi seemed quite upset that they were artistic rather than like my son, who was a lot more rough than they were.'

Sheila made it clear that her boys would receive all the love she could give, in contrast to what she felt was her own affection-starved upbringing. To some of her friends, however, the attention lavished on the boys by their mother was not conducive to a healthy upbringing: 'The boys were weak children, but they were absolute darlings. They were delicate, very skinny, fairy-like. I had a funny

73

feeling that they might grow up to be gay, they had that sort of temperament,' said Jilly. 'I very often wondered if Bambi made them like that. She was always very nervous, very protective of them – "Are you all right? Be careful", that sort of thing. Little boys need a bit of rough-and-tumble; they need to be thrown around a bit and those two never were. Their father was lovely, but he was very sensitive as well and obviously wasn't going to toughen them up.'

Care of her sons was not the only problem facing Sheila. Her financial difficulties had been steadily growing worse and in the year preceding her death they became acute. Although the flat was paid for, she still had to keep herself and the boys on a small income. Colin contributed as much as he could afford, but even with his help Sheila found it difficult to manage. While she was not extravagant, she was not used to surviving on a strict budget. Colin had handled the finances during their marriage and as a teenager working in London she had been subsidised by her parents.

'She needed to work. She was on social security, which was pretty miserable. Her parents had bought her the flat, but there wasn't a lot of money around in the last year or two of her life,' said Jilly.

There was, unfortunately, no obvious way for Bambi to make money. Her modelling career had been short-lived and, despite her good looks, there was little chance of reviving it. 'She was a pretty girl who, like most of us, looked really good when she had her make-up on,' said Jilly. 'I don't think she modelled for very long – perhaps a year or two when she was in her teens – because she had the boys when she was twenty or twenty-one. She was not really slim enough to be a model after that; her figure was getting a little bit too heavy for that kind of work.'

Modelling is an over-subscribed field and Sheila, with the upbringing of the twins absorbing her time and energy, now found it impossible to get work. Fresher, younger faces were appearing daily on the fashion circuit, girls who had no responsibilities to prevent them accepting assignments at the drop of a hat and working anywhere at any time. Sheila could not give the commitment demanded and was eventually forced to abandon any hopes of re-entering the modelling world.

Aware of her predicament, Sheila's girlfriends rallied round and tried to help her out. But it was not easy as she did not have the temperament or the qualifications which would have made her a potentially good employee. 'One of her boyfriends and I tried to get her this receptionist job with British Telecom, but it didn't work out,' said Kirstie. 'She just couldn't make it through that kind of interview. She was a bit hazy about which direction to go in, although she thought that she would quite like to be a receptionist, and she would have been good, she was sweet and friendly and pretty. Not dynamic, but always really good-tempered.'

The girls' next port of call was a far cry from the staid, respectable atmosphere of a big company reception desk. Sheila finally found work at School Dinners, a notorious restaurant just off Baker Street in central London, much beloved by ex-public schoolboys, advertising executives and scurrilous Sunday newspapers. The attraction is not to be found on the menu, which features regulation school stodge, but rather in the young waitresses who, dressed in thigh-length gymslips, stockings and suspenders, will administer six of the best to the eager clients. Not surprisingly, the restaurant features regularly in scandal sheets as yet another famous diner is photographed rounding off a meal with a good hiding after failing to finish his prunes and custard.

'We both went to School Dinners for an interview, but I decided I didn't want to do it,' said Kirstie. 'Bambi lasted about a week. She took her own school hat for the job, a straw boater that she used to wear at school and had always kept. She looked so cute in that uniform the waitresses wore.'

Sheila was embarrassed by her stint at School Dinners and mentioned it to only a few friends. 'She said. "It was awful, but what could I do? You've got to pay the bills,"' said Sonja. 'She didn't last long. It just wasn't her kind of thing.'

But money worries soon forced Sheila into an escapade that made her week at School Dinners look like child's play. It was something that she would regret almost immediately although the greatest harm to her reputation would come after her death.

It started one summer's day, when Sheila popped round to see a girlfriend to talk about a special favour. The woman thought it would be the usual request for last-minute babysitting that was made frequently in the circle of friends. But that was not what Sheila had in mind. Instead, Sheila asked if she could 'borrow' her girlfriend's garden for a photographic shoot – a nude photographic shoot.

'They were supposed to be nude pictures that would be tasteful. They were taken by a photographer who was a freelance – I think he was Australian. He was travelling around and Bambi had met up with him and somehow or other they had decided that she would do some nude shots for money. He was going to sell them to *Mayfair* or *Penthouse*, one of the more respectable nudie magazines,' recalled her friend.

'Bambi asked me if she could use my garden for the shoot. She was absolutely desperate. "Please could I do this?" she asked. "It would be perfect to take some pictures in the pool." She said that most of the shots would be of her wearing a mini-skirt or something like that. I didn't really want it happening at my house at all, but Bambi said she was desperate to do it, she really needed the money.

'I helped her by doing her make-up for the shots. Some were in the pool, some were just in the garden. I had hung sheets all round the garden so no one was aware of what was going on and I remember thinking, "God, I hope the neighbours don't see this." I went indoors once the photographing began. I do remember that the photographer brought a paddling pool and gave it to my daughter.

'I think Bambi genuinely didn't realise that the pictures would be quite as explicit as they turned out to be. I'm sure the photographer used a zoom lens and she didn't know just how close the close-ups were.'

When Sheila finally saw the results of that sunny afternoon her reaction was one of absolute horror. She panicked and demanded the immediate return of the photographs before they were published. Stricken with

77

fear and guilt, Sheila poured out her story to a sympathetic friend. 'She was really, really ashamed when she saw those pictures printed. She got hold of me straight away and said, "Oh, my God, the pictures! They are just terrible!"' recalled Jilly. 'She said she had refused to let the photographer sell them or have them published anywhere. I don't know what the arrangements were, whether she had the negatives or just the prints. It was awful for her because it was just a one-off. There was nothing lurid about Bambi. I didn't hear that she ever did any more and I'm sure she had never done anything like that before.'

Sheila gained nothing from the incident but a guilty conscience which she sought to appease by confessing the escapade to several of the gorgeous girls in Maida Vale. Gradually her friends gained an insight into what had prompted the young woman to take what appeared to be such an uncharacteristic step.

'She did it strictly to get money. I think it all went back to Bambi's uneasy relationship with her parents,' claimed a friend. 'I think she felt her father in particular was disappointed in her. Not angry, just disappointed that she hadn't done more in her life. He wanted her to make something of herself. I think that's why she was so keen on trying to get a job – apart from the fact that she had no money – it was to show her father she was managing.'

Sheila made it clear that she was horrified by the pictures but what they actually showed remains a mystery. Her friends are convinced that they were 'tastetul' pictures that went a bit too far and caught Sheila unawares showing more of her body than she intended. But a later account of the photographs by Jeremy Bamber tells of an altogether more lurid scenario. He described finding pictures of his sister caressing a 'huge' vibrator in suggestive poses which could only have been shot with Sheila's knowledge and cooperation. Perhaps Sheila, impressionable as ever, did allow herself to be persuaded to spice up the shots but hastily blocked their publication when she saw the pictures and fully realised what she had done.

A further twist to the tale is added by a former schoolfriend of Jeremy Bamber's, who remembers his classmate proudly displaying a topless photograph of his pretty sister, years before the nude session took place. Jeremy boasted about his sister's career as a model and told his jealous chums that she did not pose for girlie magazines as her ambition was to be a serious fashion model.

That snapshot may have been a one-off, taken by or for a boyfriend, and then stolen by a thrill-seeking schoolboy. No other pictures have emerged to indicate that Sheila ever took part in nude sessions during her modelling career.

The Maida Vale photographic shoot marked a significant decline in Sheila's fortunes and in her morale. The former model who had been sent to boarding school and an expensive Swiss Cottage college was forced to take on cleaning jobs to earn some extra cash. The happy atmosphere of Morshead Mansions disintegrated as Sheila's emotional stability once more began to crumble.

The beginning of 1985 saw Sheila slipping back into that twilight world of nervous tension and paranoia which had immersed her two years previously. Her temper was erratic and she began to have violent outbursts, screaming so

79

loudly that other residents were woken up by the noise. Her nearest neighbour rushed to help, but found Sheila alone apart from the twins and clearly distraught, shouting and screaming.

These terror attacks struck Sheila again and again, usually in the early hours of the morning. Her boyfriend, Freddie Emami, was sometimes on hand to calm her down, but all too often the shouting fits turned into violence. During one terrible session Sheila repeatedly banged her head against the wall. Even more disturbing were the occasions when Sheila turned on her friends. 'She became like someone possessed, ranting, raving and striking the wall with her fist,' said Emami. 'I became extremely concerned for my own safety.'

The only calming influence was Nevill Bamber. When she was feeling particularly desperate, Sheila would phone her father and talk for hours about her fears. Her old thoughts about the power of the Devil had returned with a vengeance. She was convinced that the twins and even Freddie were evil and trying to take her over.

Nevill persuaded his unhappy daughter to continue her counselling sessions, in the hope that her erratic behaviour was the result of a psychological disturbance which could be resolved through therapy. Sheila even stayed at White House Farm for a brief spell, and both Nevill and June realised that the situation was critical. Eventually Sheila's Harley Street psychiatrist was forced to conclude that she needed medical treatment as well as counselling. The only solution was to readmit her to hospital quickly as another nervous breakdown was imminent.

In March 1985 Sheila returned to St Andrew's hospital in Northampton where she had been treated two years earlier. Her admittance was traumatic; she refused to be examined by doctors, claiming that they were trying to poison her. But once inside, she seemed to respond very well to the treatment and began to make a rapid recovery free from the responsibilities and worries of her daily life. Colin had taken the boys for six months and kept an eye on the flat for her.

Within two months Sheila was sufficiently recovered to leave hospital. She was given a prescription for sedatives and also sleeping pills for the long, torturous nights. She surprised friends by declaring that during her time in hospital she had developed religious beliefs.

'I remember she was getting into religion when I last saw her, which must have been a couple of months before she died,' recalled one of her boyfriends. 'It was just local Church of England stuff, but I was surprised about that. I had no idea she came from a religious family because she didn't like to talk about her parents.'

Several of Sheila's friends were extremely worried by this new enthusiasm. Those who knew something of her background felt that Sheila was reverting to the troubled days of her adolescence, when the teenager struggled with the concept of good and evil. Religion had formerly proved to be a powerful and disturbing force in the lives of both Sheila and her mother, and it soon became apparent that this pattern would be repeated.

After leaving hospital, Sheila recuperated at White House Farm with her parents before returning to the more hectic pace of London. It was not the happiest place for her convalescence. The atmosphere was fraught and Sheila criticised her mother repeatedly, accusing her of losing her soul and neglecting her religion. There was relief on both sides when Sheila returned to Maida Vale, but the move did little to alleviate the bitterness she now freely expressed towards her parents.

'She was quite hard to cope with in those last few months. I knew she wasn't well and there was something about her that was a bit strange,' recalled Sonja. 'One day in the park she said to me, "I have been ill, you know. I went to the country to recover and they sent me to a hospital to get better." She was angry at her parents' attitude towards her.'

Sheila resented her mother's simplistic approach to the psychological crisis she had undergone. 'My mother thinks my difficulties can all be solved with this remedy or that remedy, just like taking medicine,' she complained. 'It's as if I was a problem that could be easily solved by being sent here or there. She doesn't want to listen to anything else.'

Sheila's friends felt the young woman had changed greatly during the first six months of 1985. Gone was the anxious, sweet personality and in its place was a driven, tormented creature. A friend described her state of mind: 'At that point she was even more distant than usual. She seemed as if she had been very ill. She was quite frail and I realised that the illness she had talked about was some sort of mental trouble. I remember she called me again about a month before she died. She wanted to see me and I was busy. Then, after the murders, I felt so guilty, of course.

She had wanted to talk to me and I hadn't had time for her.'

Before leaving for London, Sheila had already agreed to return almost immediately to White House Farm. The boys were due to go on holiday to Norway with Colin and Nevill and June wanted to see their grandsons before the trip. It was an unfortunate decision, given Sheila's unpredictable moods and the tension which was liable to erupt between mother and daughter at any moment. Nevertheless, Colin called for them early one morning in August and the family were driven for the last time down to White House farm.

5

The morning after
the night before

The realisation that something was badly amiss at White House Farm that morning began to filter through the surrounding countryside.

At the hub of the small, old-fashioned village of Tolleshunt D'Arcy are two pubs, The Queen's Head and The Red Lion, a post office, a tiny general store and the Bambers' church, St Nicholas. The body of the village has made few concessions to the changing years and the heart of the village is still firmly rooted in the land.

A handful of locals noticed a police car stationed in the village and it was casually remarked that there seemed to be a spot of bother at the farm. Perhaps someone had been caught poaching. By midday, most people realised that something serious had happened. The traffic through the village was unusually heavy. Cars crammed with newspaper reporters and estate wagons full of television crews circled around the centre of the village asking directions for White House Farm from bemused passers-by. Before long little groups began to move towards the outskirts of the village, pulled along by the feeling that something was happening, something was terribly wrong.

A police roadblock was hastily set up at one end of Pages Lane. Just before lunchtime a plain white undertaker's van was allowed through the cordon and down the private road. Half an hour later it made a slow return, taking its ghastly cargo of five bodies to the mortuary at Chelmsford and Essex Hospital.

The police were tight-lipped, refusing to answer any questions from the villagers or the rapidly growing crowd of journalists. There was great confusion about what had actually happened As rumour spread through the village the police had to hold back a distraught member of the Foakes family, whose parents lived in the tied cottages halfway down Pages Lane. He had rushed to the roadblock after hearing that it was his own family who had been murdered. But Len Foakes, who had worked at White House Farm for many years, and his wife Dorothy had heard nothing untoward from White House Farm during the night until they were woken by the noise of the police cars streaming past their home.

Back at headquarters, the Essex police reacted with surprise to the amount of interest the media were taking in the affair. Journalists, desperate for more information, found their inquiries were treated with indifference.

'The police had a very odd attitude,' said one of the newsmen. 'I can almost say they couldn't care less. I had

Jeremy Bamber (*Rex Features*)

Sheila Caffell (*Solo Syndication*)

The Caffell twins, Nicholas and Daniel (*Syndication International*)

Nevill and June Bamber (*Anglia Press Agency*)

had a call about the killings and I immediately telephoned the police spokesman to ask what had happened and to get an official comment. He said to me, "Oh, it's a domestic incident, you won't be bothered with this." Well, I know the press and the police have different priorities, but even so I was amazed. I said: "Five bodies and you think we won't be bothered, are you joking?" But that was how they saw it. As far as they were concerned, it was a family thing and it was all sorted out. They just couldn't understand the interest.'

Others felt that the police reaction was admirably low-key and controlled, indicating that the mopping-up operation was orderly and thorough. Word did eventually begin to seep through from behind the scenes and favoured journalists were given an unattributed briefing about the tragedy. They were told it was a family tragedy. Grandmother June Bamber had gone crazy, shooting her husband, daughter and grandsons before killing herself.

The officer whispered that there were five bodies and that no one else was being sought in connection with the crime – that meant four murders and a suicide. June Bamber was a religious fanatic who had gone off her rocker, grabbed a gun and killed everyone before turning the gun on herself.

It was only a tip-off, but it had come straight from the scene of the crime and the police were almost casual in their confidence that everything was under control. The stories were assembled and ready to go when one of the press group raced in with a tale which flatly contradicted the version they had already been given.

'I only found out by chance that the police had changed their minds about who did the murders,' recalled one of the newsmen. 'A local informant of mine was due to meet a detective for lunch that very day – the officer was organising one of those Operation Raleigh ventures for young people and my contact was helping with the publicity for it. He thought the detective probably wouldn't turn up for the lunch because he had been at the scene of the murders. But he did turn up, and the only thing he wanted to talk about was Operation Raleigh. He wasn't bothered with the murders, they had been cleared up.

'It was only through this lunch that we found out that the police thought Bambi was the murderer. The detective casually let it drop that Bambi had done it. He made some sort of comment that, oh yes, it was the daughter, of course; she had gone mad and slaughtered everyone. Of course my bloke dashed from the table and phoned me straight away, and when he returned the detective was still sitting there wanting to talk about Operation Raleigh.'

Eventually, the confused journalists managed to get official confirmation – the killer was not June Bamber, but her adopted daughter Sheila, known to her friends as Bambi.

At White House Farm the investigative team were sweeping quickly through their work. It was the bloodiest scene any of them had ever encountered, but the officers were convinced that the case was not complex. It was an extreme and tragic example of what can happen when family tensions explode.

88

Their interpretation of the carnage within White House Farm corresponded to the tale poured out during the siege by Jeremy Bamber. Sheila had evidently been pushed over the edge of her sanity. She had slaughtered her family and then turned the .22 semi-automatic rifle on herself. There was no need to look elsewhere and Chief Inspector Terry Gibbons, the head of Witham station, was able to announce that the police were not looking for anyone else in connection with the offences.

Yet the calm assurance of the chief inspector belied some peculiar scenes at the village police station. Away from the keen ears of the clamouring press, the detectives convened a conference to verify their findings at White House Farm. A couple of officers voiced concerns over Sheila's suicide, but these were swept away by the detectives in charge of the case. One of the senior officers made the men form a circle while he rolled on the floor of the station with a broom handle under his chin to demonstrate Sheila's last moments.

'He was saying "This is how she did it, just like this,"' said one officer. 'Meanwhile the cream of the Essex police force was gathered round in this room watching.'

The police were relieved to have got a 'result' so quickly. Multiple murders are rare and none of the officers had ever dealt with such a tragedy. The scene which greeted them when they finally burst into the farmhouse tallied with the scenario Jeremy had painted, and although the sheer scale of the violence had taken everyone by surprise it took little time to piece together what had happened.

Before the day was out and before the bodies had even been identified, the police had given an extensive off-the-record briefing to local journalists. The police theory was faithfully reported: Sheila had killed her mother in the master bedroom, her sons in their bedroom and shot her father after he had made a phone call to his son. Sheila had then returned to the master bedroom where she turned the gun on herself.

The bodies were identified later in the day by Julie Mugford, Jeremy's dark-haired girlfriend. She volunteered for the task, much to the amazement of detectives, who warned her that she would face a very upsetting sight. It was a brave action which spared the distraught relatives further agony. Later a mutual friend of Julie and Jeremy explained that the young woman had carried out the gruesome viewing partly through a belief in her own psychic powers. Julie was convinced she could communicate spiritually with the dead Sheila about the events of that last night in White House Farm.

Jeremy told police he could not bear to go to the mortuary. He urged Julie to go, reminding her that he needed to visit his accountant and bank manager about family finances as soon as possible. The young woman returned in a state of shock. 'Jeremy said he couldn't face it, anyway he insisted he must see his accountant about the money that was coming to him. I volunteered to go to the mortuary, not only to save him, but to convince myself that this had really happened. I don't think I really believed it until I saw those five dead bodies,' she said.

Her action also lifted the burden of identification from

Colin Caffell. He was devastated by the tragedy and police feared that he would break down completely if he saw the pathetic remains in the mortuary.

In a further statement on the evening of 7 August, police declared that drug tests would be carried out on Sheila's body. The inference was clear: Sheila must have been under the influence of drugs when she carried out the killings. It explained how the young mother could have killed her own little boys in such a savage fashion. Her sense of right and wrong, her responsibility for the two little boys had evidently been swept away by narcotics.

The speedy conclusion of the case was cause for special pride at Witham Police Station. Several of the area's top police officers were away from duty, on holiday or on training courses, but the local force had got on with the job and the top brass were pleased everything was in hand. The constabulary were still smarting from their failure to catch the murderer of Diane Jones, the wife of a local doctor, and they had received a tremendous amount of bad press. A straightforward open-and-shut case like the Bamber murders would prove that the Essex force had everything under control.

As the forensic team rattled through the bloody farmhouse, police in London called at the Kilburn home of Colin Caffell to take a statement about his former wife. Colin had driven his family to White House Farm only the day before the murders. He was due to return at the end of the week to take the boys on holiday to Norway. Officers made it clear to Colin from the outset that Sheila was responsible for the tragedy, information which he found incredible. Over and over again he protested that Sheila would not have the capacity to act in such a way; he found it almost impossible to come to terms with the violence the police described to him.

The massacre was headline news by the end of the day and came as a complete shock to anyone who knew the Bamber family. Sheila's girlfriends were stunned by the story that Bambi had shot her family. The word spread from flat to flat around Maida Vale and St John's Wood as details of the tragedy unfolded. One of Sheila's close friends remembered that day. 'As soon as we heard the news the phones started ringing and all of us kept saying, "Oh God, the signs must have been there and we ignored them. That's terrible, we just didn't notice." We all thought Bambi was a bit mad, but it was such a shock to hear she had killed all those people. But we all thought, yes, she had been upset recently.'

Some of them learned the news the following day, over their breakfast and morning newspaper. The details beginning to emerge were gruesome, but at least a handful of Sheila's friends felt astounded that the gentle, dreamy divorcee could have been driven to such lengths. 'I was horrified when I heard about the murders, it was so hard to believe,' said Sonja. 'I knew that Sheila wasn't happy but I felt she wouldn't have done something like that. There was no violence in her, none at all. She could have flipped out in other ways but not in a violent way. We were all in a state of shock. It was terrible.'

While relatives, friends and villagers struggled to come to terms with the killings, the police forged ahead with clearing up the investigation. The term was apt, for within days bloodstained carpets, furniture and clothing had been stripped out of the beautiful old farmhouse and destroyed by the police. Splashes of blood were cleaned off the walls and floors and all the paintwork was thoroughly scrubbed 'in case it upset the relatives', said one of the officers at the scene.

Jeremy was anxious that the house should be cleaned up as quickly as possible and it was at his insistence that the police burned the soiled mattresses, chairs and carpets. He asked them to make a special effort to remove all traces of the murders, to lessen the trauma when he visited the house. Jeremy made sure that all the windows and doors were flung wide open in an attempt to remove the heavy smell of death which clung to the house in the August warmth.

A few days after the murders, Jeremy visited his family home again. The young man was known to only a few people in Tolleshunt D'Arcy: his face was familiar, but he had never spent much time at home and rarely socialised in the village. Although his own cottage was scarcely four miles away, Jeremy was known by reputation only and the word was that he was a reckless and arrogant young man. Now, however, he had the sympathy of everyone in the tiny village.

Jeremy toured the farmhouse, scribbling a thorough inventory of its contents into a little pocket book and sifting through documents and bills. Returning to his own cottage in nearby Goldhanger he started to make arrangements to sell some of the family silver through Sotheby's, the famous London auctioneers. He also called in valuers to assess the antiques that his parents had collected. There was a fair number of ornaments, some good pieces of silver and a couple of heirlooms such as an antique clock. Several more items were put up for sale and he took care to reinsure the remainder.

Jeremy managed to upset his aunt, Pamela Boutflour, when she came to offer her condolences shortly after the bodies had been discovered. Mrs Boutflour asked if she could take a keepsake of jewellery from the house in memory of her dead sister, June. Jeremy refused to let her into the house and would not agree to remove anything from it. Mrs Boutflour offered her help in tidying up the house and sorting out the estate, but Jeremy did not entertain his aunt's offer for a moment. All that was his concern now, he pointed out, and it was too soon to decide what would be done with any property left by his parents.

Jeremy's behaviour may have troubled his relatives but the two Bamber children, educated away from the farm, had never been close to the rest of the family. Both Sheila and Jeremy had become even more of a mystery to the sedate Essex farmers as they grew up. The family were hurt by Jeremy's brusque manner towards them and, worse still, found themselves embarrassed by his frequent and noisy displays of grief in the days following the tragedy.

Observers had already noticed Jeremy's propensity to break down in public. They had also noticed the attentiveness of the ever-present Kiwi, Brett Collins, and drew their own conclusions. 'Bamber was a bit over the top,' recalled

94

one of the newsmen. 'But to be honest, everyone got the impression very quickly that he was a bit of a poof and I put his very emotional behaviour down to that. His New Zealand pal, Brett Collins, was around most of the time and the two looked like they were a couple. I remember going to Bamber's cottage to try to talk with him on the morning after the murders. Jeremy was leaning on a wall outside the back door, sobbing and moaning so loudly that I could hear him as soon as I got out of my car. He was being looked after by Detective Sergeant Jones, who was obviously having a weary time of it. Bamber was hustled indoors, still wailing, and Jones turned to me, as he shut the back door, and gave me a big wink.'

To most people, however, Jeremy remained an enigma. The police reported that the surviving member of the Bamber family was too distressed to talk about the killings. After much persuasion Jeremy emerged briefly from his Goldhanger cottage to tell reporters they would get the full story at the inquest.

Even less could be gleaned about Jeremy's parents. Nevill and June were routinely described as 'upright' or 'pillars of the community'. Everyone knew them, but no one could talk about them with any real depth. Instead, the full glare of publicity fell on Sheila, and the spotlight was harsh. BERSERK MOTHER BLASTS FAMILY, TOP MODEL MASSACRES HER FAMILY, DERANGED MOTHER RUNS AMOK WITH RIFLE screamed the headlines. Sheila was described as a 'frenzied woman ', a 'depressed divorcee' and was suspected by police of 'having a brainstorm' before the shootings.

All the stories mentioned her recent nervous breakdown and stressed that the involvement of drugs was strongly suspected. In no time at all, Sheila was established as a neurotic, drug-addicted socialite in the public consciousness.

No attempt was made to tone down the viciousness of the attacks on the dead woman by journalists who were taking their lead from the Essex police force. During the days immediately following the murders the police continued to highlight drugs as the catalyst that could have triggered the shootings. 'Drugs have been suggested as a possible cause of Sheila Bamber's violent outburst and we shall be investigating,' said a police spokesman.

By the time Sheila's former husband Colin Caffell spoke publicly, several days after the tragedy, it was too late to add a touch of sanity to the portrayal of Sheila or to put forward a more considered view of her character. Colin Caffell had been assured by the police that his former wife had murdered the sons he loved in the most brutal fashion, but his words were astounding in their kindness and compassion. He described Sheila as 'a beautiful and tragic woman and the loving and dedicated mother of my twin sons.

'No mother could have loved her children more. Nothing was more precious to her than Nicholas and Daniel. Yet she was a naive and frightened child herself. I don't think anyone could imagine the pain and anguish she suffered on that dreadful night.'

Colin was the only person in those early days who struggled to find a merciful explanation for his former wife's murderous rampage. He said that she had been treated for depression after the break-up of their marriage. 'She had been through a very difficult and confused time recently. The world frightened her but she tried to cover this up and only those closest to her know how lonely and vulnerable Sheila was.'

Colin's statement triggered more affectionate support for the dead model. Freddie Emami, whom Sheila had been dating shortly before her death, also tried to set the record straight by going to Harrow Road Police Station in west London to volunteer a statement. The Metropolitan police took him across the county border to their colleagues in Epping, where Emami described Sheila's state of mind prior to the murders.

'Sheila was recovering from a nervous breakdown and was on a prescription from the hospital. I can only assume she had a relapse and snapped to have done this terrible thing as she loved her twins very much. She was no junkie,' he insisted. Privately, Freddie said he was furious at the suggestions that Sheila was heavily into the drugs scene. He also scotched the idea, suggested by Jeremy and repeated to the press by the police, that Sheila had gone to White House Farm for a 'council of war' over the welfare of the children.

'There was never any danger of them being taken away,' he said. 'I respected and loved her family very much. I loved the twins like they were my own children, they were beautiful boys.'

These testaments of faith fell on deaf ears. Few people were interested in the facts that lay behind the headlines.

MURDER AT WHITE HOUSE FARM

They certainly did not penetrate the consciousness of the Essex police, who were almost ready to wrap up the Bamber case.

98

6
Amateur detectives

On 14 August 1984, just one week after the discovery of the
bodies, the inquest into the deaths at White House Farm
was opened at Braintree by Dr Geoffrey Tompkins,
assistant deputy coroner of Essex.

There was little excitement among the handful of
detectives who made the ten-mile journey from Witham to
the coroner's court. The team had cleaned up the murder
inquiry without any trouble; it was simply a matter of
putting their result on record. Of course, nothing was
absolutely official until all the lab reports were received,
but no one anticipated any problems.

The proceedings were routine. The scene at the
farmhouse was briefly described by Acting Detective Chief
Inspector Bob Miller. He said that the post-mortem
examinations showed all five occupants of the house had
been killed by gunshot wounds and offered the police
interpretation of the evidence – four murders and a suicide.

'Death had been instantaneous, particularly in the case of the two boys who were in a sleeping position,' stated the detective. 'Mr and Mrs Bamber had been shot by another person but in the case of Mrs Caffell it appears the wound had been inflicted by her own hand.'

Miller went on to ask for an adjournment of the inquest for two months to allow the police inquiry to be completed. The delay was necessary for the official technical reports to be finalised. Otherwise, there was nothing else to be done and the detective requested permission for the Bamber relatives to proceed with the funeral arrangements. Dr Tompkins gave his agreement for the bodies to be cremated or buried without hesitation.

No one doubted that a thorough examination of the bodies had been carried out by Dr Peter Venesis, the Home Office pathologist, and there were no suggestions at the inquest that anything contradictory to the police theory of the murders had been discovered.

The Essex police knew from those terrible first hours spent in siege outside White House Farm that they were dealing with a tragic case. All their forensic, medical and scientific experts were informed of their belief that it had been four murders and a suicide before examining the evidence. The force was spared the frustrating pursuit of fresh evidence or new lines of inquiry. The case had been cracked and the investigating team were glad they could ask for a speedy funeral for the victims. They had nothing else to learn from the bodies, and the case was virtually closed. There was nothing left for the police to do but sit back and wait for the laboratory reports to put the final seal on the murder inquiry.

A handful of people, however, could not bring themselves to share the optimism of the police. The relatives of the massacred Bamber family – the Boutflours (Bamber's Uncle Robert and Aunt Pamela), their son David and daughter Anne and her husband, Peter Eaton – were neither relieved nor convinced that the whole ghastly business was over. Talking among themselves, the family had already begun to feel uneasy about the speedy conclusion of the case. There was nothing specific to which anyone could point, but in general terms everything felt wrong and out of place. The violence, the frenzy and hatred – none of it gelled with their memories of Sheila and the family.

'The relatives started their stuff pretty quickly,' remembered one police officer. 'They began to look around. I don't think they suspected anyone else, they just felt Sheila hadn't done it and they weren't happy with what was going on.'

One by one, the members of the family were interviewed and most of them tried to impress on police their doubts about Sheila's capacity to murder her parents and children in cold blood. Anne Eaton found the idea of the young divorcee brutally killing four people quite preposterous. She remembered her cousin as a kind-hearted girl, unable to watch even a chicken having its neck wrung.

The concerned relatives discussed the situation again after they had finished giving their statements to the police.

Comparing notes, they all agreed that the murder inquiry officers had not paid any attention to their qualms. Anne Eaton was particularly uneasy with the police version of events and, prompted by nothing more than a feeling of dissatisfaction, persuaded her brother, David Boutflour, to accompany her to White House Farm several days after the murders.

The amateur sleuths didn't know what they were looking for until they found it – and, much to their surprise, they found several things, clues that the police in their careless survey had completely overlooked.

White House Farm was scrubbed and clean in the August sunshine when the brother and sister arrived. Harvest time was just beginning and from the front door the couple could see workmen dotted around the surrounding fields. It had been several weeks since either Anne or David had been inside the orderly house and they both felt sick with apprehension as they opened the door. At first glance nothing seemed to have changed, since the interior had already been washed down by the murder squad detectives, anxious to spare their feelings.

The hallway was scrupulously neat, just as June Bamber always kept it, and the couple failed to notice anything out of the ordinary. Turning to the left, they opened the door into the parlour. It was a comfortable room, with a sofa, soft armchairs and light curtains and carpet. A low coffee table held a stack of magazines dedicated to country matters. It was tidy but informal, as if waiting for the family to come in after dinner and settle down to watch television.

Looking round, the brother and sister spotted a couple of

102

things that made them pause for thought. The video recorder, one of Nevill's favourite toys, had been taken away. A few pieces of silver were missing from the items on display and a couple of antique ornaments kept in a glass-fronted cabinet had been removed.

Anne and David made their way through to the kitchen. It had been the cosiest room in the house, the place where everyone gathered together. Now it was practically bare. The police had removed all the debris left after the struggle between Nevill Bamber and his killer. Lamps, ornaments, even a couple of pieces of furniture had been swept up and thrown out. The stench of disinfectant clung to the air even though detectives had thrown open the doors and windows after their cleaning operation. The walls were still mottled with damp where bloodstains had been scrubbed and scrubbed again.

The atmosphere was stupefying and the pair decided to get out as soon as possible. As a final thought, Anne examined a kitchen fanlight. She knew the farmhouse had been securely locked when the police burst through the doors at the end of the siege but Anne realised that it was possible to get into the kitchen through the fanlight. She walked outside to wait for her brother and as she wandered round the outside of the building, Anne noticed marks on a downstairs window which appeared to have been made by a blade or hacksaw.

Inside the house, David Boutflour stuck his head into the room known as the study, which had been used mainly by Nevill Bamber. It was the place where the farmer kept his documents and sorted out the estate accounts. It was there

103

that Boutflour made the most significant discovery of the day, a find that was to play the pivotal role in future events.

One of the main features of the room was a large cupboard where Nevill had kept his gun collection and stored rounds of ammunition. David Boutflour looked through the cupboard and noticed a box wedged beneath one of the shelves. He pulled it out and, opening it, saw a silencer which could be fitted on to a rifle to deaden the noise of gunfire. Turning it over, the young man realised that this particular silencer had been made to fit a .22 semi-automatic rifle. David Boutflour knew there was only one such gun on the farm – the murder weapon. The silencer was a bit the worse for wear. It looked as if it had been hit against something hard and also had a blob of what looked like red paint on the outside.

'We thought every inch of the house would have been turned over,' said Boutflour. 'It was a surprise to find such an essential piece of a gun left in the cupboard.'

The brother and sister took the silencer back to Oak Farm, Anne's home, and telephoned the police. Her husband, Peter, examined the silencer and discovered a grey hair caught in the muzzle end. To their astonishment, no police officer came to collect their find. In fact, it was a couple of days before anyone from the Essex constabulary bothered to turn up at the house. After their initial wait, the Eatons wrapped the silencer in a plastic carrier bag and stored it away in their kitchen. They had to hunt for it when a detective finally arrived to take charge of the evidence.

'I rang the police immediately to the effect that we had the silencer. They didn't come for it until two or three days later,' remembered Boutflour angrily. 'I understand the police treated this as a suicide case at the time and it had little relevance to the evidence.'

One of the police officers did notice the red blob on the silencer and, looking through the photographs taken of the interior of White House Farm, matched it up with the red paint on the kitchen hearth. There was no obvious explanation as to why or when the silencer should have been struck against the mantel with sufficient force to knock off the paintwork and the officer was intrigued.

After getting permission from Jeremy to go into the house on the pretext of taking room measurements for the inquest, two detectives had another look round. Sure enough, they found a mark underneath the kitchen mantelpiece that looked as if it had been made by a blunt object. The silencer had not been found on the rifle used in the murders, but the blow to the hearth looked fresh, as if it had been made during Nevill's struggle with his attacker. At that time, the information did not amount to anything, but it was another little piece of the puzzle that did not fit.

Anne Eaton, good-naturedly nicknamed Miss Marple by the local police officers, had already dabbled in amateur detective work at the mobile home and holiday park in Osea Road owned jointly by the Eatons, the Boutflours and the Bambers.

Anne's supervision of the 400-berth site had brought her into conflict with Jeremy, who also helped to run the business. An incident at the site earlier in the year had made the Boutflours and the Eatons, especially Anne, mistrustful of Jeremy, who enjoyed antagonising his relatives by adopting and flaunting a cavalier attitude towards his job. There were disagreements between Jeremy and his cousin over the handling of the business, and the young man had accused his relatives of dismissing his suggested improvements.

The caravan site offices were broken into in March 1985, five months before the shootings, and close to £1,000 in cash had been stolen from the safe. No one could prove anything, but everyone connected with the site thought Jeremy was responsible. The theft was reported to the police but the family did not voice their suspicions about the young man and the culprit was not caught.

'The relatives were convinced that the break-in was down to Jeremy and they were furious about it,' said a friend of the family. 'Jeremy's attitude towards his work upset them all. He wanted to be made a director of the caravan site but he didn't do a thing. He thought that his family owed him a living and he shouldn't have to slave for it. Some pretty heavy hints were dropped at business meetings, but it didn't go any further than that.'

The Boutflours and the Eatons did not voice their unease about the slayings to Jeremy. Although there was no love lost between them, they did not want to add to his worries at such a time. Instead they focused their attention on the police and began to make inquiries about the progress of the investigation.

After the discovery of the silencer, the family redoubled their efforts to get some information from the police. They wanted to know more about what detectives had discovered during their examination of White House Farm

106

and were impatient for the results of forensic tests. Fed up with what they regarded as stonewalling by the police, Robert Boutflour decided to lead a group of family members in a showdown visit to Witham Police Station.

They had a meeting with Detective Chief Inspector Taff Jones to try to air their sense of unease about the whole affair. Unfortunately, the talk with Jones merely aggravated the situation rather than easing it. The detective chief inspector was a good policeman, but had a determined and unyielding character. 'Once Taff had made his mind up, that was that,' said a former colleague. 'He was usually right, but he was so set in his opinions that if he decided that a black ashtray was blue, you would have no chance of changing his mind.'

The clash of personalities could not have been more fierce. The Boutflours, Robert in particular, were equally stubborn and would not be shaken from the belief that things were not what they seemed. Sitting opposite Taff Jones, the delegation once again aired their belief that Sheila simply did not have the temperament of a killer. They had little else to offer but they hoped that their doubts might be looked into by the Essex constabulary.

But once again the police response did not change. Taff Jones reiterated the official reading of the case, it was four murders and a suicide and it was Sheila's finger on the trigger. There was no hard evidence to suggest anything to the contrary.

Yet evidence had begun to trickle through which an open mind might have found disturbing. The family were not told of a recent police discovery: Sheila had been shot twice in the neck, not once as the press had been informed. The latest medical report confirmed that the young woman had fired twice to end her life as she lay on the floor. This was the first time that many officers present at White House Farm during the siege had heard this information. Detectives reading the document paused over the section dealing with the state in which Sheila's body had been found. The corpse of the beautiful former model was remarkably clean, as if she had recently bathed. Her well-tended hands were manicured and her glossy, deep red nails had been newly painted. Apart from the terrible gunshot wounds, there was hardly a mark on her body.

Neither were the Boutflours and Eatons told that the blob of red paint on the silencer corresponded with the mark on the underside of the kitchen mantelpiece. They heard nothing further about the odd discoveries they had made but persisted in believing that Sheila simply could not have carried out the massacre. 'I said to the police, "Let's see the forensic evidence." I wanted them to show me her fingerprints on the cartridges. But they did not take me seriously and remained convinced that she was responsible,' said David Boutflour.

The relatives left the meeting feeling even more concerned than when they had gone in. Now they were convinced that the detectives responsible for the case would not even allow their misgivings a fair hearing. It was frustrating and infuriating.

Robert Boutflour was far too tenacious a character to let the matter end there. He began to ring the case detectives regularly in an attempt to badger information out of them and his probing calls were dreaded by some of the officers at Witham. It was in this atmosphere of sorrow and confusion that the family prepared to bury their dead. The police did not want to carry out any further tests on the bodies so there was nothing left to do except arrange the services, the first of which took place just over a week after the murders.

The Bamber funerals dominated British national news. The slaughter, with all its sensational ingredients, had caught the public imagination and press reports had run wild. There were rumours of promiscuous sex, of drugs, of religious mania and witchcraft. Sheila's reputation was torn apart by the mob and she was portrayed as a drug-crazed fiend who blasted apart an ideal family. Editors all over the country were grateful for such a dramatic story to enliven the usually arid holiday months and reporters were dispatched in droves to Tolleshunt D'Arcy until they almost outnumbered the locals.

Services for Nevill, June and Sheila were held on the day after the inquest, 16 August 1985. Colin Caffell had arranged a separate service and burial for the twins at London's Highgate Cemetery, but he denied speculation that he had refused to let his sons be buried with their mother. 'I want the children to be buried somewhere near me,' he said. 'Sheila's ashes are going to be buried with them.'

The tiny church of St Nicholas was packed with family relatives and locals, who filled the pews a good half-hour before the service began. More than fifty extra seats had been added to the usual 180, and even then the congregation overflowed outside, where they paid their respects in the rain.

Dozens of newsmen and women, most of them respectfully dressed in sober colours, hovered around the pale stone church, anxious for quotes and photographs. There was one 'celebrity' at the ceremony – Herbie Flowers, bass guitarist with the rock group Sky, who was a friend of Colin Caffell. During the service the photographers occupied themselves with the mound of flowers sent by mourners. Colin had sent two: a wreath from the twins with a card which read, 'We'll be together again soon, Mummy, D and N', and a ring of yellow roses and lilies with the message 'In loving memory. My dear Sheila, I will be thinking of you together with our sons forever. Love Colin X.'

Despite the best efforts of the family, the assembled journalists, photographers and camera crews gave the proceedings an air of melodrama. The star of the show was Jeremy Bamber, and all eyes were on him, noting his every movement of grief throughout the ceremony. Jeremy wept without restraint as the coffins of his parents and sister were carried out of the church and a protective circle of friends which included his former brother-in-law, Colin Caffell, closed around the young man to shield him from the glare of the cameras. The daylight revealed Jeremy looking dramatically pale and haggard as he clutched the arm of Julie Mugford.

Millions of people all over the country watched Jeremy's sorrow on the television news that evening and scanned the pictures in their newspapers the following day. Pity for the

110

'orphan of tragedy' was universal and Jeremy looked very handsome in his impeccably cut, dark designer suit, crying openly on his girlfriend's shoulder. Julie led the weeping young man to a waiting limousine for the journey to a private cremation at Colchester. Her face, partially concealed by a little hat and spotted veil, was set and grim.

Mourners who knew Jeremy were shocked by the pallor of his careworn face, but a couple of sharp-eyed friends realised there was something peculiar about Jeremy's tragic appearance. 'We noticed that Jeremy had dyed his hair for the funeral. He had dark hair anyway, but he'd dyed it a deeper shade of black and wore some white make-up so that he looked more haggard. You had to know Jeremy before you could realise what he had done,' said one of them.

Away from the cameras, Jeremy made no attempt to hide his impatience with the solemn ceremony. David Boutflour, standing near Jeremy in the tiny church, saw his cousin glance at his watch and say: 'Come on, let's get out of here. Time's up!'

When the party finally left the church and headed towards the crematorium Jeremy's spirits improved enormously. He had never shared his parents' fondness for religion and away from the oppressive atmosphere of the funeral he regained his usual, outrageous manner. He laughed and joked with friends and was as gleeful as a little boy about the smart new outfit he had treated himself to for the occasion.

'Jeremy bought this fantastic Hugo Boss suit. He actually went around the wake after the funeral showing off the

111

label,' remembered a friend. 'He was having a really good time. At the crematorium, he'd started joking. Julie had on this really slim black dress which showed her slight tummy bulge and in front of all the relatives Jeremy patted her tummy and said: "It's about time you told everyone you're pregnant, darling!"'

Jeremy was not about to waste his new suit and high spirits on a family get-together after the funerals. Accompanied by Brett Collins and a group of other friends, Jeremy dried his tears and went to drown his sorrows at a restaurant in nearby Colchester. Jeremy and his crowd ordered pink champagne and laughed and joked for a couple of hours. Malcolm Waters, a friend and former housemate of Bamber, was amazed at the scene when he joined the group in the bar. 'There was a lot of heavy drinking and Jeremy was in really high spirits. He was shouting and laughing, being cheeky to the waitresses, touching them up and slapping their bottoms,' he remembered.

Jeremy's exuberance came as no surprise to his closest confidants. They had seen other instances of his over-the-top behaviour and wrote it off as Jeremy's attempts to put the tragedy behind him. Jeremy had even insisted on returning to White House Farm on the eve of the funerals. He took Julie Mugford and some other friends with him to collect glasses and crockery which he said were for the wake. 'Jeremy spent all his time looking through the house for any cash that might have been left by his father,' said one of the friends who accompanied him to the farmhouse.

Jeremy gathered up various bits and pieces and then

the gang sped off to a local restaurant where they enjoyed a boisterous meal.

A couple of days after the service at Tolleshunt D'Arcy, a much more private funeral ceremony was held in London at St James's Church, West Hampstead. Colin Caffell was joined by Jeremy and the two men wept together as Nicholas and Daniel were buried along with the ashes of their mother in Highgate Cemetery. The spray of carnations on the single coffin read 'Thank you for all your love and for everything. We'll all be together one day. Love Daddy.'

After the pathos of the funerals, media interest waned and the villagers of Tolleshunt D'Arcy were able to get on with their lives once more. Officially, the police inquiries were still open, but there was little sign of activity apart from the odd report trickling back from the forensic laboratories. It appeared that the police had everything under control and all the routine matters were progressing at an orderly pace. But inside Witham Police Station faint murmurings of discontent had already been heard. Every member of the station was aware of the misgivings of the relatives and a small number of officers gave some credence to their doubts and had a few of their own.

'After years in the force you learn to listen to your instinct,' said one of the officers involved. 'A policeman's instinct comes from dealing with lots of crimes and lots of people and when it tells you that something is wrong, then it's time to take another look at things.'

A couple of officers decided to raise the issue with their

superiors, in the hope that there might be a review of evidence. The reaction from above was short and sharp. The inquiry was on the right track and anyone who thought otherwise was not welcome on the case. There was to be no further discussion about this issue. Such exchanges did not make for a good working atmosphere, but the officers had no option but to accept the order and carry on.

Jeremy, like the rest of the family, was not privy to the aborted insurrection within the police ranks. He expressed no doubts about the police investigation and continued to relax and enjoy life, urged on by his friends, who believed this was the perfect antidote to the shock of the murders, Jeremy also had some more pressing problems to solve. He was desperately in debt and was finding it increasingly difficult to finance his hectic lifestyle. Even though he stood to inherit nearly £500,000 – and more than likely would take over the running of the farm – ready cash was an immediate problem.

Valuers arrived from Sotheby's to look over some of the family treasures, including the antique clock, and Jeremy made arrangements for the sale of some of the more valuable property. He realised, however, that it would be months before his parents' estate would be settled and even longer before he received any of his inheritance. Jeremy's solution to his cash-flow crisis was to go though all the family business affairs in a particularly insensitive manner. A week after the funerals had taken place, he began a ruthless clean-up of the farm office that offended some of the long-serving employees.

'Jeremy came up to the office and said he wanted

everything thrown out and didn't want anything left,' said Barbara Wilson, who had worked as Nevill Bamber's secretary for seven years. 'I said there may be one or two things of sentimental value, but he said "I don't want any of it." He was a bit arrogant and a bit nasty.' Mrs Wilson said that Bamber had walked into the office, flung himself in his father's chair and put his feet up on the desk, swivelling round to give her orders. He made it clear that he needed as much cash as possible, telling her that the funerals had been very expensive and any spare money should go towards paying for them. He also awarded himself a £75 a week pay rise, to reflect his new responsibilities around the estate. Like Bamber's friends on the eve of the funeral, Mrs Wilson noticed that the young man was convinced his father had cash hoarded away somewhere. Once again he insisted on searching the house and the office for a hidden cache of money.

Jeremy was determined to get enough money to buy a good time for himself and his friends. A couple of days after his parents were cremated he and Julie, accompanied by the ever-present Brett Collins, enjoyed a long weekend in Amsterdam. The curious trio went everywhere together, staying at an expensive hotel, eating in the best restaurants and drinking champagne in the bars of the bustling city. Jeremy paid for the entire trip and returned to England just in time for the burial of his two little nephews.

Back in Tolleshunt D'Arcy, the Bamber relatives were keeping up their pressure on the police. They were furious that a special murder squad had not been formed to investigate the case, and that instead detectives from the local station, Witham, were responsible for the inquiry. The family lobbied hard for more vigour to be applied to the routine inquiries. Day after day, members of the family rang Witham to find out if there had been any new developments in the case and hounded officers with their own questions.

The most persistent caller was Robert Boutflour, June Bamber's brother-in-law. Frustrated by the lack of response from Taff Jones, he finally decided to take matters into his own hands and composed a long letter, setting out in no uncertain terms the doubts he felt about Sheila's guilt and cataloguing the clues his family had found in the farm-house. Mr Boutflour did not accuse anyone else of the crime; he just argued persuasively that Sheila could not have carried out the massacre and called for further action. The letter was sent to Robert Bunyard, the chief constable of Essex, and was sufficiently powerful for the police chief to demand a case report from his officers.

While the Boutflours were making waves in Tolleshunt D'Arcy, Jeremy stayed in London where he moved, without any hesitation, into the Morshead Mansions flat that had been the home of Sheila and the twins. Bamber not only took over Sheila's home, he also grabbed any of her belongings that caught his fancy. He wore the dead girl's sweaters and a tracksuit and rifled the flat for anything of value. He was joined there by Brett Collins and the two young men spent leisurely days shopping for clothes and went out partying at night.

Sometimes they were accompanied by Julie Mugford, who had started her first job as a primary school teacher in

116

south London. Julie realised that the buddy-buddy relationship of Brett and Jeremy was growing even stronger. Sometimes the two young men shared the twin-bedded room that had belonged to Nicholas and Daniel; when Julie stayed overnight, however, she and Jeremy used Sheila's room. But the young woman was growing increasingly irritated by the peculiar relationship flourishing under her nose.

'She knew they had been lovers and that hadn't bothered her at first,' recalled one of Julie's friends. 'But after a while she couldn't stand it. She told me they were always playing around together, wrestling on the sofa and grabbing each other. She was sick of it.'

As the relationship between the two men grew stronger, the bond between Jeremy and Julie splintered bit by bit. At first she made allowances for his lack of tenderness, attributing it to the shock engendered by the murders, but finally she was forced to concede to herself that Jeremy was growing increasingly distant. He had changed greatly from the charming, high-spirited lover who had swept her off her feet eighteen months before.

Jeremy had the ability to mentally knock people off balance. He enjoyed manipulating his friends, creating unexpected events and gauging the reaction of those around him. On one occasion he outraged farm workers by turning up to help plough his father's fields in his nightclub clothes – an outfit of skin-tight trousers, billowing silk shirt and a touch of eye make-up and lipstick. Nevill thought he had gone mad, but Jeremy just laughed.

Only six weeks before the murders Jeremy had devised a

new game and, as usual, he expected Julie to be his playmate. As usual, she had agreed. The couple were at the Essex wedding of one of their friends when they met a mutual but distant acquaintance. The young man was surprised and flattered as Julie lavished attention on him, making it clear she found him attractive. Looking around, he realised that Jeremy Bamber had disappeared from sight.

After a short while Julie invited her new-found friend to go for a walk through the surrounding fields. After a short stroll she suggested that they sit down on a grassy bank, hidden from the party by thick bushes. Lying back, she patted the grass next to her. Needing no further invitation, her companion flung himself down and put his arms around her.

Suddenly there was a tremendous shout. Jeremy Bamber leaped out of the bushes and dashed towards the couple, yelling at the top of his voice. The young man froze. Then he heard a laugh. Looking up he saw Jeremy almost choking with laughter; looking to the side he saw Julie giggling fit to burst. Jeremy pulled Julie to her feet and the couple ran off hand in hand, back to the wedding reception. Still sitting on the grass, the young man realised it had all been a warped joke staged by Jeremy and Julie.

Julie acquiesced to many hare-brained schemes in the hope that it would make Jeremy happy and keep him by her side. Ever resourceful, she had struggled to keep alive Jeremy's interest but now her ingenuity had been stretched to the limit. In the months immediately preceding the tragedy at White House Farm, Julie had suspected Jeremy of seeing other women. He denied her accusations vehemently, but now, only weeks after the murders, her doubts had come back in full force and Jeremy no longer bothered to reassure her of his love and fidelity.

Julie had hoped that she and Jeremy would announce their engagement that summer. During their first year together, she had regarded marriage as a foregone conclusion. His parents had been chilly about the relationship – in fact June Bamber had gone out of her way to express her disapproval and habitually referred to Julie as 'that harlot'. Jeremy had just laughed and enjoyed parading Julie before family and friends as his live-in girlfriend. Since the beginning of the year, however, his allusions to the future had dwindled and talk of marriage had come to a complete halt. Julie realised that the more she clung, the more Jeremy tried to shake himself free. But she could not help herself. As difficult and irresponsible as Jeremy could be, Julie wanted him; she wanted a commitment from him.

A crisis of sorts had been reached a few months previously, when Julie's parents had organised a party to celebrate her twenty-first birthday. Halfway through the evening the champagne was brought out and Julie was toasted. Then one of her girlfriends stepped forward and, raising her glass, proposed a toast to Julie's engagement to Jeremy. As the cheering died down, a red-faced Jeremy stepped forward and quietly whispered that there was no engagement and there would be no marriage. It had all been very embarrassing.

Yet her hopes had soared again when, in the traumatic

119

first days after the murders, Jeremy had leaned heavily on the support she offered. Now he took her loyalty for granted. The hours they spent together were made unbearable by unspoken accusations and Julie knew she was reaching the limits of her endurance.

The final blow was dealt at Morshead Mansions. Julie, her nerves knotted with tension, noticed Jeremy leaping to the telephone whenever it rang. She beat him to the next call and answered it herself. It was a young woman, giggling and asking for Jeremy, and making a great play of refusing to give her name. Jeremy hunched over the phone and got rid of the caller quickly, but it was all over for Julie. All the humiliation and anguish of the year turned into a white-hot rage, fiery enough to consume the love she felt for Jeremy and to reduce the awe he had commanded from her to a heap of ashes.

Jeremy did little to soothe her. He shrugged his shoulders at her screams. She hurled mirrors, boxes, ornaments, whatever came to hand; she slapped him, hard, and he pushed her away. He was no longer interested and there was nothing she could say or do that would penetrate his indifference. Julie gave up. She went back to Colchester and began to do some serious thinking.

On the evening of Saturday, 7 September, a phone call came through to Chelmsford Police Station. The caller, a young woman, was trying to find one of the detectives involved in the White House Farm murders. It was very urgent, she told the desk sergeant; she was phoning on behalf of a friend who had something to tell the detective about the case. She gave her name and number and asked the officer to pass on the message as quickly as possible to the off-duty detective.

'Should he ask for you?' inquired the sergeant.

The girl hesitated for a second or two before replying. 'No,' she said warily. 'Tell him to ask for Julie Mugford.'

7

The perfect murder

'Julie, of course, knew that Jeremy had done it. What had happened was that she had finally cracked,' explained an Essex detective.

Soon after the phone call Chelmsford headquarters were buzzing with excitement. Detective Chief Inspector Bob Miller, who was on duty that weekend, gave the go-ahead for Julie Mugford to be interviewed by Detective Sergeant Stan Jones, the officer she had requested to see. Exactly a month to the day after the massacre, the White House Farm case was blown apart.

Detective Sergeant Jones drove off to Colchester to interview Julie. At the back of his mind was the memory of her behaviour during those first terrible few days after the murders. He had suspected then that something was on her mind and he believed one day he would discover her secret. Now the time had come. 'I wasn't surprised. I knew she would have to get it out. She really and truly couldn't live with it,' said Jones. 'Julie had started talking to her friend Liz Rimington as it all got too much for her. In the end, she and Liz went to another friend's house in Colchester and rang the station to ask for me.'

Julie was nervous and upset, but she had steeled herself to go through with her story. She knew Stan Jones, having first met him at Jeremy's Goldhanger cottage on the morning after the murders, she trusted him and she had a feeling that her call was not totally unexpected. The two sat down together. Julie was pale and chain-smoking nervously. For once she had not bothered with the bold, dark eye pencil and mascara which was part of the tough persona she liked to cultivate. The grim-faced woman had been replaced by a trembling little girl, unsure of the reception that would greet her tale.

A cup of coffee in front of her and her hands twisting in her lap, Julie tried to remember how it all began, helped along by a little gentle prompting from Stanley Jones. Despite the detective sergeant's certainty that Julie would 'cough' or confess, even he was surprised at the story she had to tell.

Jeremy had first started to talk seriously about killing his parents during the last months of 1984, Julie said. Even then, some nine months before the murders, he had begun to make detailed plans for the slaughter. He told her he wanted to carry out 'the perfect murder'.

'He talked about it so often. There had been plan one, where he'd drug them with his mother's sleeping pills in their bedtime drinks, then set fire to the house by throwing a bottle of gin on the floor and putting a match to it,' she remembered. In fact he had tried out plan number one, spiking his parents' drinks with tranquillisers, but they had no effect on the couple. Julie said she put forward a practical objection – the farmhouse was too big to burn easily, and the scheme simply would not work.

'He discarded this for plan two,' Julie told the officer. 'This involved shooting them all and then letting it be thought that Sheila, who was visiting with the twins at the time, was responsible.'

It was only when Julie described the events of the day before the murders, August 6, that the horrified detective sergeant realised just how thoroughly Bamber had planned the deaths of his innocent family.

'Jeremy phoned me at my London digs where I used to spend a few days each week studying and said, "Tonight's the night." I knew what he meant,' admitted Julie. 'It was the night when he would kill his family.'

Jeremy rang her again, in the early hours of the following morning, to say that everything was going according to plan. That was the last message from the country until later in the morning, when a distraught Jeremy rang to tell her that a police car was coming to pick her up and bring her to Tolleshunt D'Arcy.

The detective said he had noticed her trauma at Jeremy's cottage on the morning after the murders. Julie confirmed that she had been almost sick with worry because she was certain that Jeremy knew all about the tragedy and it was not long before her fears were realised. Although he was surrounded by police officers, Jeremy could scarcely wait to take Julie aside to boast about his cleverness. 'Jeremy asked if we could have a few minutes alone and we went into the other room. He hugged me and said, "Do you know something ? I should have been an actor," ' she said.

It was during this incident that Stanley Jones and Michael Clark had heard a noise sounding like a chuckle. That was Jeremy laughing, claimed Julie; he was so triumphant at the success of his plan that she had to remind him that the officers were in the next room. Despite his bravado, Jeremy was well aware of Julie's distress and he did not dare risk a full explanation until the policemen had left the cottage and the well-meaning visits from relatives and friends had ceased for the day. Julie said she spent the hours in a daze, knowing that she would soon learn the truth about the massacre. 'It wasn't until nearly nine o'clock that we were alone,' Julie later told the court. 'Then I asked the question that had been practically bursting out of my mind all day: "Jeremy, did you do it?"

' "No," he said calmly. "But I did arrange it. Matthew did it for me." '

Julie said she had sat in the tiny lounge of the Goldhanger cottage as Jeremy poured out a strange story. Pacing up and down, he reassured her that he had not pulled the trigger. Instead he had hired a friend, a local plumber called Matthew, to kill the entire family for £2,000. Julie told Stan Jones that she never believed this tale of Jeremy's and when he mentioned that the pay-off was fixed for the following day she was convinced he was lying to her.

'Even I know that if you employ a mercenary you pay in advance. And, anyway, how could Matthew have possibly done it when he didn't even know the layout of the farm? How would he know, for instance, where everyone was, where the twins slept?' she pointed out.

Stan Jones sat and listened. Julie's account was more complicated than he had imagined it would be. Was she inventing this story about the mercenary or was it true? Why would Jeremy bother to confess at all unless he was telling the truth? Some time later, one of Julie's friends advanced a theory about Jeremy's revelations.

'He gave her that story about the mercenary because he wanted to calm her down and get her to go to bed with him,' claimed the friend. 'It just sort of took the edge off things for her a bit. You know, if someone said to you, "Well, of course, I didn't do the real thing, I got someone else to do it," it's somehow not as bad. And it worked. She went off to sleep with him.'

Jones was well aware of the impact these disclosures would have. If Julie Mugford was telling the truth, it meant that a crime which, for a whole month, had been regarded as the murderous impulse of a deranged woman was really a carefully premeditated and successfully carried-out act of butchery.

The officer pressed the young woman for more details of the murders, but she could tell him nothing further. Jeremy had never told her he had actually killed anyone and she had not questioned him further after his initial 'confession'. Julie said she had been aware of his determination to kill his family, but she didn't want to hear the details of what he had done.

Yet although she could not tell Jones anything more

about the murders, Julie did go into detail about the days following the slayings. The detective listened in astonishment as Julie described the behaviour of her former lover when he was away from the police and out of the public gaze. His first concern had been to search the farmhouse thoroughly for money or any items that could be sold for ready cash. He took a few things with him, including the video recorder, which he wanted for his own cottage. Jeremy spent what money he had available lavishly, buying himself an expensive suit and tie for the funerals of his parents and sister.

Julie claimed that before the church service Jeremy had fussed for nearly an hour, setting up the video to record his own appearance on the evening news bulletins. His concern was to put up the best possible show and he even followed the suggestion of a friend to make his appearance more dramatic. He bought a sachet of hair dye to turn his hair a shade darker and spread pale foundation make-up on his skin to make him look more haggard in front of the cameras. His emotional collapse outside the church was a ploy staged for the media and the police, Julie told the police officer. Once he was out of sight of the cameras the tears dried up as abruptly as they had started. 'As soon as he got into the car he started joking again. He was totally without remorse,' said Julie.

She described a drinking session at a local restaurant with all their friends after the funerals. Astonishingly, none of the group around Jeremy appeared to question his raucous behaviour or suspect that anything was amiss after the tragedy. The young man had always been a creature of extreme moods so his abrupt transformation from grieving orphan to boisterous heir passed without undue curiosity. After his parents' funerals and before the burial of Nicholas and Daniel there had been the long weekend in Amsterdam that she had shared with Jeremy and his bisexual friend Brett Collins.

During this trip, Julie experienced the first loosening of the emotional tie which bound her to Jeremy. She claimed that she was so revolted by the murders that she refused to sleep with him. Jeremy retaliated by forcing himself on her on one occasion and then neglecting her in favour of drinking with Collins.

Her disillusionment had gathered momentum in London and she told Jones about Jeremy's carefree life spent shopping for clothes, drinking and nightclubbing and the hours she had shared with him in the home of his murdered sister. But in the end, Julie said, she could not bear to keep Bamber's secret any longer. 'He knew I was under his spell. But he reckoned without my conscience. How could I let a man go scot-free when he had killed those innocent people, including two lovely little boys?' she said. 'He used to tell me, "Money's the one thing I want." To think he committed five murders for it.'

Money was the motive for murder, said Julie. Jeremy did not want to share his inheritance with Sheila and the twins and he was tired of waiting for his parents to give him some real cash. To prove her point, Julie mentioned an incident that Stan Jones had heard little about – the burglary at the family-owned Osea Bay caravan site in March earlier that year.

It was Jeremy who had decided to steal the takings, she claimed. It was the first blow he struck against what he considered to be the niggardly ways of his relatives and he got away with nearly £1,000. He had persuaded Julie to help him, telling her to keep a look-out as he broke into the offices and went straight to the safe. Julie had cowered by the sea wall, frightened of being caught but not daring to incur Jeremy's anger by running away. Jeremy anticipated the suspicions of his relatives and regarded them with contempt: they would never dare risk a family row without proof and prosecution would be out of the question.

Detective Sergeant Jones had no doubts about the veracity of Julie's confession but he knew that not everyone would be prepared to accept her version of events quite so enthusiastically. There was also an immediate problem which had to be answered satisfactorily – why had she waited so long to confess what she knew?

Then and later Julie adhered to the same explanation: she had always dismissed his murderous plans as a joke. 'You never believe in your wildest dreams that someone is actually going to murder his family. He always had to be the centre of attention and I dismissed it as something outrageous that he thought would guarantee my attention. I'd just say, "Oh yes, Jeremy, have a good night's sleep and you'll feel better in the morning." I never stopped to consider for one minute that he would ever seriously think of trying to get rid of his family.'

It was not an entirely convincing explanation. After all, Julie had just told Detective Sergeant Jones how Bamber tested out 'plan one' – doping his parents' drinks – and his

130

subsequent report to her that it had not worked. That experiment must have warned her that he really was trying to kill his family.

As Stan Jones pressed her more closely, Julie struggled to explain the predicament in which she had found herself. She had been completely in thrall to her domineering boyfriend, and described to Jones how Jeremy had threatened her to ensure her silence. He had convinced her that her prior knowledge of his intention to kill his parents would put her in terrible trouble because the police would charge her with being an accessory to murder if she said anything. Her judgement, her conscience, even her sense of self-protection, had been suspended in the face of his manipulative personality.

There was one further puzzle left which troubled Jones. He wanted to discover why Julie had decided to come forward and tell her story. He knew from experience that guilty consciences tend to flare up after a significant event and he was certain that something had happened to trigger Julie's confession. Moreover, the Essex police had to discover the crucial factor that had led to Julie's statement: there was always the chance that it might make any case against Bamber vulnerable. The prosecution did not want a clever defence lawyer unearthing damaging evidence against their own witnesses. It was vital that the police knew everything there was to know about Julie, her relationship with Jeremy and what had caused her to snap.

Julie was very tired by now and all it took was some gentle questioning by Detective Sergeant Jones before she broke down and revealed that her affair with Bamber was over. She described the violent row which had taken place at Morshead Mansions a few days before when she had been humiliated by Jeremy's mysterious female phone caller. The break with Jeremy enabled her to think independently once more and she realised that the police had to know the real story. Her motive was not revenge, insisted Julie, it was horror at Bamber's crime and disgust at his callous behaviour.

Detective Sergeant Jones believed Julie's tale but he was acutely aware of future problems with her evidence. A shrewd defence counsel could destroy the unsupported testimony of a jilted woman in court. As things stood, it would be relatively easy to undermine Julie's story and cast doubts on the credibility of her confession. The detective badly needed corroboration before presenting Julie's story to his own superiors. He pushed her harder to discover if there was anyone else who could support her accusations. It was late and Julie was weary. She sat slumped on the sofa, completely drained of feeling and devoid of willpower. It took a monumental effort to persuade her to think of anyone who could support her testimony with his or her own.

Running through all the possibilities in her mind, Julie eventually volunteered two suggestions. First of all there was Brett Collins, Bamber's New Zealand pal. She had no idea if Jeremy had talked to him about the murders, but she knew they were very close – in fact they were staying together at Morshead Mansions that very weekend. Then there was her own friend, Liz Rimington. Bamber had not confided in Liz, but Julie had done so. She had mentioned

Jeremy's story about the hired mercenary to Liz and complained to her friend continuously about Jeremy's behaviour during the past month. In fact Liz had even witnessed for herself some of the incidents Julie had described to the detective.

Liz had also been instrumental in urging Julie to go to the police. She had argued persuasively that Jeremy was a dangerous psychopath who had to be caught before he killed again. It was Liz who had suggested that the police should be contacted from somewhere other than Julie's home, in case Jeremy made an unexpected visit or tried to telephone. Liz had ushered Julie away from her home to the house in Colchester where she was loyally providing coffee and cigarettes during her friend's debriefing. Stan Jones asked her into the room and Liz did not hesitate. She was perfectly willing to make a statement.

As Julie stumbled through her first hurried account of the murder plot, a couple of senior officers sat bleakly in Chelmsford police headquarters waiting for news. Stan Jones had already warned them of the direction that Julie Mugford's statement was likely to take. They knew that she was going to implicate Jeremy Bamber in the White House Farm murders, but the exact form of her accusations and the strength of her evidence was a mystery until Stan Jones could contact them again.

The waiting officers sat in silence. They had drawn up provisional plans to deal with any possible action resulting from Julie's statement and now there was nothing left to do except keep quiet and avoid speculation. To talk would have meant discussing the likely outcome of Julie's

133

interview and perhaps the implications of what she might say were too awful for the police officers to contemplate until the last possible moment. Possibly both men shared the unspoken hope that Stan Jones would emerge shaking his head and declaring that Julie had said nothing of any value about the case.

Common sense said it was an idle wish, if wish it was. As soon as Jones had gathered enough information to make a call all hopes for a quiet life were blasted. The allegations were not completely straightforward, reported the detective sergeant, but serious enough to knock the case sideways. Detective Chief Superintendent Mike Ainsley agreed that Stan Jones should call a halt and resume the interview with Julie the following morning as it was already well into Saturday evening. The senior detectives also decided that Julie should be moved to a police 'safe house' – a place where she could stay while being questioned without fear of being discovered. The Essex constabulary could not afford anyone, whether press, public or even Jeremy Bamber, to find out what was going on. At best Julie might be harassed by the curious; at worst she might actually be in danger. The interviewing would be much easier without the telephone ringing or knocks on the front door, nor did they want to risk some hawk-eyed individual noticing Julie slipping into a police station. All detectives know how difficult it is to keep this kind of secret and they realised it would not be long before the ladies and gentlemen of the press were aware that something was up.

It took some time for Julie to get herself organised. She did not want to go into hiding, away from her family and friends, and it was with difficulty that she was persuaded that it was the only sensible thing to do. Then she had to phone her mother and break the news of what had happened. It was a painful call and Julie broke down. At last she pulled herself together and set off with Liz and a couple of women police officers. There was no turning back now.

Once Julie was safely settled into her temporary home a meeting was hastily organised at police headquarters in Chelmsford. At this point there was not a specially designated, formally ordered murder inquiry team – it had not been considered necessary to assign anyone other than the local Witham and Chelmsford officers to tie up the loose ends of the White House Farm case. But now the situation had changed dramatically. One by one senior officers were tracked down as they relaxed off duty. There had been no lengthy explanations over the phone, but by the time they filed through the dismal grey corridors of police headquarters the officers had little doubt why they were there.

The night was sticky and the warm air further tried the tempers of the tired, tense detectives. Not surprisingly, there was a strained atmosphere at the late-night conference. Round the table were ranged DCI Bob 'Dusty' Miller, DS Stan Jones, DCI Edward 'Taff' Jones, DCS Mike Ainsley, DCS George Harris and Essex Assistant Chief Constable Peter Simpson, who had been called in to review the case.

First of all Detective Sergeant Jones outlined Julie's story. There were mutterings at the end of his report –

Jones was known to be partisan, he had consistently asserted Jeremy's guilt and had repeatedly voiced his doubts about the massacre-suicide theory. But no one had chosen to take him seriously. Now, within the space of two hours, the whole picture had changed dramatically. Unlike the early days of the case, when any discussion about the massacre had been regarded as insubordination, the senior detectives were willing to discuss all and any theories about the slayings. Simply by paying heed to his own well-attuned instincts, Stan Jones had become the unlikely Cassandra of the Essex constabulary.

It was a moment of humiliation for the assembled detectives. If Julie Mugford was telling the truth, they had been well and truly duped by Jeremy Bamber and everyone in Britain would know it – just as they thought they knew that Sheila Caffell, a schizophrenic divorcee, had gone mad and shot her entire family and then herself.

For a few minutes the calmly delivered address of Stan Jones held sway in the room, but as detectives digested the new information, the tension was screwed up a notch by the intervention of Taff Jones. The detective chief inspector was not prepared to jettison his solution of the massacre so quickly, particularly on the say-so of a young, emotionally distraught girl. Furiously, he ran through his opposition to the proposed new interpretation of the murders and a couple of officers nodded their agreement. They were yet to be convinced by Julie's accusations and voices rose as officers began to argue points with each other.

There was little time for exhaustive debate. A brief, vigorous discussion took place about which course of action to adopt but the officers had no real option: they could not afford to disregard Julie's story. Despite lingering reservations the decision was made. Jeremy Bamber was to be arrested on suspicion of murder.

According to Julie, her former lover and his friend, Brett Collins, were in London staying at the Morshead Mansions flat which had belonged to Sheila. A call to nearby Paddington Green Police Station secured the cooperation of the Metropolitan police and a small team of detectives set off from Chelmsford at about five o'clock on Sunday morning to bring Bamber in for questioning.

The debriefing of Julie Mugford continued in the meantime. It would eventually take three days to complete her statement as she searched her memory for anything that might help convict her former lover of his atrocious crime. Copies of the question-and-answer sessions were rushed back to Essex police headquarters where they were anxiously studied by the senior detectives. Julie's accusations were winning more and more converts there, but even the most devout believers knew there were very real problems with the information. Julie had to admit that Jeremy had never actually confessed to carrying out the murders; instead, she claimed, he had fabricated a tale about hiring a mercenary who had carried out the killings for £2,000.

Detective Chief Superintendent Mike Ainsley and Assistant Chief Constable Peter Simpson realised they were in an acutely embarrassing situation which had to be handled with a great deal of care. They knew the inquiry team would be severely criticised for originally naming Sheila as the killer – there was no way that could be avoided. But just how strong was the evidence against Jeremy Bamber ? If he denied the murders, which was more than likely, there was not yet any direct evidence linking him to the crime. They simply could not afford to get it wrong.

All the available evidence would have to be thoroughly re-examined and, sitting in the neon-lit office gazing out into the dark night sky, Detective Chief Superintendent Ainsley felt his heart sink as he realised just how much evidence was no longer available to his team. The farmhouse had been scrubbed down and the bloodstained carpets and furnishings burned only a couple of days after the murders. Three of the bodies had been cremated within a week – one of them the body of the supposed murderer. There would be very little chance of finding any forensic evidence to link Jeremy with the killings – the police would have to build up a case of convincing circumstantial evidence.

Mike Ainsley and his men knew that Jeremy's arrest would bring the media down on them like a ton of bricks. The police believed they had been duped by Jeremy but the press would feel they had been duped by the police. It would mean pursuing inquiries under the scrutiny of hostile reporters, eager to pounce on even the slightest mistake. The complications of opening up the case and rebuilding it from scratch were awful to contemplate. Potential witnesses would be more difficult to trace and win over and the reactions of the family and friends were not to be guessed at. Confidence in the Essex police would be greatly shaken.

Julie Mugford had already confirmed that her hesitation in coming forward had been partly due to the open-and-shut attitude to the case exhibited by the police. Their automatic assumption that Sheila was to blame for the murders, coupled with Jeremy's insistence the matter be allowed to rest, kept her quiet in the days immediately following the murders. 'The police had been round and spoken to Jeremy saying that things were as they looked and it was four murders and a suicide. I didn't think at that stage that anyone would believe me because it was obvious that I was so terribly shaken up by the affair and Jeremy was so terribly confident,' she admitted.

Her reasoning had the detectives squirming in their seats. Their enthusiasm to wrap up the case had prevented a key witness from coming forward. Their own mistaken certainty about the murders had forced Julie to keep her secret.

Reactivating the case would be a tortuous process but to let Jeremy go free while discreet inquiries were carried out was unthinkable. He had already made one trip abroad, and he might take off again at any moment. In any case, it was only a matter of time before one of the newsmen got a hint that something was happening. It was impossible to keep inquiries secret and there were already two girls who knew what had happened. It wouldn't be long before they told other friends and the news would get out. The police had no choice but to grab Jeremy and do their utmost to extract a confession before the storm of adverse publicity hit them.

Meanwhile, detectives began to question Liz Rimington about Jeremy and Julie. The young woman, who was studying catering at a college in nearby Manningtree, provided good third-hand knowledge of the events. She had no direct evidence, but there was sufficient corroboration to support some of Julie's claims.

'Julie wanted to tell somebody, but she couldn't bring herself to do it. She was so in love with him. I told Julie that she had to go to the police because he was a psychopath who could murder again and it would be forever on her conscience. It was a big game for Jeremy. He enjoyed it,' said Liz Rimington.

The words were salt to the wound for the inquiry team when they read the statement. A good few people had clearly harboured suspicions that Jeremy Bamber was responsible for the massacre, but no one had thought to let the police into the secret. Liz Rimington had an interesting story to tell. She had known Jeremy for a number of years and had seen him become more and more frustrated with his family and his lifestyle. 'Jeremy had told me he hated his mother. He'd say "She's such an old cow." He would rage on about Sheila's twins, saying they were spoiled to death and could never do a thing wrong in his mother's eyes. He gave me the impression he was incredibly jealous,' recalled the young woman.

'Every morning he would be at work on the farm. During harvest time he'd work from six in the morning till eight at night. He felt very embittered that he wasn't getting the recognition and the reward. Jeremy would get about £80 a week, but for his kind of lifestyle that wasn't enough.

Drinking champagne every night was his ideal. He wanted to be out there getting in on the London scene. He wanted a flat in London, he wanted to go out drinking, take people out to dinner, go abroad. He hated having to run to his parents every time he wanted some extra cash. I remember we were talking about money once and he said "It's important to have money when you're young." I said: "You'll get your money eventually."'

Liz Rimington was one of the party of friends who helped Jeremy and Julie at the funeral service. Although she did not suspect him to be the murderer, Liz was outraged by Jeremy's behaviour and added more details and bizarre stories to those that Julie had already related to the detective. She described his tasteless jokes after the ceremony and his attempts to upset the rest of his family. 'The relatives carried on as though he was acting normally. I was shocked. Jeremy said, "The only reason they're being so bloody pleasant to me is because they're a pack of vultures, all waiting to see what they're going to get out of it." He laughed and said, "If they think they are going to get a bloody thing, they're joking."'

Liz also knew about the trip to Amsterdam that Bamber had made with Julie and Brett Collins. The threesome had taken the short break after the Tolleshunt D'Arcy funerals and got back in time for Jeremy to attend the burial of little Nicholas and Daniel in London. She explained why Jeremy had wanted to take the holiday so soon after the cremation of Sheila and his parents and before the children had even been buried. 'His purpose was to buy cannabis. His supply had run out. He took several toothpaste tubes, scooped out the contents and packed them with the cannabis he'd bought in a café. Before he made the purchase he tried out several brands for quality. He was a great cannabis smoker and would grow marijuana plants on the farm,' she claimed.

Liz was aware that the relationship between Julie Mugford and Jeremy was deteriorating and Julie frequently poured out her troubles to her friend. But Julie never hinted at Jeremy's involvement in the murders until the day he finished their affair and a distraught Julie telephoned her best friend for consolation. Julie broke into floods of tears as she described the end of her relationship to Liz and then added a shocking aside. Jeremy's behaviour was completely callous, she told her sympathetic friend, but that wasn't all: he had hired someone to kill his family for £2,000. It was then that Liz decided enough was enough and persuaded an hysterical Julie that it was time to tell Stan Jones what she knew.

Back at police headquarters in Chelmsford, the final preparations were being made for the swoop on Morshead Mansions. Several of the detectives waiting for the command to arrest Bamber had taken part in the White House Farm siege. Sipping coffee to chase away any remaining tiredness, they remembered their wait outside the farmhouse a month previously. Then everything had seemed very straightforward. Now no one was quite sure what would happen. But everyone involved in the operation, from those at the very top of the Essex constabulary to the least experienced detective on the inquiry team, prayed that Jeremy Bamber would confess to the murders. That was the stroke of luck the force needed. It would not prevent criticism being hurled at them and awkward questions being asked, but it was easier to admit an error on one hand when you could produce the correct solution on the other.

It was 5 a.m. on Sunday, 8 September 1985. Time to get on with the job. Time to talk to Jeremy Bamber.

8
Sufficient evidence

Jeremy was in one bed and Brett in the other when the detectives burst through the door. It was 7.30 a.m. – the very hour at which the officers had broken through the back door of White House Farm a month previously.

The two bewildered young men were ordered to get up and dress as quickly as possible. Watched closely by the officers they grabbed clothes from the piles heaped on the bedroom floor and, without stopping to wash, they were bundled out of the flat. Only a couple of churchgoers on the way to early-morning service saw the strange little procession march down the path to a convoy of waiting cars which then drove away in formation. A small group of detectives remained behind in Morshead Mansions to search the untidy rooms of Sheila's once immaculate flat.

Jeremy was in a police car travelling at high speed towards Chelmsford before it finally sank into his consciousness that Julie must have gone to the police. Her name had not been mentioned by any of the detectives but it was obvious that she was behind all this. It was a ghastly, unbelievable thought and for a few minutes he resisted the idea, reassuring himself that she would never dare to extract her revenge in such a way.

It only took a few moments for logic to reassert itself. He knew the police had not been pursuing any active inquiries; all the funerals had taken place, the only difference between this week and last was that he had dumped Julie. She had to be at the bottom of this ridiculous episode. Regretfully, Jeremy acknowledged to himself that he had treated her rather carelessly. He had trusted too much in Julie's faithful stoicism which she proudly exhibited as a token of merit, like a Girl Guide's badge. Now the worm had turned and he was being well and truly punished for his complacency.

Jeremy pulled his thoughts together, psyching himself up for the reception committee that would greet him back at police headquarters. Lack of sleep made him paler than usual and his dark hair was unruly. He glanced at the detectives crammed into the car beside him. Bloody stupid village Plod! he thought angrily. The oiks start running around like headless chickens as soon as that stupid girl decides to get her own back.

He decided to keep quiet until he could get a firmer grasp on what had happened. He had to try to figure out how far Julie had gone in her little chats with the Essex constabulary. The police said 'suspicion of murder' – that didn't sound very substantial. Perhaps Julie was just trying it on a little, hoping a touch of blackmail would frighten

146

him back into her arms. Slumping down in the back seat he ignored the banter of the accompanying detectives and refused to respond to any remarks addressed to him. The journey back to Chelmsford passed rather too quickly for Jeremy.

A much livelier scene was taking place in the second car of the convoy, where Brett Collins was jumping up and down and making as much noise as an excited puppy. Unlike Jeremy he would not keep quiet and pestered the detectives around him about what was happening to him and his friend. The chubby, rumpled young man quickly threw off his tiredness and, clearly unintimidated by the police, bombarded them with questions. It was not until they reached the murder squad interview room that the blond-haired New Zealander realised the seriousness of the allegations he was facing.

'I was told I was suspected of withholding information about the killings,' said an outraged Collins, shocked by the reception which greeted him at Chelmsford. 'I told them I didn't have a clue what they were talking about.'

The two friends were kept apart and hustled into separate interview rooms. Detectives soon realised that Collins would be of little help to them as far as the murder inquiry was concerned. He maintained he had been on holiday in Greece when the massacre took place and the discovery of his passport in Morshead Mansions corroborated his story. But he was not yet off the hook. The detectives persisted with their questioning, hoping that he would let slip something that could be used to put more pressure on Bamber. 'One of them said to me: "Come on Brett, you know he's done it." I told them there was no way that Jeremy carried out that terrible act,' said Collins. 'They said to me, "OK, we know you were both on it – but we can't prove it."'

Privately, the detectives acknowledged that they would get little information of any use from Collins. It was a blow to the Essex force: they had hoped the mercurial Kiwi would collapse under pressure and confirm Julie's story. If Bamber had talked to her, he had probably talked to Collins as well, the detectives had reasoned. Regretfully, they were forced to concede that Collins was telling the truth.

'It was obvious from the first minutes of the interview that Brett knew nothing,' said an Essex detective. 'I think he actually believed Jeremy didn't do it and had no idea about it at all. Collins is the kind of guy who would have sold his story if he had any idea about what had gone on – "How Killer Told Me of His Plans," that kind of thing. He couldn't have kept it to himself.'

Collins was not released immediately. Instead the detectives turned their attention to the relationship between Bamber and his best friend. Julie Mugford's statements about the pair and their own observations had aroused the interest of the detectives, ever alert to what they regarded as potential weak spots in Bamber's character. 'I told them I was not gay and nor was Jeremy. I often stayed with Jeremy and we are very, very good friends. But there it ends,' said an indignant Collins.

While Brett parried questions about his sexual habits,

Jeremy refused to answer any prayers for the Essex constabulary. Destroying their hopes of a quick solution to the case, he did not confess to the killings but simply asked to see a solicitor. Hoping to shake Jeremy's calm demeanour, detectives revealed that Julie Mugford had named him as the killer and was prepared to give detailed evidence against him.

Bamber did not miss a beat. This was what he had been waiting for, this was the point of the whole charade. They expected he would crumple over Julie's tittle-tattle. Well, the detectives had decided to back the wrong horse and they would regret it. Calmly he replied that Julie was embittered because he had dumped her and this was her way of getting revenge. He looked straight at each officer in turn, showing them he had nothing to hide. Outwardly keeping his cool, Mike Ainsley was inwardly cursing his misfortune. This was the worst scenario the police could have imagined.

Taff Jones was the first detective to interview Bamber. The detective chief inspector was undoubtedly an experienced interrogator, but it was an appalling mistake on the part of the Essex police to give him first crack at Bamber. As head of the Witham station team handling the White House Farm murders, Jones had been largely responsible for wrapping up the case within hours of the killings. His belief that Sheila was responsible for the murders remained unshaken by Julie Mugford's story. He was convinced the police were being led on a wild goose chase and this attitude spilled over into his dealings with Bamber. It was peculiar that more thought had not been given to the execution of such an important interview: despite Jones' stance and the extreme precariousness of the police case, no change was made to the handling of the interrogation.

During the initial period of interrogation, when Bamber was unsettled and ill at ease with the procedure, it would have been better policy and may have yielded more positive results if the questioning had been carried out by an officer who was not so convinced of the suspect's innocence. It gave the young man a breathing space in which to regain his self-assurance and muster his defence. Jeremy was sharp enough to spot and take advantage of even the slightest ambivalence of manner. It was clear to him before the first round of questioning was over that Taff Jones maintained an open mind on the issue of his guilt.

'Taff Jones knew I was innocent. I could tell that straight away,' Bamber said later. 'It was obvious he was going through the motions from the way he phrased his questions. He wouldn't accuse me of anything, he'd say things like "You're accused of doing so-and-so but you say you didn't do it, is that correct?" He knew the police didn't have a case.'

The first session of questioning on Sunday produced two minor results: Bamber wrote a reconciliation note to Julie Mugford and finally admitted to burgling his family's caravan site. His prison-cell message to Julie read: 'Hi darling, hope this gets to you from Stalag 13. Thinking about you. Sorry for splitting up, I love you, Stinko.'

Police cars surround White House Farm on the day the murders were reported (*Express Newspapers*)

The coffins of Nevill and June Bamber at their funeral at Tolleshunt
D'Arcy (*Anglia Press Agency*)

Girlfriend Julie Mugford supports the ostentatiously grieving Jeremy Bamber at the funeral of his parents (*Anglia Press Agency*)

The exhibits officer holds the .22 rifle and silencer which Bamber used to murder his family (*Press Association*)

Detective Inspector Taff Jones who led initial inquiries into the murders (*Anglia Press Agency*)

Essex police's Assistant Chief Constable Peter Simpson (*Anglia Press Agency*)

The transparent motives for the friendly note were later spelled out by Jeremy. 'I had been told by the police of the allegations that Julie was making against me and I believed she was doing that out of spite because we had split up. I wrote the note believing she would take everything back,' he admitted.

During one exchange with Taff Jones, Bamber admitted that he had burgled the jointly owned caravan site earlier in the year. This admission gave the police a lever in their attempts to keep Jeremy in detention – they were all too aware that the suspect could not be held indefinitely without charges being brought against him. As Monday morning passed without any indication that Jeremy would crack and confess to the killings, the murder squad knew that they would have to either release him or charge him and bring him before a magistrate. There was uncertainty among the detectives about exactly how Jeremy should be charged.

'Jeremy didn't cough to the murders, but he did cough to the burglary and they decided to hold him on that,' said one of the detectives. 'Now, some of us were against holding him on a burglary charge. He had a clean sheet, no previous and it was only £900 odd – we knew we couldn't keep him on that. We should have gone on suspicion of murder and rearrested him outside the court on a murder charge if he was released.'

The police hierarchy, however, felt they had no option but to gamble on Jeremy's charge. If they accused him of murder and were successful in presenting their case, it meant Jeremy would be remanded in prison custody and

151

would have the right to refuse to answer any further questions about the alleged crime. On the other hand, a minor offence such as a £900 burglary committed by a man with no previous criminal record would not normally warrant the offender being remanded in police custody. For a first-time offence of burglary the magistrates would be just as likely to free the defendant on bail. That meant Bamber could walk away from the intensive police questioning and have time to get his thoughts together and prepare his defence for the next round of questioning. Detective Chief Superintendent Ainsley did not want to lose what little advantage he had gained by the surprise arrest. It was still early days, another few sessions of interviews and Bamber might begin to open up.

The murder squad finally decided on the burglary charge and instructed their solicitor to press for a remand because of the special circumstances of the case. They were well aware, however, that it was a gamble and there was no guarantee of the bench agreeing to hold Bamber in custody.

A special magistrates' court session was hurriedly arranged at Chelmsford after the courts had closed on Monday evening. The schedule was planned to ensure secrecy: it was unlikely that any court reporters would be hanging around at that time. The detectives knew, however, that it would be impossible to keep the hearing under wraps indefinitely. Someone would find out what was going on.

Magistrate Mrs Eileen Hance was not the sort of woman to waste time. She listened to the charge against Bamber, which accused him of burgling the offices of the Osea Bay caravan site on 25 March and stealing £980, and she heard the arguments for and against bail. The JP made up her mind quickly and remanded Bamber in police custody for three days. Jeremy, who had been hustled into court wearing the skin-tight blue jeans and white Arran sweater he had pulled on in Sheila's flat the previous day, appeared calm and in control.

He was represented by Tim Stone, a member of a well-established Chelmsford firm of solicitors, Hilliard and Ward. Stone, a recent recruit to the firm, had been on weekend duty when the call from Bamber came through to his office. Hastily apprised by Bamber of the more serious subtext to the burglary charge, Stone was determined to do battle. Despite his strenuous objections to his client being remanded on such a minor charge, there was nothing further Stone could do except begin work on the next application for bail, which would be heard later in the week.

The police had won themselves a few days' grace, but they knew that Jeremy's appearance in court would be common knowledge by the next morning and the press would bay for news. On the advice of their press office, they tried to pre-empt the speculation that Jeremy's remand would cause by issuing a brief statement late that evening:

'As a result of further information relating to the incident which occurred at White House Farm, Tolleshunt D'Arcy on the night of 6 and 7 August, further inquiries are being made by Essex police. A number of persons, both male and female, are assisting with these inquiries.

'Jeremy Bamber of Head Street, Goldhanger, Essex, has been charged with an offence of burglary, allegedly committed prior to August 1985.'

The carefully worded statement had the desired effect – it threw the press and the public off the scent of what was really going on at Chelmsford headquarters. The official lead set by the police was accepted and no connections were made between Jeremy's burglary charge and the renewal of the murder inquiry. Attention centred on the 'reopening' of the murder investigation, and the burglary was relegated to a minor news item. A discreet leak from an unofficial but authoritative source revealed that two men and a woman were helping police with the murder inquiries. But there was no clue as to the identity of the mystery figures.

A frisson of excitement was created by the new developments and the realisation that the biggest murder case of the year was far from being over as everyone, including the police, had assumed.

At the end of the Monday evening court session Jeremy was rushed back to police headquarters, where questioning was due to resume the following morning. Mike Ainsley decided on a change of tactics in an effort to get Jeremy to open up. He instructed Detective Sergeant Stan Jones to take over the interviewing. The detective sergeant was convinced of Bamber's guilt and confident of his ability to coax a confession out of the arrogant young man.

However, none of the detectives who questioned Bamber during those first days could get even the slightest admission about the murders from him. The confident young man proved expert at stalling whenever he was pushed into a tight corner by the interrogators. The sessions quickly became a war of nerves between the detectives and Jeremy, boosted by the suspect's knowledge that some officers did not regard his guilt as a foregone conclusion. He managed to goad experienced detectives to a state bordering on frenzy. Officers used to coaxing confessions from the most hardened old lags were bemused as Bamber stole a psychological advantage in the interview room. His supreme self-confidence infuriated his interviewers and he treated them with scarcely concealed contempt. The questioning was conducted at Bamber's pace and if a line of inquiry proved to be difficult, the young man would ask for a glass of water or slowly light up a cigarette to give himself time to think about his answer. He refused to be hurried or pressurised, slumping in his chair and replying to questions in an indifferent, affected drawl. His most maddening habit was to pull strands of wool from his white Arran sweater and chew them thoughtfully or hold the threads between his teeth, flicking them up and down in the face of the questioning officer.

Jeremy's arrest took place before the introduction of PACE – the Police and Criminal Evidence bill. Often criticised by the police for being too helpful to suspects, it regulates, among other things, the conduct of interviews and ensures that all question-and-answer sessions are taped and can be used as evidence. As news of Jeremy's behaviour spread through police headquarters many detectives felt that on this occasion the PACE

155

regulations would have ensured Jeremy's conviction without a confession.

'I think if the interviews had been taped under PACE, we would have had him. He was arrogant and cheeky and if a jury had heard a tape of how he was answering the questions they would have had no doubts about his guilt,' said one of the detectives. 'He would say "noooo, yeeeeess", drawing the words out as if we were absolutely stupid and the whole thing was a joke. I mean, we were talking about the murders of five people and he was playing the fool and taking the piss out of us. It was just unbelievable.'

With his delaying tactics and his confident manner, Bamber was proving impossible to shake. There was only one point on which officers managed to crack his composure.

During a lengthy session of questioning Jeremy had become confused over the timing of the various telephone calls he made to Julie Mugford and to the police on the night of the murders. The interviewing officers were themselves unsure about exactly what time Jeremy had spoken to Julie that night. He claimed he rang to tell her about the trouble at White House Farm after he had phoned the police for help, but could not remember exactly what time the call had been made. Eventually, Julie was able to bring forward a flatmate who remembered a call coming through just after 3 a.m. That meant the call to Julie had been made before Jeremy phoned the police, not afterwards as he claimed. It was a small point, but it helped to rattle the arrogant suspect.

In the end, the detectives were forced to admit defeat. Jeremy stonewalled all attempts to make him 'cough'. Hostility left him unmoved; appeals to logic were treated as an invitation to a game and a sympathetic approach was greeted with disdain. There was no way of getting through to him. He was either very determined or completely innocent.

While Jeremy parried questions with the confidence an experienced criminal might envy, the police themselves were coming under considerable pressure to produce some answers about the White House Farm murder case. In a gesture of goodwill, the county's assistant chief constable, Peter Simpson, had a quick chat with waiting journalists on Tuesday afternoon, nearly three days after the arrest of Jeremy Bamber.

'At this stage we have no reason to change our theory that Mrs Caffell killed her family,' he said. 'Obviously the investigation is continuing and at present a number of people are helping with inquiries. A number of other matters have come to light.'

It was a desperate show of bravado considering that only yards away from the conference room the assistant chief constable's finest officers were trying their best to prove that Sheila Caffell had not killed her family. The disingenuous statement offered no new facts, but it did provide a flimsy base on which to build speculation.

The Bamber case was back in the news and any story, no matter how wild, could be seen as the cause for the renewed police interest. A day after Simpson's briefing, headlines screamed that the Bambers had been slaughtered by a

157

Mafia-style 'hitman' after Sheila reneged on a £40,000 drug deal. The story hinted that the Essex police had cracked a drugs ring of epic proportions as a result of inquiries in Britain and Holland. The insider who leaked the information had been creative with the truth. The police were, of course, investigating Bamber's trip to Amsterdam, but the 'drug trafficking' involved a couple of toothpaste tubes filled with marijuana.

The newspaper story was ridiculous, but unwittingly, it played into the hands of the police by diverting public attention away from the arrest of Jeremy Bamber.

An official police statement issued later that September day did nothing to clarify the incredible story in the morning's press: 'In relation to the deaths of the Bamber family the inquiries into these deaths have continued since the date of the tragedy. As a result of these inquiries a number of persons, both male and female, have and are assisting us. In addition to this tragedy we are also investigating criminal and drug-related offences. It is intended that a team of officers will carry out house-to-house inquiries in the Tolleshunt D'Arcy and Goldhanger areas and local people are asked to cooperate fully with these inquiries.'

The bulletin had been prepared with great care by the Essex constabulary. With an eye to forestalling future blame over the handling of the case, Assistant Chief Constable Peter Simpson was careful to stress in this statement that the murder inquiry had never been closed. Senior officers had noticed with concern references in the press to the 'reopening' of the inquiry and Simpson would later deny that the police had ever closed it. Technically, of course, the inquiry had not been officially closed. The coroner had yet to receive all the requisite reports from police labs which would allow him to conclude his part of the proceedings. However, it came as a surprise to those still interested in the case that the police claimed to have been actively pursuing the inquiry ever since the day of the murders. At that time, just after Bamber's arrest, this was a small issue, but it was one that was destined to grow into a full-blown argument.

The statement also revealed that house-to-house inquiries in the villages surrounding White House Farm had not yet been carried out. That form of intensive questioning usually takes place as soon as possible after the discovery of a serious crime when memories are still fresh and unbiased, and it might have been expected immediately after the violent deaths of five people.

Jeremy was due back in front of the magistrates on Friday, 13 September, charged with burglary, and the police hoped he would remain in their custody. They had interviewed 'Matthew', the plumber mentioned by Julie Mugford as Bamber's alleged hired hitman. The young man was completely bewildered by the questioning. He confirmed that he knew both Julie and Jeremy but that was as far as it went. After checking his alibi, the police let him go. Julie's story had not been substantiated, yet she herself had always claimed it to be a smoke-screen fabricated by Jeremy to put him at arm's length from the actual bloodshed.

Jeremy had not yet been publicly linked with the

murders but time was running out for the Essex force. The days of interviewing had resulted in very little in the way of new evidence against Bamber. The only incriminating facts to emerge were related to minor offences such as burglary and possible drug possession. Police attitudes towards Bamber had hardened – most of the officers found his sneering manner insufferable – but there still remained a hard core, notably Taff Jones, who had yet to be convinced of Bamber's guilt.

As Jeremy kept his own counsel in Chelmsford police headquarters, his new solicitor, Bruce Bowler, was working feverishly on the defence submission. Bowler knew the strategy of the police was to keep Bamber in custody for the burglary until they could get a confession from him or collect enough evidence to support a murder charge. Bowler was determined that Bamber should be given bail, which would normally be awarded for a minor burglary charge. He felt the police were unfairly trying to hold Bamber. 'The burglary gave the police the ability to arrest Bamber. It was on that basis that they tried to keep him in custody. The real reason was that they were trying to interview him about the murders,' recalled Bowler.

Friday, 13 September, the day of Bamber's second court appearance, proved to be doubly unlucky for the Essex police force. The first blow came with the morning newspapers. The cover was finally blown on the real reasons behind Jeremy's arrest, thanks to the irrepressible Brett Collins. THEY ARE TRYING TO PIN THE KILLINGS ON HIM announced the headline in the *Sun*, Britain's most popular tabloid. Collins had slipped quietly out of Chelmsford after being released on police bail. He made his way back to London and then decided to return to Chelmsford to lend Jeremy moral support at the scheduled bail hearing. Collins was broke but, ever-resourceful, he rang a reporter to cadge a lift to Chelmsford. In return, he offered him a very interesting story: the secret questioning of Jeremy and the determination of the police to charge him with the White House Farm murders.

The day got even worse for the Essex detectives. Once again Mrs Eileen Hance was chairman of the magistrates' bench, but police solicitor Peter Boeuf found the attitude of the court very different from what it had been the previous Monday evening. As far as the magistrates were concerned, the police had been given an extra three days to prepare a case against Bamber. Despite many more hours of questioning they could produce no new reasons for keeping him in custody on anything but a burglary charge. They had had their chance and to give them any more time would be unfair to the defendant. The police were horrified and Peter Boeuf argued desperately for the remand order to be renewed.

The hearing turned into an hour-long marathon (a routine application would usually take a matter of minutes). Bruce Bowler was determined that his client should be allowed out on bail and countered every point put forward by the police. Peter Boeuf told the magistrates that the police were continuing inquiries into 'drug-related matters', but Bowler insisted that drugs had not been mentioned during the eighteen hours of questioning and no charges were pending. The magistrates were becoming

161

visibly impatient with the police procedure and retired to consider the application.

After a twelve-minute recess, the magistrates returned and awarded Jeremy Bamber unconditional bail until 16 October, when he would have to appear in court at Maldon. The police were dumbfounded as Bamber walked from the court, pulling his white fisherman's sweater over his face to avoid waiting photographers and television cameramen. He did not stop to talk to anyone, leaving Bruce Bowler to face the press. 'He has been questioned for the past three days about the murder of his parents, sister and nephews. He has denied all this vehemently. There has been a lot of speculation about the killing by the police which has been put to Mr Bamber, but I don't want to go into details as investigations are still continuing,' Bowler told the waiting journalists.

The game was up as far as Essex police were concerned. They had failed to crack Jeremy and would now have to find evidence to support Julie Mugford's claim under the gaze of a hostile press and a concerned public. Questions about their handling of the case began as soon as Jeremy walked from the court.

Later that day Assistant Chief Constable Peter Simpson was forced into an embarrassing admission at a news conference. 'I don't know how those five people died,' he confessed in response to the clamour for details about the murder inquiry. Exactly one month after police had told an inquest that Sheila had apparently killed herself and then asked permission for the bodies to be cremated without delay, Mr Simpson revealed the true state of the inquiry.

They had no idea if the killings were murders, or murder and suicide. They did not know who was responsible for any of the deaths.

'I am keeping my options entirely open,' declared the assistant chief constable. 'There is a possibility that Sheila Caffell was killed by somebody else and there also remains the possibility that she committed suicide. It is those two lines that our inquiries are following. I have a responsibility to the coroner's court to establish to his satisfaction the cause of death of those five people found inside the farmhouse. I don't know how those five people died.' He added some reassuring words which, given the performance thus far of the investigating team, the public may have failed to appreciate. 'I do not think that the people of Essex need fear that we have someone running around intent on indiscriminate killing.'

As he spoke, murder inquiry detectives based at the incident room at Witham police station had begun to make the first house-to-house inquiries in Goldhanger and Tolleshunt D'Arcy. Neighbours of Jeremy Bamber were asked if they had received any letters to be forwarded on to him or had seen Bamber with large packages. Through this peculiar line of questioning the police were trying to verify a tip-off that Bamber had run a marijuana mail-order service from his Goldhanger cottage.

White House Farm was subjected to a vigorous re-examination by forensic officers, led by Detective Chief Inspector Wright from Chelmsford. While the experts worked away at the scene of the crime, at the press conference Peter Simpson was angrily denying that the hasty burning of furnishings after the crime would handicap the revitalised inquiry: 'The samples we have needed we have got. There is no question of those being destroyed,' he maintained.

While the police top brass and the press sniped at each other, the murder squad faced yet another stumbling block: how could they keep an eye on Jeremy Bamber? His bail had no conditions attached to it other than the appearance at Maldon Magistrates' Court on 16 October. Bamber was out of reach as far as the police were concerned; they would have to rely on their background inquiries to build a case against him.

Jeremy himself was determined to make full use of the forthcoming month's freedom. Pausing only to join in the attack on the police who, he claimed, had 'bungled' the investigation, he dashed back to the comforting welcome of Sheila's flat and Brett Collins.

The two young men decided that they deserved a break after their ordeal. Jeremy fancied the south of France and Brett agreed; after all, if you wanted diversion, where better than St Tropez? Jeremy wanted to get out of the way of the Essex police for a couple of weeks until all the fuss had died down. He was not due in court on the burglary charge for another month and he knew it would intensely annoy the local bobbies to see him taking off right under their noses without them being able to do anything about it. He was not going to wait around until they devised some other charge on which to drag him in for questioning.

As the pair were gathering their bits and pieces together for a quick visit to the Goldhanger cottage and White

House Farm, Jeremy decided to take one last look around Sheila's flat. The difficulties of laying his hands on ready cash were still bothering him. Money was a problem and it looked as if the settlement of his parents' estate could take a considerable amount of time. Just on the off-chance he decided to see if his sister had hoarded anything away. It would be just like Sheila to have hidden a little windfall somewhere.

There was no money to be found, no antiques; there were a few small pieces of jewellery but hardly anything of value. Drawers and a desk were searched and finally Jeremy came across something which he realised he could exploit: the pictures from Sheila's regrettable nude photo session.

On their way back to Tolleshunt D'Arcy, Jeremy and Brett discussed what they should do with their find. Jeremy was certain that the photographs would prove to be the little gold mine he needed to carry him through the next few months. The two friends decided that the quickest and most profitable way to cash in was to sell them to a newspaper. Brett suggested the *Sun* – it was reputed to be one of the best payers on Fleet Street and the Kiwi had already had dealings with one of the reporters.

Collins rang the newsdesk and asked to speak to Michael Fielder, the paper's crime reporter. Fielder had followed the White House Farm story closely, and was naturally intrigued by the offer that the young man put to him. 'Collins had been in touch with me before. He had first rung when Bamber was arrested on the burglary charge. I think he just wanted a free ride down to Essex, where the police

165

were then holding Bamber. Of course we took Collins with us because he could give us stuff about Bamber that no one else could,' recalled Fielder.

'At that time I did a piece on Bamber's arrest with Collins saying that the police were harassing them.

'By the time of the second call the Bamber story had been running for quite a while and it was just beginning to emerge that it was not all that it seemed. I knew that the police were after Jeremy for the murders. It was then that Collins contacted me and asked if I would be interested in doing a deal for some photos of Bambi. Of course I was very interested to meet Jeremy because of what I knew about the police investigation. I arranged a lunchtime meeting in The Nag's Head pub in Chelmsford.'

The three met up and Fielder was amazed at the attitude displayed by the young men. 'Collins and Bamber turned up and we had a few drinks and a snack,' remembered Fielder. 'They were sniggering and giggling together like a couple of schoolboys. I asked them about the photographs and Bamber said, "Oh, they are really good pictures of Bambi – with the biggest vibrator you ever saw." They gave me the impression that the pictures showed Bambi doing things to herself with the vibrator. The two boys were just laughing and sharing in jokes.'

But Bamber and Collins went one step further with their scandalous hints, according to the reporter: 'They were definitely trying to give me the impression that Bambi and Jeremy had been with each other. There was loads of innuendo about Bamber and his involvement with her. It was all crude suggestiveness and snigger, snigger.'

166

The trio discussed the proposed sale for an hour. Bamber was asking a price of £20,000 for about twenty topless and nude colour transparencies. 'They show everything, right down to the last detail. They are really good pictures,' said Jeremy. He also discussed the possibility of selling unpublished pictures of his parents and his murdered twin nephews, Nicholas and Daniel, to the newspaper. Bamber mentioned he would be looking for a 'substantial sum' for the pictures and would be prepared to sell his own life story – at the right price. According to Fielder, all the discussions and dealings were conducted in a very polite and gentlemanly fashion. It was obvious that Bamber and Collins meant business.

Fielder was amazed at the complete callousness displayed by Bamber and was keen to follow up this incredible turn of events to see where it led. As the couple had not brought any photographs with them, he began to make arrangements to view the collection at the Morshead Mansions flat. 'I phoned the *Sun* newsdesk from the pub. As it happened, the editor was standing by the news editor when my call came through. His view was that Bamber trying to sell dirty pictures of his dead sister was utterly appalling. He said: "Tell the bastard to stick his pictures", and told me to write the story about what Bamber was trying to do,' said Fielder. 'I did what he said, but I think it was a mistake. I would much rather have bought the pictures or gone along with the pretence of buying them so that we could have checked that they did actually exist.'

That closed the episode as far as Bamber and Collins were concerned. Fielder's story on the attempted sale of the soft-porn photographs appeared in the next edition of the newspaper. Discouraged by the failure of their venture, the pair made no further attempt to peddle their find around Fleet Street. Back at the *Sun*, Michael Fielder reflected on the episode he had just witnessed. 'I have been in this job for twenty years and I have seen a lot of terrible crimes, but this one sent a chill down my spine. It was really incredibly bad and Bamber himself sent a shiver through me when I was talking to him. Of course I knew that the police were almost sure he had done it so I went to the meeting with a certain view of him. I found it amazing that he could be so self-assured and arrogant, not caring at all about what had happened.'

The whole sordid business reflected Jeremy's complete disregard for the precariousness of his position. His contemptuous attitude towards the police and his failure to acknowledge the importance of public opinion was foolhardy in the extreme. Jeremy was on a high – he had thumbed his nose at the police and was determined to live exactly as he chose after the trauma of the past month. There were no restrictions on his behaviour, all his close friends were in thrall to him and Jeremy believed he had won the game.

'I couldn't believe that Bamber tried to sell those photographs at that time,' said Michael Fielder. 'He knew the police were interested in him. I had to give them a long statement about Bamber trying to sell the photographs. I was even asked to be available during the trial in case I was needed to give evidence. It was only second-league evidence, but I was surprised I wasn't called, because it was actually more damning to Bamber than some of the evidence the prosecution did use.'

Their hopes of quick money dashed, the unrepentant pair collected their suitcases and set off to catch the ferry to the Continent. Anji Greaves, the new girlfriend who had precipitated the final row between Julie Mugford and Jeremy, was not invited on the holiday. Instead she was left behind in Chelmsford as Bamber and Collins went off to celebrate their freedom in style.

'The police were furious, but they could do nothing,' said Bruce Bowler. 'They had to step back and watch Bamber go off to France.'

The odd couple – slim, pale-faced, dark-haired Bamber and chunky, tanned blond Collins – began to drown their sorrows as soon as they arrived in the expensive resort of St Tropez. According to Collins, Bamber did not appear to have been affected by his experiences with the police. 'While we were in France, Jeremy fell in love with a Swiss millionairess and she fell for him. He had a great time making love to her, sunbathing and drinking,' he said. 'I warned him he was number one on the police list for the killings, but he wasn't bothered. He just wanted to enjoy himself while he could. But I knew a storm was brewing for him at home.'

Collins was right. A big case conference was held before Jeremy had even been released from police custody to decide what new course of action should be taken. All the senior officers gathered at Chelmsford police headquarters for a showdown on the case. Was Jeremy guilty or was he innocent? Was he telling the truth or was Julie Mugford?

Taff Jones remained convinced of Jeremy's innocence and put his case in the strongest possible terms. He reiterated his belief that Julie Mugford was not a reliable witness. He felt she was over the top, an hysterical, jilted woman out for revenge. It would be madness, he argued, to turn the case upside-down on the word of such a character.

But more of the officers involved in the investigation had begun to believe the case against Jeremy, and those detectives who had spent time with Julie found her testimony convincing. Every detail suggesting Bamber's guilt was outlined and considered. It was left to the most senior-ranking officer present, Assistant Chief Constable Peter Simpson, to make the decision about what direction the investigation should take. Simpson did not hesitate: 'It's Bamber,' he said.

Jeremy had disappeared from view but the Essex police were not unduly worried. They had traced the Maldon travel agency where Bamber had booked his earlier trip to Amsterdam. The staff confirmed that he had left for France and although they did not know when he would return, they knew he would have to sail to Dover. The murder team contacted Special Branch officers at the port and waited for news.

They had to wait some days for the call but finally it came through on Sunday, 29 September. Special Branch officers were holding Jeremy Bamber and his friend Brett Collins at the port and they agreed to detain him until Essex police could get there.

A group of detectives piled into a car and tore off to Dover, making record speed through the evening traffic.

170

The approach to the port was busy and the tension was sky-high as the officers reached the little room where Bamber was being held. The young man looked up as the policemen walked in. 'Hello Stan, hello Mike,' he said casually, recognising two of the officers he had met before. The reply came swiftly.

'Jeremy Bamber, I am arresting you on five charges of murder.'

9

On remand

Jeremy and his escort arrived back at Chelmsford Police Station just before 10 p.m. A quarter of an hour later he was officially charged with murdering five members of his family at White House Farm. It was exactly three weeks since his first arrest. But for the murder squad detectives the expected feeling of triumph froze with the coolness of Jeremy's demeanour. There was no reaction from him at all. He accepted his arrest without a murmur of protest.

'He didn't bat an eyelid,' remembered an officer at headquarters. 'I thought he'd start screaming his innocence, or take a swing at someone, or call us all bastards, or something. Not a word. It was such an anti-climax. We had been so worked up and there was nothing from him at all. We couldn't believe it.'

Jeremy kept his composure after being charged. True to form he quietly denied everything and immediately

contacted his solicitor, Bruce Bowler. A special sitting of
the magistrates' court at Maldon was arranged with some
difficulty for the following day and Jeremy was allowed to
get some sleep before beginning the next round in his battle
of wits with the police.

After an anxious start which saw the venue for the
hearing switched twice within an hour, things began to
fall into place for the Essex police. Once again they
had the advantage of surprise in the remand hearing. There
were strenuous objections from Bruce Bowler, who had
not had time to prepare an application for bail and asked
instead for Bamber to be remanded for only two days – the
length of time it would take him to draw up the requisite
document. Nevertheless, it was scarcely eight minutes
before Bamber was remanded in custody for ten days, until
9 October.

Jeremy appeared relaxed and smiled at the small crowd
which had gathered as he left the court. He was dressed in
casual holiday clothes and his dark hair was fashionably
slicked back, showing off his smoothly tanned face. As his
client was bundled into a waiting police van, Bruce Bowler
made a statement on his behalf: 'In view of the wild
speculation which has surrounded this case, my client
wishes it to be known that he is completely innocent on all
five charges of murder now made against him.'

The second arrest of Jeremy Bamber, coming only weeks
after his release on bail, unleashed a torrent of criticism
directed at the Essex constabulary. The force hastily
announced a review of the investigation due to commence
on the conclusion of the case. It would determine what

lessons could be learned from the conduct of the case and, more importantly, it would decide whether to launch an internal inquiry.

The murder squad had plunged into a frenzy of work during Bamber's jaunt to St Tropez. All the evidence was re-examined and lab reports were studied for clues that would lead to a murder conviction. It was not long before the police admitted that Sheila's body had been found with two shots to the neck, although the Essex spokesman informed his audience that this was not unusual in cases of suicide.

The police desperately wanted to get on with their investigation unhampered by outside criticism. There was a lot of ground to cover if they were to make a charge of murder stick against Jeremy Bamber and the hostile attitude of the media was an irritant and a distraction. Despite their best efforts more and more vital information seeped into the public domain and became cause for embarrassment.

Caught on the hop by persistent questioning, a spokes-man dismissed the rumour that a mystery woman was under police protection as 'pure speculation'. The officer declared that there was nothing in the story at all, obviously forgetting that Julie Mugford had been under protection for a week.

The police were also forced to admit the existence of the infamous silencer at White House Farm, although their somewhat disingenuous explanation made no mention of the role played by the Bamber relatives in the discovery:

'At an early stage in the investigation a silencer was taken away from White House Farm for forensic examination,' read their report. 'The police do not consider it unusual to have found a silencer in the house but until the results of the scientific tests are to hand it will not be possible to confirm whether or not it was used in connection with the deaths.'

Pressure to consolidate a case against Jeremy Bamber grew in direct proportion to the revelations about the investigation which continued almost daily. There was speculation among the officers involved in the case that some of their colleagues might be responsible for the leaks. Suggested motives for this disloyalty ranged from dissatisfaction with the conduct of the case to a determination that facts could not be ignored or swept under the carpet.

But the worst was yet to come. Nearly six weeks after the killings, information allegedly gleaned from yet-to-be-released pathology reports found its way into the public domain. According to the new revelations, Nevill Bamber had been savagely beaten before being killed. The farmer was a tall, well-built man, still physically fit at the time of his murder. It would have required a great deal of strength and ferocity to bludgeon such a man before his death. It also emerged that all but one of the bullets fired had found their target and that the killer had reloaded the rifle during the slaughter. These points threw doubt on the police 'theory' that Sheila was the killer. It seemed unlikely that the former model had been sufficiently expert with weapons to shoot so accurately and coolly reload the rifle during the massacre.

176

The following day brought an outright attack on the Essex police and their conduct of the inquiry. Headlined A SHUT AND OPEN CASE, a page-long editorial in the *Daily Mirror* declared that the force had 'disgracefully mishandled' the investigation. The Essex force had made up their minds about what had happened almost from the moment the five bodies were discovered, claimed the article. 'For them it was an open-and-shut case. Now it is open again.' The editorial highlighted some of the facts that had recently emerged and pointed out that the hasty cremation of the bodies and the burning of furniture might have destroyed vital evidence. All that was bad enough, but the comment got worse.

'This was not the bungling of some bumbling fictional detective. Even Inspector Clouseau could not have made such fundamental mistakes. An immediate investigation by a senior Scotland Yard officer is needed into the handling of the case. One investigation has already been appallingly mismanaged. Another must bring those who blundered to account.'

Officers arriving at Essex police headquarters that Wednesday morning need not have even glanced at a newspaper to know that something was terribly wrong. The usually noisy corridors were silent – the affair had become too serious for jokes and banter between the detectives. Most officers were bewildered by the turn of events. They could not understand how the top brass had let things reach a stage where they had become the subject of public humiliation. The rank and file had been kept in the dark – they had no idea what was going on – and

177

they were angry with the press and angry with their own chiefs.

Peter Simpson realised he had a crisis on his hands as soon as he saw the morning's papers. He knew that he had no choice but to respond. Every police force is subjected to sniping from the press at some time or another, but this was all-out war and the battle had to be joined. Although several officers advised a low-key approach and a positive effort to get back on good terms with the press, Simpson felt a cease-fire was out of the question. The only way to silence the critics was to come out with all guns blazing and make the strongest statement possible.

The assistant chief constable carried his point and later in the day read out an angry reply to his critics. He declared that contrary to stories in the press, the Essex police were never convinced that Sheila was the murderer. 'From the morning of 7 August this has been an ongoing inquiry and we have kept our options open, albeit that initially there was the probability that Sheila Caffell had committed suicide,' he stated. 'But there was also the possibility that she had been murdered. We have been following those two lines of inquiry all the time. I have a very professional team of detectives examining every aspect of those tragic circumstances.' He pointed out that the inquest had yet to be completed because murder had not been ruled out.

Simpson also attacked reports that Nevill Bamber had been beaten with a rifle butt and which stated that nearly all of the bullets fired had found their target. The police chief dismissed the stories on the basis that the pathology, forensic and ballistics experts had not yet delivered their findings. 'Any suggestion that someone else knows the content of those reports can be nothing but speculation. There has been a lot of speculation by certain newspapers and I think they have indulged in kite-flying,' he said scornfully.

The assistant chief constable won no friends with his performance that day. His claim that Essex police had kept their options open ever since the morning of the murders was at odds with the statement made by Chief Inspector Terry Gibbons on the very morning of the murders – 'At this stage we are not looking for any person in connection with possible offences,' Gibbons had told the press in the first official comments about the massacre.

Police thinking had still not changed a week after Gibbons' pronouncement when Bob Miller put the 'murder-suicide' theory on record at the Bamber family inquest. The large farmhouse had already been scrubbed down and aired for Jeremy by obliging police officers by the time the bodies were buried or cremated. If the police had really been actively pursuing the possibility that Sheila had also been murdered it left many question-marks hanging over the conduct of the case.

It was particularly unfair of Simpson to sneer at 'kite-flying' over the pathology, forensic and ballistic reports. The stories he dismissed with such contempt would shortly prove to be accurate. Nevill Bamber *had* been beaten before his death, nearly all of the bullets *did* find their targets and the rifle *was* reloaded during the massacre.

The furore surrounding the case introduced a completely

179

different atmosphere to the proceedings relating to the second arrest of Jeremy Bamber. At the time of his first detention for questioning, no doubts had been publicly aired about the solution of the White House Farm murders. Any implied connection between Jeremy and the massacre was treated with caution or scepticism. But the inept police handling of the affair and the flow of new information created a different climate for Jeremy's second brush with the courts. The evidence presented against Jeremy might still have been circumstantial, but this time everyone was aware that something was badly amiss with the case and that knowledge was helpful to the prosecution.

Detectives had failed yet again to break Jeremy, so no confession was forthcoming, but the bench were sufficiently impressed by the evidence before them to place Jeremy on remand for a short while. The last great battle to win him bail took place in the middle of October.

Once more the hearing lasted over an hour as Bruce Bowler provided lists of people ready to stand bail for Jeremy and offered to surrender his client's passport as added proof of his good faith.

For this appearance Jeremy was smartly dressed in a grey pin-striped suit and looked much more subdued than at his previous remand hearing. His St Tropez tan had faded and he fidgeted nervously as he stood in the dock. He managed, however, to show a glimpse of his familiar careless style, smiling directly at two blonde women sitting in the public gallery at the Maldon courtroom, who giggled and whispered behind their hands. Bamber seized every opportunity to cultivate a reckless, rakish image, regardless of his surroundings. On his way out of the hearing he turned away from the escorting policemen to blow a kiss at a third young woman, another blonde dressed in a grey suit and fingerless black lace gloves. It was the most exciting thing to have happened all morning and the following day's papers were agog with news of 'the mystery blonde'.

The lady in question was Angela Greaves, who had supplanted Julie Mugford as Bamber's main girlfriend. Anji and her younger sister Virginia had known Jeremy for some time and both had occasionally dated him in the past. Anji, like so many before her, had become infatuated with Bamber and was prepared to give the handsome young man her unstinting support. Jeremy seemed capable of inspiring tremendous passion in his girlfriends and Anji was only the latest in the line of long-suffering women prepared to sacrifice their own best interests for the young man. The thirty-year-old-beautician was upset by the attention of the press and tried to hide her face from photographers behind a magazine as she left the courtroom. Anji managed to evade the crowds and left immediately for London, where she began her own efforts to help Jeremy with his defence.

This hearing marked the beginning of a year spent shuffling Jeremy in and out of magistrates' courts for the requisite remand formalities. Sandwiched between Jeremy's court appearances was another necessary legal formality – the completion of the Bamber family inquest. There was little choice but to officially adjourn the proceedings until after the murder trial. Nothing new

181

emerged at Witham Coroner's Court; it was just an uncomfortable reminder of the first hearing, two months before, when Detective Inspector Bob Miller had confidently stated the police theory that Sheila had killed herself.

The rumour-mill was still working at a furious rate, much to the annoyance of the murder squad. Even the most routine matters became sensational. When police sought to re-interview the plumber, Matthew MacDonald, who had sensibly been allowed to disappear from sight after his initial questioning, the minor incident exploded as a major story. It was claimed that police were hunting a cold-blooded professional hitman who had been interviewed but released in a major blunder on the part of senior officers. The former mercenary had been hired by a drugs syndicate for his ruthlessness as a gunman and headed up a three-man hit squad. It was alleged that the intended victims were actually Nevill and June Bamber, and that the gang slaughtered Sheila and the twins because they were potentially dangerous as witnesses.

A game of Chinese whispers between the police and the reporters had been played with one little point of information resulting in an embarrassing fiasco. But not all the mistakes could be attributed to bad relations between the press and the police. One officer recalled that the press, ever eager to get a scoop, were being unintentionally led astray by the local Essex farming community.

'Most of the journalists did not appreciate the people they were dealing with,' he said. 'This is a very quiet part of the county and any little thing out of the ordinary is noticed. It only needed a helicopter flying overhead one day and the torches of a poacher to be found in a hedge and immediately the story became a tale of a drug consignment being landed on an improvised runway in a field by White House Farm. No one was lying – the locals were simply being helpful by telling the story and the journalists were imaginative.'

The Essex constabulary knew that keen attention would be focused on their handling of the murder inquiry. Chief Constable Robert Bunyard was reported to have ordered a low-key internal inquiry into the conduct of the investigation. A senior assistant was reportedly given the job of pinpointing any errors in the investigation, particularly those made by supervising officers. The announcement was made so quietly that it was hardly noticed by the press. There was even less publicity a few weeks later when a small news item reported that the inquiry had been shelved. Chief Constable Robert Bunyard did little to throw light on the matter: 'Now that a man has been charged with the murders, no further comment will be made,' he said.

There was a feeling prevalent among onlookers that there was confusion within the ranks of the police. The more cynical bystanders suspected that false 'leads' were being suggested by senior officers and passed on by juniors who believed them to be true pieces of information. 'I don't blame some of the police on the murder squad, although I'm sure they felt we were all very difficult,' said one national newsman. 'I think that they genuinely didn't know that the men at the top were covering up for what they

realised were terrible mistakes that they had made. So what
happened was that lies began to be told about what had
been done and what was being done. I think some of the
more junior officers were led up the garden path by their
superiors.'

Acting Detective Chief Superintendent Mike Ainsley
found himself in a particularly difficult position. Although
Ainsley led the investigation, Assistant Chief Constable
Peter Simpson was the man in overall charge. Ainsley faced
the press with mixed feelings. He was a good detective who
believed in fair play, but he had come off very badly in his
dealings with the media over an earlier case, the murder of
Diane Jones, a doctor's wife from Coggeshall.

The hunt for the missing woman and the subsequent
murder investigation had been a fraught time for Mike
Ainsley. The crime attracted a great deal of attention
nationwide and there was immense pressure on the police
to 'get a result'. Despite repeated questioning of the dead
woman's husband no charges were ever brought and the
case was left unsolved. It was not the constabulary's finest
hour.

'I remember the press conferences held during the search
for the doctor's missing wife,' said a reporter. 'Ainsley has
a very good sense of humour and tried to liven up the
question-and-answer sessions as much as possible. There
was one particular incident where he held up cards marked
"yes" and "no" for the questions put to him. In some ways it
was a good idea, because there was very little he could say
and the conferences were desperately boring. Unfortunately, the joke tell flat – most of the journalists didn't

appreciate it and tore a strip off him in the stories they filed. That left Ainsley feeling that he had been taken advantage of by the press and he was never really at ease with them after that.'

The murder squad detectives were as busy as they had ever been during the two-month inquiry. Their best leads came from the forensic laboratories, where every new report offered fresh evidence of Sheila Caffell's innocence. There was still little to implicate Jeremy, but by now the detectives had come up against an unavoidable question: if Sheila could not have done it and if Jeremy had not done it, then who had? There were no other potential suspects – no one appeared to have any motive for the killings. It really was a two-horse race, Sheila or Jeremy.

That line of reasoning had already occurred to Jeremy, who was puzzling over his defence case while on remand at Norwich jail. As the weeks of his custody dragged on and on, Jeremy became increasingly worried about the investigation. At first he was convinced there would be almost no case to answer. It would be a straightforward contest between himself and Julie Mugford, his word against hers. Julie was an embittered, jilted girlfriend and he was an innocent man who had never confessed. But Jeremy's thinking had changed since that first, abortive arrest by the Essex police. They certainly now had enough evidence against him to make his regular remands in custody a mere formality.

Just how seriously Bamber regarded his position was revealed at his next remand hearing. In a move that took the magistrates and the police by surprise, Jeremy announced that he wanted to be represented by a top London lawyer, Sir David Napley. Any change of solicitor had to be approved by the court and George Ginn, chairman of the bench, was not at all happy at the request. 'It's not your right,' he snapped at Bamber. 'You're on legal aid. We can appoint you a solicitor.'

But Bamber had come well prepared and correct legal advice was delivered by Paul Terzeon, a solicitor in Sir David's practice. Terzeon reminded the magistrates that it was the basic right of any defendant to choose their own court representative. The angry magistrate adjourned the hearing for seven days and declared that he was not convinced by Bamber's reasons for requesting a change.

Sir David Napley was then seventy years old and a former chairman of the Law Society. His track record was second to none. He had successfully represented Jeremy Thorpe and *Coronation Street* star Peter Adamson, and had acted in the Helen Smith case, where his bill of £164 an hour for appearing at an inquest caused outrage among West Yorkshire ratepayers. Napley's reputation was as imposing as his gold-coloured Rolls-Royce, and the news that his firm had agreed to handle Jeremy's case signalled to all that the trial would be sensational.

The magistrates had little choice but to allow Bamber to appoint Sir David's firm. His Chelmsford solicitor, Bruce Bowler, withdrew his own representation of Bamber with good grace and after the hearing was over, he read out a letter which Bamber had sent him. Bamber wrote that his change of solicitor was prompted by the 'seriousness and unusual, if not bizarre, circumstances surrounding the case'. He added that he was entirely innocent of the charges and that his desire to obtain Sir David's representation was not based on a whim or fancy.

Bamber owed the acquisition of such a top-notch lawyer to the determination of his girlfriend, Anji Greaves. From the outset, the young woman had taken a far less sanguine view of the case than Jeremy. She decided he must have a lawyer with a reputation to be reckoned with and, after a council of war with Brett Collins in London, she had decided that Sir David was the man for the job.

The only problem was that neither she nor Jeremy had access to any substantial sum of money. Yet Anji was undaunted. Her tactics were straightforward – she walked into the Gray's Inn offices of Kingsley-Napley and told them that they had to take the case because of its public importance. The firm was attracted to the case, despite the fact that Bamber was receiving legal aid, which had a maximum payout of £30 an hour. It was too intriguing and too high-profile a trial to turn down and after several days which saw Anji on the office doorstep every morning, Kingsley-Napley added Jeremy Bamber to their list of 'celebrity' clients. Anji's persistence was rewarded when, on his way out of court following the successful application to change his legal counsel, Jeremy turned to her, and with a clenched-fist salute and a broad smile, whispered a victorious 'Yeah'.

That was the last real development in Jeremy's case for a long while. He stopped attending court for the monotonous remand hearings – even his new solicitor, Paul Terzeon from Kingsley-Napley, knew there was no chance that his

187

client would win bail – and agreed to be continually remanded in his absence.

Anji's determination and hard work were not forgotten by Jeremy, who sent her a constant stream of letters from his prison cell. Confident of his eventual release, he told her he wanted to 'make babies' – his shorthand for having sex – after his trial was over. A more explicit letter was signed 'I.C.W.T.G.Y.T.B.', which stood for 'I can't wait to get you to bed'. The besotted girl even sent one of Jeremy's poems to BBC Radio 1, where the saccharine little rhyme was broadcast as a request – 'Time and space may keep us apart, but you are always in my heart.'

Some of the letters took a more serious tone. Bamber never failed to maintain his innocence and always stressed that in his notes. 'I am depressed but I know 100 per cent I am not guilty,' he told Anji. 'So why should they convict an innocent man of such a terrible charge? It will not happen. Put your trust in me,' he urged.

He also confessed to her that he had even considered killing himself during the early days of his spell in prison: 'I was feeling very close to the edge, as I know you understand that suicide is a simple answer to all of life's traumas and this is the truth. If I hadn't had your love and knowledge that soonish I would be out to give some of myself back to you I would have called it a day.'

Anji also managed to visit Bamber in prison several times during the long year on remand. The young man looked forward to her appearances in short skirts and high heels and urged her to wear the most daring outfits possible: 'Dear darling, a note to say how incredibly desirable you were on Thursday, for all your bashfulness,' read his letter after one of her visits. 'You exhude [*sic*] sex appeal. I feel really proud when I sit in the visiting room.'

There was hardly any festive cheer for Jeremy during the Christmas of 1985. There was little to do except help in the preparation of his own defence and worry about what evidence the police might have gathered for the prosecution. Life in prison was grim and Jeremy was not popular with his companions. They thought he was arrogant and stuck-up and there was always tension in the air when some of the more violent prisoners were around. Jeremy found it hard to settle down and his insistence that he had been unfairly imprisoned was irritating to some of the more world-weary convicts. Bamber complained to Anji Greaves that all the inmates knew about him from press reports and that some of them resented his wealthy background. His family circumstances, his privileged education and his posh accent made him an outcast in prison.

Shortly after the New Year it was reported that Jeremy had been transferred to the hospital wing of Norwich Prison. The Home Office refused to comment on suggestions that doctors were keeping a watch on Bamber's mental condition. Some months after this incident, Bamber told Anji he was afraid of being harmed in prison. There was always someone eager to provoke a fight with the notorious remand prisoner. 'You know how sensitive and non-violent I am, but what can you do?' he wrote. 'I told the governor and he laughed at me.'

But there were still flashes of humour. In a letter to Brett Collins Bamber joked that the one good thing about being

189

inside was that it was helping him save for his gas bill. He was adamant in his protestations of innocence, both to fellow inmates and to friends. Letters and conversations all reflected Jeremy's absolute certainty that he would not be convicted. Brett Collins said Bamber was convinced there was light at the end of the tunnel. 'He wrote to me and it was always when – not if – he was found not guilty. He had everything planned: he was going to sell up, have a good time.'

The wherewithal to provide that 'good time' looked to be on the way. June Bamber's will, published at the beginning of 1986, showed that Jeremy stood to inherit nearly all of the £229,790 left by his sixty-one-year-old adoptive mother. Apart from a couple of small bequests, the money was to have been shared between her husband, her daughter Sheila, her twin grandsons and Jeremy, who now looked set to gain the lot. Immediately, speculation broke out about Jeremy's right to the money. Even Mr Basil Cock, a friend of June Bamber's and the executor of her will, admitted that the unusual circumstances of the case would render his duty a very complicated affair to administer.

A week later the complications were multiplied when Nevill Bamber's will was published. He had left almost £400,000, and again Jeremy was the main beneficiary. By now, however, legal experts had been consulted on behalf of Nevill and June's other surviving relatives. The considered opinion was that, if convicted, Jeremy would lose all claim to the money.

In May the police finalised their case against Jeremy

Bamber and went to Maldon Magistrates' Court to commit him for trial. The 'old-style' committal proceedings were avoided at the last minute, to the relief of everyone concerned. That form of committal can last for days, as statements from leading witnesses are read out to the court in an attempt to persuade magistrates for or against sending the defendant to the crown court. Not only is it a lengthy procedure, but it also lets both prosecution and defence assess the strengths and weaknesses of the opposing evidence and gives them an insight into how the opposition might approach the case. As it was, the magistrates took only five minutes to commit Bamber for trial at Chelmsford Crown Court, accused of murdering five members of his family.

There were strong protests over the selection of Chelmsford as the trial venue. Bamber's solicitors argued that it would be impossible for their client to have a fair trial anywhere within the Essex boundaries. They claimed that Jeremy 'might have a legitimate grievance if he was tried locally in view of the publicity and the high respect in which his father, a local JP, was held.' Mr Justice McCowan, who heard the application for the trial to be moved outside the county, rejected the plea on the grounds that jurors could be drawn from other parts of Essex rather than from the east of the county where the Bambers were known. The trial date was set for October.

Briefings for the defence and prosecution counsels were begun. The defence solicitors, Kingsley-Napley, brought in Geoffrey Rivlin QC as Jeremy's counsel. Rivlin, a small bespectacled man, was a stranger to the law-court circuit of south-east England. Queen's counsel tend to have a particular area of the country in which they work and they become known in the courts of that region. Geoffrey Rivlin's home ground was in the north of England. He had a reputation as a QC with an especially good grasp of the facts of a case. His persistent chasing of facts during cross-examination led him to be swiftly dubbed 'a Jack Russell with glasses'.

For the prosecution, Anthony Arlidge was a familiar face on the Essex legal scene. He was a counsel with an excellent track record in prosecuting difficult cases. One of his great strengths was the ability to make his case sound as simple and straightforward as reading a story. He was also famous for a clinically ruthless cross-examination manner and the Essex force were relying on this skill to shake Jeremy who, after a whole year spent on remand, had still given nothing away. The circumstantial evidence was looking good, but the murder squad detectives knew that this case, one of the largest multiple-murder charges ever brought in England, required cast-iron evidence. They had Julie and they had a lot of people who felt Jeremy could have done it, but no one, not even Julie, had seen him do it or even heard him say he had actually pulled the trigger. It would be touch and go.

As both sides were putting the final touches to their cases, the press scuffled to sign up the leading players in the drama. The *News of the World* scooped up Julie Mugford and her story for serialisation after the trial was over. Fortunately for the newspapers, Jeremy had been a compulsive womaniser. There was a former girlfriend available for just about every newspaper who cared to have one on their books. The *Sun* put together a delicate deal with Angela Greaves, who was still hovering in the background, doing her best to help Jeremy and his defence. Said one of the paper's reporters: 'The deal was that if Bamber was innocent, we would pay him a certain amount of money, whisk him off to a suite in a London hotel, he would tell us his story and then we would take him away on holiday where no one else could get to him. I even had the route from the court planned out. I was going to have two cars waiting: one would have Bamber in, the other one would follow. We would go down a little country lane and the second car would block the entrance so we couldn't be chased and no one would know where we were going. Then it was going to be straight to London and to the hotel suite where Anji was waiting.'

The press agreed between themselves that the outcome was going to be a close thing. No one knew just how strong the case was against Bamber. But they were all aware that the police had been caught red-handed in a series of blunders which might seriously undermine their prosecution. The two legal teams arrived and set up headquarters, and the trial was about to begin.

10
In the dock

There were five charges of murder and the young man in the dock denied each one.

'Not guilty, not guilty, not guilty, not guilty, not guilty.'

It was Thursday, 2 October 1986 and the trial of Jeremy Bamber had just begun at Chelmsford Crown Court.

Outside the court, press and public had mingled in a constantly growing crowd ever since breakfast-time, hours before the day's session was due to begin. It was soon impossible for any resident of Chelmsford to be unaware of what was going on in New Street. The narrow road leading to the law courts was virtually blocked off as the mass of people spilled over the pavement. Every car park was filled to overflowing and local teashops enjoyed a sudden boom in their trade. Television crews jostled for position, determined to snatch what film they could of the witnesses and legal teams entering the building to take part in what had already been dubbed 'the case of the decade'.

Unfortunately, the setting for the case of the decade reflected none of the town's charm. Although built near the beautiful old church of St Mary the Virgin, St Peter and St Cedd, the crown courts are housed in a modern building, with a shiny dark brown brick exterior. A shallow flight of steps leads though large glass doors and into the yellow-brick ground floor. The six courts are grouped on the first floor and lead off from a large communal waiting space, which resembles the departure lounge of a shabby airport. The soiled orange seats are interspersed with upright ashtrays and the air is heavy with smoke as nervous participants sit and wait to enter one of the six doors that lead to the courts.

The courtrooms are all alike and are surprisingly small for such a modern building. There are no windows, and that, coupled with the neon panel lighting, makes the courts claustrophobic after a while. The dull red leatherette seats swing up like those in a cinema and their colour clashes with the orange-brown veneer of the woodwork.

There was a mad scramble for seats as soon as the door leading to Court 2 was opened. Journalists shoved and pushed desperately to grab one of the thirty places reserved for them, determined to get a good seat that would become theirs for the duration of the trial. Then it was the turn of the public, and a carefully counted number were allowed through the main doors and upstairs to the courtroom. The court ushers anxiously restored order before the judge, Mr Justice Drake, swept in with a nod and a smile to the waiting legal teams and assumed the judge's bright red padded seat on a raised platform, directly underneath a bilious yellow and grey coat of arms that read 'Dieu et mon droit' – the traditional emblem of the crown court.

Jeremy, dapper as ever, dressed in a navy-blue pinstriped suit, a crisp white shirt and a striped tie, was brought up from the holding cells directly underneath the dock to deny the five charges in a low, firm voice. He appeared very calm and composed, well aware that every move he made, every blink of the eyes and gesture of the hands, would send pens scurrying over paper.

Jeremy was convinced he would eventually walk out of the court a free man. A few days before the start of the trial he had written to Anji Greaves from his remand cell, telling her to keep her spirits up and scribbling a snatch of schoolboy Latin, which translated into 'Don't let the bastards grind you down.' He added a more typical Bamber touch, rounding off the letter with a schoolboy rhyme: 'Three more weeks to go, three more weeks of sorrow. Three more weeks in this old dump and I'll be home tomorrow.'

His high spirits well under control, Jeremy sat back in the elevated dock and listened intently as Anthony Arlidge QC outlined the case for the prosecution.

Arlidge did not deviate from his usual no-nonsense delivery. The tale he told on the first morning of the trial needed no embellishments to shock and horrify. There wasn't a rustle or a cough as, in his well-bred voice, Arlidge explained to the court just how Jeremy Bamber had carried

197

out the crime which he had allegedly described to Julie Mugford as 'the perfect murder'.

It was the first time that the public had ever heard such an authoritative account of the ghastly scene that greeted police officers at White House Farm the previous August.

Arlidge recounted that the first body found was that of farmer Nevill Bamber. His corpse was in the kitchen where he had been savagely beaten and fragments from a rifle butt were scattered on the floor. His arms were injured as if he had tried to defend himself from the blows and his head and body were punctured with eight bullets. 'It suggests that he was shot and wounded, beaten unconscious and then finished off with four bullets, carefully and calculatedly shot into the head.'

He went on to describe the carnage in the upstairs bedrooms. June Bamber and her daughter Sheila were both in the master bedroom. June's bed was peppered with bullets and she lay slumped in the doorway. Sheila was stretched out on the floor, a rifle slung over her body and a blue, leather-bound Bible by her side. Her two little boys heard neither the blows nor the bullets in the desperate struggle for life that raged in the farmhouse that night. The twins were found in a nearby bedroom. Five bullets had been pumped into Daniel and three into Nicholas. They were both shot in the back of the head. 'It appeared that these two little boys had been shot in their sleep. There was no sign of resistance,' said Arlidge.

The jury of seven men and five women looked shaken and upset as they studied photographs taken by police of the bodies inside White House Farm. A particularly

198

distressing picture showed one of the twins who had been blasted in his sleep. He lay with his head on the pillow, his thumb still in his mouth.

The murderer was Jeremy Bamber and his motive was almost £500,000 in inherited money and property, claimed Arlidge. The QC proceeded to outline to the jury just how and why this handsome, privileged young man had destroyed his entire family.

Bamber's first plan, claimed Arlidge, had been to drug his family and burn down the farmhouse in a blaze that would be faked to appear accidental. But he abandoned the idea after deciding that the house was under-insured. Instead, he decided to shoot everyone – and put the blame on his sister. Detectives at White House Farm found all the doors and windows locked. This, coupled with Jeremy's description of his sister's mental illness and his story about a family row over the welfare of the twins, made it appear that Sheila was the murderess. 'On the face of it, it would appear more credible that she shot her family and then herself,' said Arlidge. 'But the plot thickens.'

He went on to outline a series of 'clues', which made it unlikely that Sheila had been responsible for the killings.

She had no experience with guns, but each of the twenty-five shots fired that night found their mark. Witnesses would say that Jeremy Bamber had been in a shooting competition and was an accurate shot.

The gun had been reloaded twice, and in attempting to repeat this, a police officer had broken his nails on the stiff bolt. But Sheila's long nails were in perfect condition, newly manicured and painted bright red. There were no traces of lead or gun oil on her hands or her nightdress and her bare feet were absolutely clean – unbelievable if she had walked from room to room on the trail of slaughter.

The 'fatal flaw' in this perfect crime was the silencer, which was later found at the back of a cupboard in the farmhouse, said Arlidge. Specks of blood inside the silencer matched the blood group of Sheila Caffell. How could the silencer have got into its hiding place if Sheila had killed her parents and little boys and then shot herself? 'It must mean that she had shot herself once, injured herself, decided that she did not want the sound moderator on the gun and put it in a wrapping in a box at the back of the gun cupboard and then walked upstairs to shoot herself again. In human terms that would not make any sense, would it?' scoffed Arlidge.

He then described the suspicious behaviour of Jeremy Bamber after the massacre. Before the victims had even been buried, Bamber had begun to spend lavishly, taking Julie Mugford for a weekend in Amsterdam and buying new clothes. 'He was doing everything in deluxe style,' the QC pointed out.

Concluding his opening remarks, Arlidge briefly mentioned that Julie Mugford would give evidence for the prosecution. Her testimony would include the accusation that Bamber had hired a mercenary to carry out the killings.

His speech over, Arlidge sat down to an outbreak of frenzied whispering. This had been the first-public disclosure of many details of the case and the allegations surrounding it. That, coupled with the news that Julie

Mugford was definitely going to appear as witness for the prosecution, delighted the excited crowd.

A good proportion of the courtroom spectators were stunned by the opening address. Before that morning not even the most cynical had envisaged anything more complicated than a slaughter carried out in a spur-of-the-moment frenzy by either Sheila or Jeremy. The tale that now unfolded before them sounded as tortuous and deeply laid as a plot in a Hollywood film. There was a touch of macabre, movie-style extravagance about the events which Arlidge claimed had happened. But the QC's manner was impressive and, to many, convincing and credible.

The revelations did more than whet the appetite of the courtroom spectators for the forthcoming drama; they were delivered with a ring of authority that proved to be very persuasive in establishing the manner in which the press and the public would henceforth view the case.

'The atmosphere in the court was pretty strange,' remembered one of the daily spectators. 'I think most people felt a bit like I did at the start – pretty unsure of what was going on. We were all aware that the police seemed to have made a mess of things, kept changing their minds. So no one was sure if Bamber really had done it or if it was just Plod looking for a result. But for me everything changed with that opening speech of Arlidge's. He was great, he set everything out logically and by the end of that I was sure that Jeremy had done it. I think other people were convinced too.'

The court adjourned after Arlidge set out the prosecution case. The opening session had proved to be a triumph for the Essex force, as the powerful prosecution speech carried the day. The police chiefs hoped their success would continue on the following day, when the officers who laid siege to the farmhouse would be the first prosecution witnesses to take the stand.

The Friday hearing passed smoothly as Arlidge carefully took the detectives through their accounts of the night of the murders. Several officers recalled conversations they had shared with Jeremy outside the farmhouse as they waited for a sign of life from within. This testimony proved very little in factual terms, but chipped away at Jeremy's character. The only piece of evidence to make any real impact on the court was a description of Jeremy's cool behaviour despite the gravity of the situation. One of the detectives claimed that Jeremy 'seemed remarkably calm considering the information relayed to us at the time. His demeanour never changed dramatically.'

The jury heard that Bamber chatted about the harvests and discussed his hopes of getting a new car. One by one, the officers with their thick country accents recounted Jeremy's comments about his sister and her disturbed state of mind.

Dr Iain Craig took the course of events onwards. He told the court about Jeremy's tale of a 'council of war' over the welfare of the twins on the eve of the massacre. He also explained that he broke the news to Bamber of his parents' deaths and gave the young man a dose of whisky to counteract the shock of the tragedy.

So far, the testimony had not been greatly harmful to Jeremy Bamber. But Arlidge then called to the stand a witness who disagreed with the picture of Sheila that Jeremy had painted to the police. Neighbour Julie Foakes described the dead woman as 'a loving mother' and told the court she had seen Sheila and her two young sons skipping hand-in-hand down Pages Lane only hours before the killings.

Julie's mother, Dorothy Foakes, followed her daughter into the witness box and also contradicted Jeremy's portrayal of Sheila as a profoundly disturbed young woman. Mrs Foakes implied that Jeremy had a sinister motive for portraying his sister in a bad light and recalled a conversation about his sister with Jeremy a year before the murders. 'He said he didn't get on with her and would not share his money with her,' said Mrs Foakes.

The testimony of the neighbours concluded the second day of the trial and ended the business of the court for the first week. It had been a successful beginning for the Essex police. But nearly all the officers due to give evidence knew that they faced a rough ride when the court resumed on Monday, 6 October. One by one they would have to explain the errors which led them to publicly blame an innocent victim for the farmhouse massacre and which allowed the man they were now accusing of the murders to go free for a month.

Even the most apprehensive officer was unprepared for the strained feeling of expectation in Court 2 on Monday morning. The air was electric with a tension that the detectives found hard to stomach as they waited to be called to the witness stand: 'The atmosphere in that court was unbelievable,' remembered one of the officers. 'I've been in the force for many years and it was easily the worst atmosphere I've been in. It was so tense you felt nervous and sick as soon as you walked in. I actually had to go on sick leave after it was over because it got to me so much, and I wasn't the only one. It was terrible.'

Detective Inspector Ronald Cook, the scenes-of-crime officer at White House Farm, was one of the first detectives to take the stand. This was the moment of truth as far as the press were concerned. Infuriated after months of what they regarded as half-truths and cover-ups they were eager to see the errors of the murder squad exposed in court. They sat on the edge of their seats, poised for the kill.

'The police were really on trial,' said one member of the Essex force. 'Everyone was dying to have a go at us and poor Ron Cook really got it. Of course, the papers made us look like idiots and we all hated it.'

Unfortunately, the detective inspector did not help his own cause. He was forced to admit that officers at the scene had missed a whole group of clues which indicated that Sheila Bamber could not possibly have committed the massacre. His own investigation of the farmhouse had been conducted in the belief that Sheila had committed the murders. Mr Cook said this theory persisted after the examination of the farmhouse and no one doubted it: 'At the conclusion of the post-mortems nothing was said to me to alert me to the possibility that this may have been anything but a case of murder and suicide,' he protested to the jury.

Cook was forced into an embarrassing series of revelations about mistakes made by himself and other officers.

The miserable litany of errors was exacerbated by his lengthy answers, in which he managed to confuse himself as well as the rest of the court. The beleaguered officer was in the unenviable position of having to flay himself mercilessly in order to substantiate the police case. The court sat and watched as the prosecution threw their own man to the wolves.

The defence wasted no time in adding to Ronald Cook's woes. An astonished jury heard that detectives in the farm on the morning of the massacre did not wear gloves when handling evidence. Cook admitted he himself had removed the rifle from Sheila Caffell's body without putting on protective gloves to prevent fingerprints. He also told the court that it took the murder squad eleven weeks to match Jeremy Bamber's fingerprints with a print found on the butt of the murder weapon. Cook admitted that he had failed to get specimens of Jeremy Bamber's clothing for analysis after the murders but could give no explanation of why this basic procedure had been neglected.

Pressed hard by Geoffrey Rivlin, Cook admitted that the Bible lying at Sheila Caffell's side had not been dusted for fingerprints, nor had anyone noticed that the model's feet were perfectly clean, making it extremely unlikely that she had walked through the farmhouse that evening. Photographs taken at the scene of the crime showed the pristine appearance of Sheila, but it was not until several weeks later that this fact was spotted by the murder squad.

Worse was to come. The court heard that it was Bamber's cousin David Boutflour, rather than the police, who had found the silencer used in the killings at the back of a gun cupboard when he and his sister searched White House Farm some three days after the murders. Detective Inspector Cook admitted that the cupboard had not been thoroughly examined by detectives in their initial exploration of the farm. He protested that at that time there had been no particular reason to search the cupboard for any evidence.

The comedy of errors surrounding this vital piece of evidence continued to unfold. Cook told the court that a grey hair found inside the silencer had gone missing in transit between the police station and the forensic laboratory where it was to be analysed. The embarrassed detective explained that the hair must have somehow become detached during the journey.

This error had been compounded as not one of the detectives had thought to warn scientists at the Huntington laboratory of the items being sent to them. The experts had no inkling that the blood-spattered silencer had a hair stuck to it, and therefore may not have handled it with the required delicacy. It was too much for judge Mr Justice Drake, who had listened to the series of mishaps with growing disbelief. His mounting frustration finally exploded. 'They should have been told, shouldn't they? You know they should,' he snapped at the detective inspector.

But there was a much more painful moment to come for the rattled detective, and one which was gleefully remembered by all those present in court. One of the spectators recollected: 'Ronald Cook had just been torn to pieces by the defence and frankly made to look a total berk. Then he was handed a rifle to demonstrate some point about Sheila and the firing of the gun. There was a big build-up, he's handed the rifle, he juggles with it desperately and he drops it. The whole court just burst out laughing. It was as if he proved himself what a berk he was.

Mr Justice Drake did not forget his outrage at the slack behaviour of the police. In his summing-up at the end of the trial, the judge slammed their search of the farmhouse, saying it 'completely lacked care and thoroughness'.

The incompetence of the investigation became headline news at the end of the third day. Stony-faced Essex police chiefs left the court precincts refusing to answer any questions until the trial was over. They also angrily declined to comment on the possibility of an internal inquiry being launched to find out just what had gone wrong.

The following day saw the first of several lengthy arguments between prosecution and defence counsels concerning the admissibility of evidence. The jury was ushered from the courtroom as Geoffrey Rivlin and Anthony Arlidge fought over the testimony of Robert Boutflour, Jeremy's uncle.

Boutflour alleged that in a conversation a year earlier Bamber had claimed he could kill anyone, even his parents. Rivlin objected to the court hearing this testimony, claiming that it was not relevant to the case. After more than an hour of fierce argument, he lost the point. The jury were called back in and Boutflour gave his damning account of the conversation.

Boutflour said that he and his nephew had begun to discuss the mental attitude required to fire a gun. Jeremy had boasted that he was not troubled by the act of killing and that he would be able to kill anyone, even his own parents.

Other relatives of the family gave evidence that day, much of their testimony concentrating on the character of Sheila Caffell. Anne Eaton declared that she had never seen Sheila with a gun and added that the young woman probably did not know one end of a gun from another. Mrs Eaton described Sheila as a nervous young woman who had little ability to cope with demanding physical acts. Sheila had such poor coordination that even routine tasks were difficult for her. 'She couldn't even put baked beans on toast and if she poured a cup of tea she would miss,' claimed Mrs Eaton.

The testimony of the Boutflours and Eatons brought a little colour into the proceedings and made a welcome change for the courtroom spectators after the wooden replies of the embattled police officers. The session was livened up even more by Mr Justice Drake, who clearly enjoyed a joke and several times took it upon himself to relieve the mounting tension with a bit of humour. When Robert Boutflour admitted he was unable to read out a document because he had forgotten his spectacles, the learned judge interrupted him. 'Here you are,' he said, whipping off his own glasses and holding them out to the astonished farmer. 'Try these. They'll probably do.'

This piece of banter was to be the last flash of wit for quite a while in Court 2. The trial had been in progress for a week before the journalists and sensation-seekers finally got what they had come to see.

Julie Mugford, the girl who had lived with Bamber on and off for two years and whose confession had led to the arrest of her boyfriend, took the stand as witness for the prosecution.

Millions of television viewers and newspaper readers had already seen pictures of Julie comforting Bamber as he wept hysterically at the funeral of his parents. Then, in her black dress and veiled hat perched on top of her dark hair, she was the sole supporter of the distraught young man. Now the tables had turned and the supporter had become the accuser. Julie Mugford held the key to the outcome of the trial and to the fate of her former lover.

Forensic evidence could take the blame for the killings away from Sheila Caffell, but only Julie could persuade the court that the finger on the trigger was that of Jeremy Bamber. If Julie's testimony failed to convince the jury, it was almost certain that the prosecution case would collapse. Julie's importance to the case could not be underestimated and Jeremy Bamber was acutely aware of her pivotal role. A couple of days before Julie's appearance in court, Bamber wrote to his girlfriend, Anji Greaves: 'Keep your spirits up and your fingers crossed for Wednesday, when Julie goes into the box. Hope she tells the truth.'

Dressed in a print blouse and a dark skirt, Julie was led into the court building by police officers. The little procession stopped briefly to allow the jostling photographers to get the pictures they were after and then disappeared inside. There had already been a certain amount of friction between the prosecution and defence over Julie's testimony. Jeremy's legal team protested that Julie had sold her story to a Sunday newspaper and this could conceivably influence her evidence. Mr Justice Drake reminded the media of the etiquette necessary to the proceedings.

'The judge was very funny and gave the press a big lecture about not approaching Julie to try to sign her up until after the trial,' explained one reporter. 'He had this ruling written on a sheet of A4 paper and tacked up on the noticeboard outside the court. I remember him saying something along the lines of, "Well, lads, it's very important that witnesses aren't induced to tell their story a certain way." It was all a bit silly as the *News of the World* had been talking to Mugford already.'

Julie was white-faced and visibly shaking as she stepped into the witness box. At first she was hesitant and her voice could scarcely be heard, and Anthony Arlidge had to repeatedly implore her to speak louder. But as soon as Julie's replies began to flow the court were riveted by what they were hearing – it was a sensational tale and, if believed, would surely condemn Bamber.

The young woman began by describing how her former lover had plotted the killings for months. At first he had only intended to kill his parents, she said, but then he had expanded his plans to include Sheila and his two little nephews. Julie said that terrible tensions within the family had led to Jeremy dreaming up his diabolical scheme.

There was constant trouble between parents and son. Nevill and June felt Jeremy did not work hard enough on the farm, while for his part, Bamber resented the way his

210

parents controlled his life. Julie claimed that Jeremy began to talk to her about the unendurable problems he was experiencing at home: 'He said his parents were getting down his throat and he often wished he could get rid of them,' testified Julie.

Studiously avoiding direct eye contact with the accused man sitting in the dock, Julie described the rationale underlying Jeremy's murder plot: 'Basically, the reason behind it was that his father was getting old and his mother was mad anyway and he would be putting her out of her misery. Sheila was mad as well and had nothing to live for and the twins were emotionally unbalanced.'

First of all he toyed with the idea of drugging the family and burning down the farmhouse. He rehearsed his plan by spiking his parents' drinks with tranquillisers prescribed for his mother. 'Jeremy told me he was going to take them in a drink and see what effect it had and whether the tranquillisers could be detected by taste. Later he told me they were no good because they had no effect whatsoever,' she claimed.

Julie said that Bamber ditched the scheme once he realised that the house and some of its more valuable antiques were under-insured. Instead he decided he would shoot his family and told Julie that he had a way to get in and out of the house without anyone discovering him. He planned to set up Sheila as a scapegoat by telling the police about her history of nervous breakdowns and her incarcerations in a mental hospital.

The court was agog as Julie described how Bamber had put himself through a bizarre test of nerve to see if he was

capable of murder. 'Jeremy told me that he had killed some
rats on the farm with his bare hands to see if he could kill his
family. Having done so he said he didn't think he could do
it,' she claimed.

That was the last statement of the day and the press
rushed out of the courtroom to telephone over their
gruesome copy. The honest citizens of Chelmsford sitting
in the public gallery were stunned by the revelations. What
kind of madness was this? A cold-blooded, deeply laid
murder plan, a handsome young man killing rats in a trial
run for a planned atrocity? It was strong stuff.

Opinion was divided over Julie's performance on the
witness stand. Some found her testimony overwhelming
and utterly convincing: 'Julie was very strong. I thought she
was pretty impressive. It was a terribly strange atmosphere
– one of the most tense courtrooms I have ever been in,'
remarked one of the reporters.

Others felt that Julie overplayed her hand in delivering
her testimony: 'Mugford was not impressive for the
prosecution. She came over as being very silly and
immature. She was a bit unreal, pretending to be very
innocent and shocked by everything, but I don't think that
worked with the jury,' said a local journalist.

Geoffrey Rivlin QC faced a formidable opponent in
Julie Mugford. His first task was to remove the ghastly
images of Jeremy slaughtering rats from the minds of the
jury. He went straight on the attack when his turn came to
re-examine the witness on the following day. Unfortunately he succeeded only in making matters worse for his
client. 'Rivlin tried to ridicule Julie's story by asking her

how Jeremy caught these rats,' grinned one of the Essex detectives. ' "Well," she replied, "he fed them marijuana first and they slowed down enough for him to catch them." It created just as much sensation as her first statement.'

Rivlin did manage to score one small point against Julie by getting her to admit she occasionally smoked marijuana, although she did claim that Bamber nearly always supplied her with the drug.

Julie had started the day with noticeable composure, but as she recalled the eve of the murders, her nerve cracked and she began to cry. Grasping the edge of the witness box, Julie said Jeremy Bamber had rung her at her London flat around 10 p.m. on 6 August 1985 – just a couple of hours before the massacre. He told her he had been thinking about the shootings all day and, in his words, it was 'tonight or never'. He rang again at 3.30 in the morning to give her a report: 'Everything is going well. Something is wrong at the farm.'

A further call came several hours later. Bamber told her that Sheila had gone mad and a police car was coming to collect her from London. When Julie arrived at the cottage in Goldhanger, Bamber told her he had promised a mercenary, Matthew MacDonald, £2,000 to carry out the killings.

'I asked him if he did it. He said he couldn't have done it, but he got Matthew to do it. Bamber said he told him what was to be done and gave him details of how to get into the house and where people were sleeping,' Julie told the court. According to Bamber, the mercenary had to struggle with the extremely strong Nevill Bamber. 'But,' said Julie, 'he added that as instructed, Sheila was told to lay down and shoot herself last and Matthew placed a Bible on her chest so it looked as if she had some sort of religious mania.'

Handed over to Geoffrey Rivlin for cross-examination, Julie began to cry so violently that it was difficult to hear her answers. She rejected his claim that her evidence had been gleaned from newspaper cuttings. 'I didn't become aware of what I knew because of that. Jeremy told me, not the press. I was aware the press had printed things, but I was not sitting down reading them. Jeremy read them, not me. I knew what I knew because of him,' she protested.

The next questions she had to face were the most difficult of her entire testimony. Why had she not gone to the police as soon as Jeremy began to plot the death of his family? Why did she not alert the police on the night of the killings when Jeremy rang to tell her it was now or never? Why had she not immediately informed the police after Bamber told her about the mercenary he had hired? Her credibility as a witness rested on her answer and Julie took her time before replying.

'I loved him. Initially, I didn't want to believe that he had got rid of his family in that way. I was scared myself to believe it. Jeremy said if anything happened, it would also happen to me because I knew about it. He said if I ever said anything I could be implicated in the crime as well as him,' she stammered.

Rivlin pressed her harder. He wanted a more thorough explanation. The court was completely silent as Julie continued to flounder. 'When someone you love tells you something like that, you don't want to believe it,' she wept.

Bamber's former girlfriend Suzette Ford leaves Maldon Magistrates Court (*Anglia Press Agency*)

Detective Chief Superintendent Mike Ainsley on his way to Chelmsford Crown Court for the Bamber trial (*Anglia Press Agency*)

Bamber's close friend Brett Collins with Jeremy's girlfriend Angela Greaves (*Press Association*)

Bamber leaves Maldon Magistrates Court in handcuffs (*Anglia Press Agency*)

Bamber is taken away in a prison van after receiving five life sentences for the murder of his parents, sister and twin nephews (*Press Association*)

'In my subconscious I believed that Jeremy was plotting to kill his family. My subconscious was telling me something that my consciousness didn't want to believe.'

While Julie's subconscious waged war with her consciousness, she joined her lover in a money-spending spree after the killings. She told the court that Bamber bought himself a designer suit and an expensive tie and that together with friends they drank champagne and cocktails at a local restaurant on the eve of his parents' funerals. When they returned to his cottage he joked about the media attention he was bound to receive the following day, saying that he hoped the cameras got his good side. He then programmed the video recorder in an attempt to film his appearances on the evening news programmes.

Despite three days in a luxury Amsterdam hotel, Julie claimed she could not stand the pressure of being with Bamber when he was living a lie. 'I said how could he do it and I couldn't cope with the fact that he was being so normal and living a charade and why he had told me and why was he doing it to me?' she sobbed.

Julie described how her horror over the murders led to the breakdown of her relationship with Bamber. She admitted that an argument provoked by a phone call from one of Jeremy's other girlfriends proved to be the final straw. A few days later Julie went to the police and made a statement.

Once again, Julie was on shaky ground and Geoffrey Rivlin did not hesitate to question her motives for finally contacting the police. 'All this business about him planning murders and doing these terrible things came into your

215

mind when it was apparent that he was no longer going to be with you,' he demanded.

But despite her tears, Julie was not about to crack. 'I am afraid you are totally incorrect. I haven't rehearsed what I was going to tell the jury. I didn't want to believe it, I have tried to put it out of my mind. The reason I went to the police was because I couldn't cope with the guilt I felt for Jeremy. I wasn't trying to hurt Jeremy, I was trying to make Jeremy understand what he had done,' she sobbed. 'That was the only reason why I went to the police. Not because I thought he was slipping away from me.'

The young woman was too distressed to answer any more questions immediately. There was a short delay while she tried to pull herself together, gulping a glass of water and dabbing at her eyes with a tissue. Geoffrey Rivlin made no attempt to hide his frustration. He could barely wait for another chance to snap and worry at Julie's heels.

After five minutes, questioning resumed. Julie bounced back, reacting angrily to Rivlin's accusation that she was trying to make her evidence sound as black as possible for Bamber. 'I am only telling you what he told me. The evidence *is* black. I don't mean to do anything. I have no intention of saying anything. I don't like saying anything at all,' she snapped.

There was nothing more to say. Her ordeal was finally over and Julie left the witness box.

The police were overwhelmed with relief at Julie's performance. They believed she would prove to be a case-winner for them. 'Julie was petrified of giving evidence but she did a great job,' said one admiring officer. 'She was shaking a lot and had to sit down, but she didn't let Rivlin rattle her. She stuck to her guns and at times I thought she wiped the floor with the defence.'

A fellow officer put it more succinctly: 'A court appearance is a performance. Julie performed well.'

Julie's place on the witness stand was taken by her mother, Mary Mugford. Like her daughter's, Mrs Mugford's testimony did not augur well for Jeremy Bamber. She testified that she had got on extremely well with her daughter's boyfriend, who even began to call her 'Mummy' and confided in her about his sad home life. 'Jeremy disliked his mother immensely and I thought he was more affectionate towards me. He resented his mother because she had sent him away to boarding school and he never forgave her for that. He couldn't see the point of adopting a child and sending it away to boarding school. He said he didn't speak to his mother, he didn't speak to her ever. He would just ignore her, which I thought was very hurtful,' she remembered.

Bamber told Mrs Mugford that his mother was a religious maniac who had driven Sheila into mental illness. A few months before the murders he said his mother was thinking of changing her will in favour of the twins. 'She doted on them all the time, which got on his nerves a bit,' said Mrs Mugford.

That was the final contribution to the proceedings from the Mugford family. Next into court was the mysterious mercenary who had carried out the killings for £2,000, according to a story allegedly told to Julie Mugford by Jeremy Bamber.

217

The ruthless would-be killer was Matthew MacDonald, a bespectacled plumber from Colchester. His testimony was an anti-climax. Mr MacDonald said he had never been a mercenary, but there had been local gossip about his supposed exploits five years before the killings. He knew Bamber, but had not seen him for some years. He had stayed with a woman on the night of the murders.

After this brief appearance, the level of tension in the courtroom dropped considerably. It plummeted even further when a troop of forensic experts followed each other into court. Scientists and pathologists tiptoed through a bewildering maze of evidence relating to blood tests in an effort to establish the order of the shootings.

After a lengthy examination the most important fact to emerge was that Sheila Caffell could not have fired the murder weapon with the silencer in place. The five-foot-seven mother did not have sufficient arm reach to have grasped the trigger once the rifle with an attached silencer was placed under her chin. But specks of her blood found inside the silencer suggested that Sheila had been shot with it attached to the muzzle. Therefore it was fair to conclude, argued the prosecution, that Sheila had been shot by someone else using the rifle with the silencer affixed. That person had then removed the silencer and hidden it in a downstairs cupboard.

For the first time in the trial, empty seats were visible in the courtroom. But the media and the spectators would be back in full force the following day to see Jeremy Bamber take the stand.

218

11
Actor or actress?

The defence of Jeremy Bamber began on 16 October 1986.
His counsel, Geoffrey Rivlin, knew he faced an uphill
battle. Anthony Arlidge QC had built a strong case for the
prosecution, despite the blunders of the police. Not only
would the defence have to be equally impressive, but
Jeremy would have to go one better and completely
outshine Julie Mugford as star witness if he was to go free.
It was his word against hers. At 9.55 a.m. the courtroom
was crammed full of people desperate to catch a glimpse of
the debonair young man.

'The defence is that Jeremy Bamber did not commit
these killings. It is for the prosecution to prove that
he is the guilty party and they need to do that with
good and relevant evidence,' stated Rivlin in his opening
speech.

The defence felt they had to address the question which
had become the crux of the trial: if Jeremy had not carried

out the killings, then who was responsible? Despite his opening words, Rivlin believed it was really up to the defence to prove that someone else had committed the murders, otherwise the jury would undoubtedly convict Jeremy. 'There really wasn't a great deal of hard evidence against Jeremy. I think it was more a case of if he didn't do it, who did?' commented one of the spectators.

The myth of the 'mysterious mercenary' had collapsed after the appearance of Matthew MacDonald in the witness box, which left only one suspect other than Jeremy Bamber. The defence team had no alternative: they would have to put the character of Sheila Caffell on trial.

Rivlin's opening speech concentrated more on Sheila's possible guilt than on Jeremy's innocence. He outlined her history of mental illness and described her mental state some months before the murders, in March 1985, when the former model was hospitalised with her second nervous breakdown. 'She was then suffering from bizarre religious, paranoid and illusory ideas. She said she thought she was a white witch and that she had to get rid of the evil in the world.'

Rivlin told the court that during this terrible period Sheila was convinced that her sons were being taken over by the Devil. She felt herself compelled to somehow stop this evil and her suspicions spread to include other members of her family in her delusions. 'She expressed certain morbid thoughts that she was capable of murdering them or that they were able to become evil and murderous themselves,' he said. 'She felt locked in a coven of evil and she held very strong views about her mother. She thought her mother was deeply involved in this bewildering complex of evil and influence.'

He stated that on hearing of the deaths, Sheila's psychiatrist found it believable that she might have killed her mother and herself, but found it difficult to believe she had killed her father and her sons. But, Rivlin suggested to the jury, something may have triggered the catastrophe that fateful night in White House Farm, and it was up to them to decide if Sheila had been pushed over the edge into a madness that resulted in the deaths of all her family.

The small, bespectacled counsel treated his evidence about Sheila with tact and couched it in sympathetic rather than accusatory terms. His manner changed and became more aggressive as he moved on to the evidence given by Julie Mugford. Preparing the ground for his client to take the stand, Rivlin rubbished the testimony of Bamber's former girlfriend. He described her evidence as 'so badly flawed that you will find that in many respects it is demonstrably unreliable and unacceptable'. Rivlin had heralded the start of an all-out attack on Julie. The stage was set, and it was time for Jeremy to make his grand entrance.

The twenty-five-year-old was dressed as smartly as ever in a suit, a crisply pressed shirt and a tie. His dark hair was still quite long but was neatly combed back from the thick dark eyebrows that almost met over the bridge of his nose. In a soft, well-bred voice Bamber described himself as a farmer and gave his address as Head Street, Goldhanger.

221

Jeremy's usual self-assured demeanour had deserted him. His statement was scarcely audible and his skin was deathly white, making his large blue eyes appear even more prominent.

He began his testimony in a whisper which had reporters and spectators craning forward to hear until judge Mr Justice Drake intervened and told the young man to speak up.

Describing his feelings towards the rest of his family, Bamber said he had shared a very loving relationship with his father and also with his mother, although he acknowledged that with the latter there had been what he described as 'a lack of understanding on both sides'.

His relationship with Sheila was very good but he found it difficult to understand her mental illness fully because 'it came out in some bizarre things'. But he had no problems with her sons, the twins; he enjoyed their visits to the farm and often gave them rides on his tractor during their holidays.

Prompted by Geoffrey Rivlin, Bamber talked through the events surrounding the massacre. He told the court that on the day of the murders he worked in the fields and then returned to the farmhouse in the evening, where a family conference about his sister's future was taking place. Their parents had been very worried about her welfare and were discussing the possibility of Sheila and the twins coming to live near the farm and also proposing a form of fostering for the boys. Bamber said that Sheila's attitude was vacant and she did not participate in the talk. 'I heard her say, "Oh no,

I just want to stay in London." I left and didn't pay too much notice,' he claimed.

Bamber took a rifle, later identified as the murder weapon, and went rabbit shooting in the surrounding fields. He returned to the farmhouse without having fired the gun and left it leaning against the kitchen wall before going home to his cottage in Goldhanger. The rifle was unloaded, and the silencer was not fitted to it, but Jeremy left a magazine of ammunition nearby – a detail which caught the attention of prosecution QC Anthony Arlidge.

'It was obviously most unfortunate that you should have left this weapon with a magazine close to it on the very night that your sister decided to kill her family, was it not?' demanded Arlidge.

Bamber was upset and showed it. Fighting back the tears, he took a drink of water before replying quietly, 'Yes, it was.'

Jeremy thought that although his sister had little experience with guns, she had been on family shoots. He said that he would not have been surprised if she had used a gun at some point in her life and that that particular model, a .22 rifle, was not a difficult gun to handle.

Jeremy continued his story of the fateful evening. He had returned home with no inkling of the tragedy that was about to take place. His next contact with the farm was not until the early hours of the morning, when his father had phoned him at his cottage in Goldhanger. Jeremy briefly broke down once more as he described the frantic message from Nevill Bamber. 'He said: "Sheila has gone crazy – she has got a gun." I don't remember the exact words. It just ended after that. There was just no more. I didn't have a chance to say a word. It just went dead. I telephoned back two or three times. It was engaged each time. Then I called the police.'

Bamber said he rang Chelmsford police station but it was some time before he could get the desk officer to take him seriously. He was not sure if the policeman had actually believed what he was saying so, desperate for a word of comfort, he telephoned his girlfriend, Julie Mugford, at her London flat. 'I needed a friendly ear. I told her there was trouble on the farm. She said: "Go back to bed." She thought it was a practical joke,' he recalled.

On the evening following the murders Bamber was interviewed at length by two policemen from Witham, Michael Clark and Stanley Jones. The discussion took place at his cottage in Goldhanger. He claimed the officers had asked for a drink before they left and had drunk half of a litre bottle of whisky. Bamber said he had been shocked by the behaviour of the policemen and that one of the officers was drunk when he left the house. Despite his obvious discomfort, the officers did not appear to think that they had acted in any way out of the ordinary, claimed Jeremy.

But the focus of his testimony was Sheila. The questioning turned once again to his sister and Bamber elaborated on his earlier statement about her bizarre behaviour. He said that Sheila was prone to sudden, inexplicable bouts of violence and recalled an incident in which she had punched one of her sons in the face after the little boy had interrupted a conversation. He also told the

224

court about the paranoias which plagued her life, citing one occasion when his father had been forced to talk all night to Sheila on the telephone because she was too disturbed by her fears to sleep.

Jeremy had regained his confidence and composure during his early testimony and it was now time to address the most serious issue of his defence. Guided by Geoffrey Rivlin, Bamber began to explain the complexities of his tortuous relationship with Julie Mugford, the girlfriend who betrayed him a month after the murders were committed. Bamber told the court that he and Julie had been going out together for nearly two years, but his own feelings towards Julie had started to cool before the killings. 'I had ended the relationship in my mind but I did not say that to her. She got the idea I was not going to be her boyfriend any longer,' said Bamber.

He told the court he felt guilty about Julie because he had leaned on her for emotional support. Because of this and because he knew Julie wanted to continue their relationship, he asked her to remain friends with him after he 'dropped' her. Bamber described Julie's passion for him as overwhelming but at the time, despite his not inconsiderable experience with women, he did not appreciate the strength of her emotion. 'She is not the only girl I have been out with. But I am not a judge about a girl's feelings. I suppose she did love me, but it is difficult to distinguish between lust and love,' he declared.

Bamber described the telephone call from Anji Greaves which led to the final confrontation between Julie and himself. She slapped his face and there was a tussle as

225

Bamber tried to restrain her. Jeremy claimed that Julie threatened to go to the police if he hit her, but he did not retaliate and the matter was temporarily dropped.

A few days later, Julie did go to the police and accused Bamber of the murders. After his arrest Bamber tried to explain to his interrogators that Julie had a fertile imagination and was just as capable of telling lies as she was of telling the truth. He suggested there were a number of reasons why Julie should tell such dreadful lies about him: 'Jilted love being the main one,' he maintained. 'She had lost me and if she could put me behind bars nobody else could have me either.'

His statement was pure melodrama; nevertheless, it was well received in the courtroom. Many spectators found it hard to believe that the handsome, well-spoken young man could have had anything to do with such a vile crime. What did appear eminently feasible was the notion that Jeremy was capable of inspiring jealous passion in his girlfriends. Proof of his charisma could be seen in the courtroom as crowds of women, young, middle-aged and old, jostled for the public seats on those days that Bamber gave evidence.

Much speculation surrounded the immaculately groomed defendant. Coverage of the trial had sparked huge interest in Jeremy and it was rumoured that in his cell he had a carrier bag crammed with love letters from women around the world. It was said that a lucky few had already been promised a place at his celebration party planned for after the trial.

His testimony had flowed fairly smoothly, and many spectators compared it favourably to the performance of

226

Julie Mugford. It was generally agreed that Jeremy had been precise and factual, although a little more emotion would not have been amiss. So far so good, but now Bamber had to undergo the true ordeal – the prosecution's cross-examination led by Anthony Arlidge.

Bamber's credibility was dented straight away as Arlidge forced him to admit he had burgled the Osea Bay caravan park, run by his family. Jeremy reluctantly admitted the theft but declared the reason he stole nearly £1,000 from the office safe was to demonstrate the lack of security at the site to his parents. Anthony Arlidge was not about to let Jeremy off the hook so easily.

Pressed hard by the QC, Bamber conceded that the burglary was also partly inspired by sheer greed. He said he had simply wanted some ready cash to spend although he had no desperate need for money and there was nothing in particular that he wanted to buy with it. His motivation for the theft was more concerned with his status at the camp than with his desire for profit. He worked hard at the caravan park for his parents and felt he should have been made a director.

Bamber's mendacity established, Anthony Arlidge then returned the questioning to the night of the murders. He asked Bamber why he had rung the number of Chelmsford Police Station when he could simply have dialled the emergency services direct. 'If you rang 999 it's quite possible the police would get to the house sooner and maybe it would not be long before a doctor got there, and if a doctor got there he might be able to say how recently the people were dead. Was that your problem?' he demanded.

'Not at all,' Bamber replied.

'You murdered them all, didn't you?' Arlidge snapped.

'No, I didn't,' Bamber answered coolly.

They crossed swords again on the issue of Julie Mugford's evidence. Arlidge suggested to Bamber that Mugford had shown she loved him. 'If she loved you that much she is hardly likely to tell dreadful lies about you,' declared the QC.

'Well, she has told dreadful lies about me,' retorted Bamber.

'It's you that's the dreadful liar, isn't it?' shouted Arlidge.

'That's not so,' Bamber snarled.

Again and again, Jeremy was hauled over the coals. Arlidge questioned him about the timing of his telephone calls on the night of the murders, analysed his behaviour during the funerals and exposed his cavalier misuse of his parents' house and his sister's flat. By the end of the day, the critical observers felt that the balance of the case had been redressed by Anthony Arlidge's ferocious cross-examination. One admiring police officer remembered: 'It was quite remarkable. Arlidge literally dissected Bamber and his testimony, piece by piece. It was like a surgical operation.'

There was nothing more Jeremy could do now to help himself. It was left to his defence team to convince the court of the young man's innocence – and that meant proving Sheila Caffell's guilt.

Harley Street psychiatrist Dr Hugh Ferguson, who had begun to treat Sheila two years before the killings, was called to the witness stand. He confirmed that Mrs June Bamber had also been one of his patients and, like her adopted daughter, had suffered two nervous breakdowns. The psychiatrist said he was horrified when he heard that Sheila was thought to have murdered her family. 'It did not fit my concept of Sheila Caffell. I did not feel she was someone who could be violent to her children or to her father, although I was aware that she was a fairly disturbed woman and had fairly disturbed feelings towards her mother,' he acknowledged. 'Mrs Caffell had a very strong belief that she had evil in her mind and her adopted mother also had evil in her mind and they both needed the evil to be cleansed.'

The psychiatrist went on to describe how Sheila had told him that the belief she was evil stemmed from the ghastly confrontation which had occurred between her and her mother when she was in her teens. 'The essential theme was that the concept emanated from or was connected with her mother. At the age of seventeen her mother found her in a rather sexually provoking incident and called her the Devil's child, and that concept of being the Devil's offspring lingered with her,' said the earnest Dr Ferguson. 'She was particularly caught up with the idea that the Devil had taken her over and given her the power to direct the Devil's evil not only on to other people but particularly her twin sons.

'Sheila believed that the twins possessed an evil adult intelligence and thought that she was constantly at risk of being compelled to have sex with them or to join them in some sort of violence.'

The psychiatrist said that Sheila was first hospitalised for treatment in August 1983. At that point she had become completely overwhelmed by the struggle within herself between good and evil. She spent just over a month at St Andrew's Hospital in Northampton and on her release Dr Ferguson diagnosed her as a schizophrenic.

But Sheila's condition worsened over the following year and she was readmitted to hospital in March 1985. She was convinced that her boyfriend, Freddie Emami, was the Devil and that she herself was in direct communication with God. Dr Ferguson reported that Sheila responded to treatment and was released at the end of March. Her monthly medical prescription was halved shortly before the murders and the psychiatrist felt this would have made her particularly vulnerable to mood changes of an excessive degree.

The press loved it all, but the spectators were baffled. The bizarre psychology, with its witches and devils and indecent sexual connotations, was a bit too rich for the blood. It certainly proved that Sheila was barmy but, on the whole, they were not yet convinced she was a murderess.

Iranian-born Freddie Emami, who described himself as Sheila's 'confidant', did not attend the trial but his statement was read to the court. Emami recalled Sheila's difficult relationship with her mother. 'When she visited her father she used to return depressed because of her mother. She said her mother was always quoting religion at her and telling her it was wrong to make love to her boyfriends and how she should always remember God,' it read.

230

He remembered that Sheila had become increasingly hysterical before her readmittance to hospital in March 1985. Minor incidents could trigger violent reactions and Sheila would declare that, despite what her mother might say, God was sitting near her and loved her.

Several of Sheila's girlfriends also spoke of her instability and the problems with her mother. Sheila had confided to one friend that her mother was an interfering woman who criticised her and said she was unfit to look after the twins.

Helen Grimster, a relative of the Bamber family, visited White House Farm at the time of Sheila's release from hospital in March 1985. Miss Grimster said Sheila was convinced she was a white witch whose job was to rid the world of evil. 'She asked me if I had ever thought of killing myself and she said that she had contemplated suicide on more than one occasion. She said her mother said she had lost her soul and should be more religious,' recalled Miss Grimster.

Geoffrey Rivlin QC closed the case for the defence by calling expert medical testimony to prove that Sheila Bamber had been capable of murder. He re-examined Sheila's own psychiatrist, Dr Hugh Ferguson, who came to no definite conclusion on the issue of his patient's capacity for murder. During his initial testimony the psychiatrist felt the idea of Sheila as a murderer did not fit the concept he had formed of her and her illness. He felt she could not have murdered her father and her sons because she did not bear them the hate she bore her mother. Questioned once more, Dr Ferguson admitted that there were scenarios of family murders followed by suicide which had been triggered by feelings more complex than hatred.

This theory was picked up by consultant psychiatrist Dr John Bradley. The doctor had never met Sheila but commented generally on the case. He told the court of many situations where mothers had killed their children for reasons other than the straightforward desire to inflict great harm. These 'altruistic' killings were usually carried out in the belief that it was for the good of the victim. The psychiatrist said that such paranoid mothers tended to 'overkill' their victims and reminded the court that Sheila's sons had each been shot several times in the back of the head and that her parents had been peppered with bullets.

When he was informed that medication for Sheila's schizophrenia had been halved before the murders, Dr Bradley declared there was no guarantee that she was free from the illness and a relapse was most likely to occur after a highly emotional incident.

The defence case also received an important boost from the testimony of pathologist Bernard Knight. The professor said the Bible found near Sheila's body was typical of a suicide scenario. He then commented on her injuries, saying he would have expected the two gunshot wounds on her body to have been different if they had been inflicted by a third party rather than by her own hand.

'Sheila's is the only shooting of the five where the bullets have gone upwards and to shoot upwards one must put the gun under the chin,' he declared. 'For a third person to do this seems extraordinary. It would be difficult for someone else to have done it without her objecting.'

His testimony closed the case for the defence and allowed Geoffrey Rivlin to end on a high note. Dr Knight's expert opinion had restored a great deal of credibility to the much-maligned murder-suicide theory. There were no more witnesses to come. It was now time for the closing speeches of the prosecution and the defence, their last chance to persuade the judge and jury in their favour.

Anthony Arlidge QC was typically forthright. He began his summing-up of the prosecution case with the claim that Jeremy Bamber had made one fatal mistake in his plan to murder his family and inherit a fortune. The error was Bamber's allegation that his father had telephoned him in the early morning to say that Sheila had gone berserk with a gun. 'If the telephone call occurred, it meant Sheila was running amok with a gun. If he didn't get the call and he was lying, it means it was Jeremy Bamber who did it and was trying to cover it up,' insisted Mr Arlidge.

The killings had to be carried out either by Bamber or his sister, the QC continued. There was no evidence that anyone else had been involved and the claim about the phone call tied the defence to the suggestion that Sheila was responsible. He then turned to the question of Sheila's two-shot suicide. Arlidge reminded the jury that a spot of blood identified as Sheila's had been found inside the silencer, which was hidden at the back of a downstairs cupboard. 'Sheila can't have taken off the silencer because she would have been dead after the second shot. It's far more likely that someone had shot everyone with the silencer on, then when he tried to fake the suicide by placing the rifle on the body, realised she could not have shot herself,' suggested

233

Arlidge. 'So he removes it because there is only a small amount of blood on the outside – he wouldn't have appreciated the give-away, damning piece of evidence on the inside. If it was fitted to the gun when Sheila Caffell was shot and you are satisfied it was, then that really is the end of the defence case.'

He added that even if the jury was not convinced by the silencer, there was still an 'overwhelming' case against Bamber. He claimed three vital elements pointed to Bamber's guilt: there was the evidence of Julie Mugford, whom Arlidge described as a 'compelling witness'. Julie testified that Bamber had plotted the murder for months and then told her he had hired a mercenary to carry out the killings, a story she didn't believe. There was also a good deal of circumstantial evidence which pointed to Bamber's guilt and then there was also his own version of events, which was unconvincing.

'But,' concluded Mr Arlidge, 'the jury has to face the fact that either Bamber was lying or Miss Mugford was lying.'

Finishing his speech on this strong note, he sat down to the congratulations of his team. In the back of the court, the relieved expressions on the faces of half a dozen Essex police officers proved that he had done a thorough job.

Geoffrey Rivlin QC gamely tried to return the ball that Arlidge had thrown at him. He opened his speech on the attack and Julie Mugford was the target. 'The evidence of the ex-girlfriend, Miss Julie Mugford, has been unreliable, untruthful and poisonous,' he claimed. 'Almost as soon as I started to cross-examine her, she was crying and she carried on crying and protesting and let slip droplets of poison into

234

this case all that afternoon. Julie Mugford is an intelligent young lady. She knew, she must have known, that in those circumstances it was almost impossible to cross-examine her.'

Rivlin complained that Julie's attitude changed abruptly when she was questioned by the prosecution. 'Quite quickly, as if by magic, those tears dried. She answered the questions that were put to her. Who are we dealing with in this case, a consummate actor or a consummate actress?' he asked.

Moving on to his own client, Rivlin said that Bamber had no reason to kill his family. 'The case of financial motive is pathetically weak,' he declared, dismissing claims that Jeremy hated his parents with the declaration that they 'did not get off the ground'.

He reminded the court that after the murders, witnesses testified that Bamber was 'stunned, deeply shocked and unable to communicate'. If he had 'taken drink', bought a new suit and gone to Amsterdam and France, it was only his way of trying to cope with the tragedy. As Rivlin ended his speech, Mr Justice Drake decided to postpone the start of his summing-up until the following day.

The judge's summing-up brings together all the evidence which he considers vital for both prosecution and defence cases. Although the speech must be balanced it is often all too clear which side of the case is found to be more credible by the judge. Gathered over their cups of tea at the end of the session, the pundits of the press benches felt that the outcome of the case rested on Mr Justice Drake's speech. On balance, they thought Jeremy was guilty. But if the judge stressed the lack of direct and forensic proof and pointed out that the evidence against Jeremy was largely circumstantial, he might well walk free.

Mr Justice Drake was in a brisk, no-nonsense mood at the start of the following day's proceedings. Beginning his speech, he came straight to the point. There were, he declared, 'three crucial questions' for the jury to face in deciding whether to convict or acquit the defendant. 'Do you believe Julie Mugford or do you believe Jeremy Bamber? Are you sure Sheila Caffell did not kill her family and then commit suicide? Was there ever any telephone call in the middle of the night to the defendant?' he asked. 'The answer to each of these can, independently of each other, lead you to the decision to find the defendant guilty or not guilty.'

The judge then began to piece together the story of murder that the court had heard over the past sixteen days. He pointed out that Bamber and Julie Mugford, lovers for nearly two years, had 'flatly contradicted each other'. He warned the jury that Julie's evidence should be treated 'with a great deal of caution' because of the uncertainty which shrouded her reasons for making the statement.

'Why did she go to the police? The defendant says it was because he had clearly finished with her and that she made up the whole tissue of lies in detail because she felt she had been jilted,' Mr Justice Drake reminded the jury. 'Julie says that is not true and that she was very much in love with Jeremy Bamber. It's for you to decide which of them you believe. It's entirely a matter for you.'

Although the judge would not give his own opinion on

236

the credibility of the two witnesses, he did have some praise for Julie Mugford. Referring to Geoffrey Rivlin's accusation that Miss Mugford had proved almost impossible to cross-examine, he declared: 'Julie has answered every question that was put to her. Perhaps the complaint is that the defence was unable in the course of a full cross-examination to get her to vary the story she told.'

There was a distinct shift in the atmosphere of the court. Both prosecution and defence teams had, up to this point, looked equally strained. Now the expressions on faces around the room changed. Anthony Arlidge and his team relaxed ever so slightly, one of his junior barristers leaned back in his chair and stretched out his legs, aware that the tension had lifted. In contrast, the defence team wound themselves up even more tightly. They knew that the speech was not going their way. Super-sensitive to courtroom atmospheres, they smelled the first whiff of defeat.

Mr Justice Drake moved smoothly on to consider one of the pillars of the defence case – Sheila Caffell's possible guilt. He told the jury they had to consider whether the idea of four murders followed by suicide was anything more than 'a fanciful theory' and detailed the evidence involved.

The judge pointed out that Sheila bore no marks from a fight with her father and was smaller and slighter than the powerfully built six-foot-four farmer. 'These things are not conclusive but point to it being very, very unlikely indeed that she fought and overcame that tough farmer, who apparently managed to go on fighting even with a number of wounds,' he remarked.

He also mentioned the contention of Julie Mugford's London flatmate that Jeremy Bamber had telephoned the flat at 3.12 a.m. on the morning of the murders – which meant he made the call before his father had rung him and before Jeremy phoned the police. 'If Jeremy Bamber is wrong in his evidence and he phoned Julie first, well before his father telephoned him, and he immediately telephoned the police, it makes a nonsense of the whole of his evidence about the call from his father and it would surely undermine the whole of his story,' suggested the judge.

Before the jury retired to consider their verdict, Mr Justice Drake gave them a further piece of advice, one which stung the ears of the Essex police present in the court. He told them to dismiss the initial police belief in Bamber's story that Sheila carried out the killings, as it was wholly irrelevant. 'It is quite clear that the police search and investigation at White House Farm on 7, 8 and 9 August completely lacked the care and thoroughness which would have been used if the police had not believed that the killings were an open and closed book,' he commented grimly.

The jury went out on 27 October 1986. The press contingent rushed outside to file their stories from their car phones, then it was back into the court to retreat upstairs to the second-floor cafeteria. No one dared to wander far from the court as most reporters felt it would be only a matter of hours before the jurors returned with their verdict.

'The judge made it pretty clear that Bamber had done it,'

said one journalist. 'That seemed to be the opinion of everyone in the courtroom. No one imagined there would be any doubts.'

But there were doubts. The first report that the jury were filing back into the courtroom came after only a couple of hours. There was pandemonium as the press and public scrambled to regain their seats, only to find the foreman putting questions of law to the judge. Annoyed at the false alarm, the weary journalists trooped back upstairs where they could amuse themselves by staring into the windows of Chelmsford Police Station right next door to the court. By the end of the day, nearly all the officers had realised they were being watched from the opposite windows and had lowered their blinds to ensure privacy from the bored reporters.

At the end of the first day, Mr Justice Drake sent an usher to the jury, closeted in their windowless room, to see if there was any possibility of a unanimous verdict being reached before the evening. The answer was no. He was also told there would not be a majority decision before the evening. The judge had no choice but to order the jury to spend the night in an hotel and resume their deliberations the following day.

The hours while the jury was out were the most frustrating of the case. Spectators remained in the courtroom, reluctant to leave their grandstand seats in case they could not reclaim them when the verdict was announced. The press were itching to get on with the final story, having already written background articles on Jeremy, Sheila, the Bambers and the Essex countryside. In the meantime, rumours about the defendant were spreading around the building.

A member of the court staff reported that Jeremy was amazingly calm and that he had been so all the way through the trial. He was convinced he would walk from the court a free man and assured the prison officers he would be leaving them soon. He was content to spend hours in his holding cell reading novels or flicking though the scores of letters that came pouring in for him. There were whispered details of the huge party Bamber had asked to be organised to celebrate his expected release. The defendant's legal team became increasingly annoyed as they were asked to confirm the story and tried their best to quash it. Bamber's friends said it was going to be a wild extravaganza but confided that they had been asked to keep quiet about the affair.

There were a few more false starts as the jury returned to ask the judge for clarification on certain points of evidence. In the end spectators were caught unawares when word came through that the jury were, at last, ready to return and give their verdict, two days after they had retired to consider the evidence.

The packed courtroom watched in silence as Jeremy Bamber was ushered up from the cells below the court which led directly into the dock. He stood there, ghastly pale but very calm, with his hands clasped behind his back. As usual he was smartly dressed in suit, shirt and striped tie. There was still a palpable air of confidence about him despite his surroundings.

The jury filed in and the foreman, standing bolt upright,

confirmed that the jury had at last made up their minds.

The verdict was by majority, ten to two – guilty on all five counts of murder.

Mr Justice Drake wasted no time on consideration and pronounced sentence immediately. Bamber's only reaction was a slight gulp as the judge imposed life for each of the five murders.

The judge told the young man he had 'a warped and callous and evil mind concealed behind an outwardly presentable and civilised appearance and manner'.

'Your conduct in planning and carrying out these killings was evil almost beyond belief. An individual who can shoot to kill five members of his family – including two little six-year-old twins – in cold blood must be put away for a long time,' he continued. 'I recommend that you serve a minimum – and I repeat, a minimum – of twenty-five years.'

Mr Justice Drake then summarised the events that led to the deaths of the Essex family. Speaking directly to Bamber in the dock, he declared: 'In March 1985, you stole nearly £1,000 from the caravan site owned by other members of your family. Then you told your girlfriend, Julie Mugford, "I shall be the prime suspect, but they will never be able to prove it."

'When you planned the killing of five members of your family, you went one better. You used the mental illness of your sister and planned matters so she became the prime suspect. I don't doubt that you thought that your sister's illness would be such that it would be difficult for people to be aware of your guilt. It is clear from what we heard of

241

Sheila being a prime suspect that your ideas and plans came somewhere near to success,' he stated in a voice that made clear his disgust.

'I believe that you did it partly out of greed, because although you were a well-off young man for your age, you were impatient for more money and possessions. But I take the view that you also killed out of an arrogance in your character which made you resent any form of parental restriction or criticism of your behaviour.

'I believe at once you wanted to be master completely of your own life as well as to enjoy an inheritance, much of which would have come to you in any event in the fullness of time.'

Mr Justice Drake finished his remarks and turned pointedly away from the defendant. The court was absolutely still as the gravity of the judge's speech sank in.

Bamber shut his eyes briefly, swallowed hard and then, without a backward glance, was led out of the dock to begin his sentence.

12

To do a Bamber

One trial was over, another trial began. As the prison van taking Jeremy to begin his twenty-five-year sentence swung out of the court precincts, the Essex police began a press conference to answer their critics.

It was a well-timed move. The press had to be faced at some time and tactically there was no better moment than the day the television and newspapers were already dominated by the story of Jeremy Bamber. The police knew they would still be heavily criticised, but most of the column inches would be devoted to the guilty man and to accounts of the trial. It was better to draw the fire of censure now and get it over with.

No matter how clever their manoeuvres, the police chiefs gathered for the conference knew they were in for a grilling. They had been nicknamed 'the Clouseau squad' and there were jokes about a new saying which had entered police vocabulary nationwide, courtesy of the Essex force.

'To do a Bamber' was now the slang expression for making a mistake, or as one officer might say to another, 'It's been Bambered', meaning 'It's been messed up'. Already on the news-stands was the latest edition of the *East Anglian Daily Times*. The local paper had provided sober coverage of the massacre and the trial and their editorial was one of the more restrained articles on the affair. It still made heart-stopping reading for the police of Essex county, however. Entitled 'A Grave Warning', the editorial summarised the investigation.

'In detective stories, amateurs are always coming across vital clues that the police have managed to overlook. In real life, we were given to understand, such a thing was quite impossible; real policemen were never as incompetent as all that.

'In the Bamber case, though, the Essex police were every bit as incompetent as all that. They made the most elementary mistakes of jumping to easy conclusions and of failing to carry out a thorough search of the scene of the crime. Their embarrassment will be prolonged, for the case is likely to be quoted for many years as a classic example of how not to conduct an investigation.

'Had Jeremy Bamber not boasted to his girlfriend, there is no certainty that justice would have been done. It is a very grave warning against trusting too much to superficial appearances.'

The showdown took place at police headquarters, a modern, octagonal building near Chelmsford prison on the outskirts of the town. It was a short drive from the crown court and the journalists gathered in packs. The police team sat on a raised platform at one end of the room. They were led by Ronald Stone, deputy chief constable of Essex, and Detective Chief Superintendent Jim Dickinson, head of the county's CID.

It was an interesting choice of spokesmen on behalf of the Essex constabulary. The press conference was to be the last official duty for Mr Stone, who announced that he was to retire that very day. He was succeeded by Peter Simpson, the assistant chief constable who had been in overall charge of the murder inquiry. Although he was the most senior officer involved in the case, Simpson was not present at the conference to answer for his team. If Simpson's absence was a startling omission, then Jim Dickinson's participation was a puzzling addition. He had played no part in the early stages of the case nor in the subsequent murder inquiry. Although he had been briefed on the conduct of the investigation, it was difficult to see how he could have sufficient knowledge to give detailed answers to the questions thrown at him.

Deputy Chief Constable Stone opened the conference with one of the few admissions he or his colleagues would make over the next couple of hours. 'We were duped by a very clever young man,' he conceded. 'The senior officers who attended this tragic scene took note of all it presented and deduced precisely what had been intended, namely murder followed by suicide. With the benefit of that perfect science, hindsight, it could be said that the judgements made at the scene of the crime by senior officers were misdirected, but I must again emphasise the careful way in which the whole affair had been planned,' he added.

Stone admitted that Jeremy's appearance as a grieving relative and the description he gave of Sheila's mental state helped convince officers at White House Farm that the former model had gone berserk and killed everyone before shooting herself. But eyebrows were raised and whispers of disbelief buzzed around the room at the deputy chief constable's next statement: 'Whilst assumptions were made, no firm conclusions were initially drawn and the evidence collected eventually enabled the investigating team to pursue what proved to be the final line of inquiry,' he asserted.

He added that the emergence of Julie Mugford as a witness, together with scientific evidence, caused the police to doubt their previous assumptions and to open new lines of inquiry.

The sceptical journalists were not prepared to let the deputy chief constable off the hook quite so easily. They concentrated on the search of White House Farm, immediately after the bodies were discovered – the examination which had been severely criticised by trial judge Mr Justice Drake as perfunctory and completely lacking care and thoroughness. The charge of police negligence was a thorny issue, but the early handling of the case also involved a sensitive personal subject. The officer in charge of the farmhouse search, Detective Chief Inspector Taff Jones, had died earlier in the year after falling off a ladder at his home. His colleagues were anxious that his hitherto excellent track record as a detective should not be marred by blame over the Bamber murders. 'It is no

246

criticism of Taff Jones that the killings were initially misinterpreted as murder and suicide,' said Stone. 'He was a thoroughly competent officer who made a judgement that proved wrong.' He then went on to tackle another incident concerning the former officer – the allegation that Detective Chief Inspector Jones had played in a charity golf tournament only hours after the bodies had been discovered.

'He in fact went to play golf two and a half days later, something which I endorse as a method of relieving the pressure that inevitably builds up in an investigation of this kind,' countered the deputy chief constable. Quite what kind of pressure he was referring to, in a case considered to be solved, was not disclosed.

The Essex police refused to make any straightforward admissions of negligence. Jim Dickinson came close when he was forced to concede that, 'with hindsight', it was regrettable that the funerals had been allowed to take place before the investigation was fully completed.

The stonewalling continued as Detective Superintendent Maynard Cartledge contributed what reporters regarded as the most defensive answer of the day. Responding to queries about negligence at the scene of the crime, Cartledge admitted that not all the officers in the farmhouse had used gloves while handling objects. But, he added, he would not criticise them for this failure as gloves were more likely to destroy the evidence. The experienced reporters could not believe their own ears. Wearing gloves is standard procedure, invaluable for the later examinations made by the forensic scientists. This was the first time anyone had heard the claim that protective gloves could destroy vital evidence.

The obstinate attitude of the police spokesmen infuriated the listening journalists and tempers began to rise inside the conference room. Determined to force some concessions from the officers, the press asked one awkward question after another, beginning with the suggestion that the police handling of the case had been 'sloppy' – a charge answered by Ronald Stone with a simple 'no'. He refused to elaborate but was forced to comment on Mr Justice Drake's scathing criticism of the search of White House Farm: 'Whilst I would say his lordship is entitled to form his views, I find it difficult to reconcile that with my view of the examination by scenes-of-crime officers.'

But Jim Dickinson added a note of compromise: 'In future we will provide police at the scene with all the available assistance so that they can make a more considered judgement.'

This led to the questions that everyone wanted answered. Would there be a review of procedure and when would the Essex force begin an internal inquiry into exactly what went wrong? To the absolute astonishment of the press, Stone refused to commit himself to the inquiry which all the journalists had expected to take place as a matter of course. He said no decision had yet been taken on whether or not to hold an internal inquiry, but police procedures would be looked at to see if improvements could be made. 'It may well be, having suffered the criticism we have, we will ensure to the best of our ability that things like this do not happen again,' Stone added.

248

The conference wound up on a sour note, with little having been achieved in the way of press and police relations and even less for any member of the public who might have wanted to learn exactly what went wrong and why.

The following day's papers proved that few journalists had been impressed by the performance of the Essex spokesmen. TWENTY INCREDIBLE POLICE BLUNDERS screamed the centre spread of the *Daily Mail*. London's *Evening Standard* was even more direct: HOW DID HE FOOL YOU? asked the banner headline – a question that Deputy Chief Constable Stone had failed to answer. The Sunday newspapers continued in the same vein. A cartoon on the *News of the World* editorial page summed up the press and public reaction to the events. Officers with a patrol car marked 'Essex Police' stand by a corpse which has just been hauled out of a river, its feet embedded in a huge block of cement, an axe buried in its skull, a gag in its mouth and its arms bound securely with rope. One detective turns to his constable and says, 'It's an open-and-shut case – suicide.'

It was not only the press and public who had an interest in the mysterious inner workings of the Essex police force. While Deputy Chief Constable Stone and his colleagues were fending off charges of sloppiness at their press conference and prevaricating over whether to hold an inquiry, Home Secretary Douglas Hurd had no doubts about what he intended to do. The morning after the press conference he ordered Essex chief constable Robert Bunyard to produce a report on the murder investigation within the next few days. A spokesman for the Home

Office stated: 'There have been doubts expressed as to what the police actually did and didn't do. The first job is to find out exactly what the position is. The report from the chief constable will be a fact-finding report.'

The spokesman added that the Home Secretary would discuss what action to take with Sir Lawrence Byford, chief inspector of constabulary. The most drastic step would be to order a full inquiry into the handling of the case. The last time such an inquiry had taken place was into the handling of the Yorkshire Ripper case in 1981.

Chief Constable Robert Bunyard reacted to the news that the case was being taken out of his hands and examined by his superiors with a confidence that was considered courageous by his beleaguered officers and brazen by those who felt the Essex police to be at fault. The chief constable said he welcomed Mr Hurd's demand: 'It will give me an opportunity to correct false impressions that he may have formed as a result of incorrect accounts which have appeared in the press and on television. In my view, although at an early stage in the inquiry the investigating officers appeared to have been misdirected by a plausible villain, the position was recovered through the skill and dedication of a large number of members of the Essex police, who produced enough evidence to secure a conviction.'

The chief constable did have his supporters. Some were already staunch allies; some came from rather more unexpected quarters. The Essex Police Federation – in effect, the policemen's trade union representing officers up to the rank of chief inspector – approved the proposal of changes in police procedure. 'As far as our members are concerned, we wouldn't want to think of anybody being disciplined,' they commented. 'We would be opposed to any measure that seeks to lay the blame on any individual – it was an organisational problem, really.'

This declaration was completely routine. What did come as a surprise was a statement from Robert Boutflour, Jeremy's uncle, praising the force which had branded his niece a suicide and a murderess and had paid little attention to the doubts of the remaining family. Mr Boutflour said of the Essex police: 'I have nothing but admiration for the painstaking and diligent manner in which I believe they set out to achieve the task that was assigned to them. I consider it was to the highest standards of their profession.'

That vote of confidence came as a great relief to the force, who must have lived in dread of the family approaching the Police Complaints Authority or calling for a public inquiry. Behind the scenes a great deal of work had been done to repair the relationship between the Essex constabulary and the relatives of the murdered family. Shortly after the trial, the relatives had attended a meal with some of the highest-ranking officers from the Essex force and whatever disagreements had once existed between the two groups were clearly at an end.

Plans for the traditional 'wrapping-up' party for officers, usually held on the completion of a case by the investigation team, were abruptly scrapped. The order came from senior officers, who were worried that news of it might leak to the press and generate further bad publicity. There was to be no consolation for the foot soldiers of the force who had worked hard to build a successful case and had suffered humiliation carrying the can in court for their superiors.

Detective Chief Superintendent Jim Dickinson was given the task of compiling the report demanded by Douglas Hurd. Helped by a couple of colleagues, he interviewed all the officers who had been involved in the case. His findings were assembled quickly – too quickly in the opinion of some of the more junior officers who referred to the document as 'the whitewash report'. 'It left out a lot. It didn't go into the early bits – the detective work done by the relatives and some of the early indications that all was not as it seemed. It would have been impossible to criticise anyone on the basis of that report,' said one man who was privy to Dickinson's findings.

The 'findings' were on their way to Whitehall within a week. Officially, the force declined to comment on their contents but it soon became known that the senior officers in charge of the case had been strongly defended. The document also contained support for the assertion made by Ronald Stone at the post-trial press conference that although Julie Mugford's evidence was a breakthrough, the murder squad were already beginning to suspect Bamber due to the forensic evidence they had begun to receive. In short, it sought to prove that the police would have found the real murderer without the help of Julie Mugford. This line of reasoning was quickly adopted as the standard retort to criticism.

Before Douglas Hurd had made up his mind about whether or not to order an inquiry into the conduct of the case, Chief Constable Bunyard was forced to fend off censure in his own backyard. The Police Federation magazine, *Police*, published a stiff assault on the chief for not appointing an officer from another constabulary to investigate the handling of the case. Never one to suffer in silence, Bunyard hit back, describing the article as out of date and ill judged. 'A report of the case has been submitted to the Home Secretary and everything is currently being done in liaison with Her Majesty's inspector of constabulary to ensure that any lessons which can be learned from the case are passed on to the police service so as to minimise the possibility of anything similar happening again,' he said.

But it was nearly three years before any lessons from the Bamber case were passed on to the police service. Sir Lawrence Byford retired and a new chief inspector of constabulary, Sir Richard Barratt, took over the Essex dossier and tried to analyse the inquiry. He managed a fairly thorough job, highlighting no fewer than eighteen points of police procedure which needed to be corrected or tightened up. By this time the scandal had lost some of its notoriety, but the report still made dismal reading for the Essex constabulary. Accepting Sir Richard's recommendations in a written reply to the House of Commons, Douglas Hurd also included a brief survey of the major errors committed by the Essex murder squad. 'It is clear that errors were made in the early stages of the police investigation. First the senior investigating officer, having assessed the scene of the crime and considered the information provided by Jeremy Bamber, wrongly concluded that Sheila Caffell had taken her own life after shooting her parents and her twin sons.

'In consequence of this error of judgement, he did not follow normal procedures of potential murder cases and was reluctant to take account of information which challenged his original assessment.'

The Home Secretary also declared that there had been inadequate supervision of the senior investigating officer by his superiors. Mr Hurd managed to save the blushes of the Essex force somewhat by playing down the impact of the recommended points. He said that the eighteen 'improvements' which would be implemented were not radical changes to existing police procedures, they were simply a means of ensuring that existing methods were properly followed.

The safety-check measures included the closer involvement of senior officers, one of whom should examine the scene before any bodies were removed; the inspection of the scene with a non-suspect familiar with the premises to look for anything unusual; more attention paid to the fears, suspicions or concerns of people interviewed; that bodies should not be disposed of following a post-mortem until a pathologist had sent a written report to the coroner; that detectives should be careful to differentiate between actual fact and theory when briefing scientific experts and the attendance of ballistics and pathology advisers at the scene of multiple deaths.

All in all, the recommendations added up to a damning analysis of the Bamber murder inquiry. But their impact amounted to nothing worse than a rap on the knuckles for the constabulary. None of the police chiefs were criticised, and any blame was directed at the less senior-ranking officers. There was no internal inquiry and no pressure from the Home Office for the force to institute such an inquiry. No matter that public confidence, particularly in Essex, was shaken and that press scepticism of the police was increased – the force was officially in the clear and would not take the matter any further unless forced to do so.

Little was done officially, but unofficially the rank and file knew they had lost a great deal of credibility in the eyes of the public. That feeling grew to paranoia in C Division Chelmsford and could be narrowed down to the Witham sub-division. Within the space of two years, this tiny area had produced two of the most sensational murder cases of the decade – the murder of doctor's wife Diane Jones and the Bamber murders. The Diane Jones case was still unsolved and the White House Farm fiasco, with its undiscovered and mislaid clues, mistaken murderess, destruction of evidence and almost accidental discovery of the real murderer, either amused or distressed the public.

The Essex police were not quite out of the woods. From his prison cell, Jeremy Bamber was determined to expose the police mishandling of the case which, he claimed, had resulted in the conviction of an innocent man. Jeremy succeeded in obtaining a Police Complaints Authority investigation but, after an inquiry which lasted nearly two years, the report provided no new revelations about the case. It did, however, spark another investigation of the Essex constabulary, this time led by officers from the Metropolitan police. Once again, Bamber was dis-appointed. Another lengthy inquiry concluded that there were no grounds for disciplining any officers and found nothing fundamentally incorrect about the outcome of the White House Farm investigation.

A favourite local joke among locals was an idea to set up a murder mystery tour of the Witham area: 'It would start in Chelmsford, perhaps at the gun shop where Jeremy Bamber bought the undiscovered silencer for his rifle,' said a local shop-owner. 'Customers could then stop for a drink in the wine bar where Jeremy celebrated after his parents' funeral, then carry on to Coggeshall to see where Diane Jones lived and the driveway in which she disappeared. They could refresh themselves in the pub where she had her last drink and then travel a couple of miles to Tolleshunt D'Arcy and walk round White House Farm, where the police laid siege for several hours. Finally, they could stop at Jeremy's cottage at Goldhanger, which the police didn't search, and chat to the neighbours who were not questioned for eight weeks. A tour of the police mistakes in the Witham division could easily take up a whole day.'

Local authors deluged the county's newspapers and magazines with stories of 'the curse of Coggeshall' and traced back every murder in the vicinity over hundreds of years. A popular theory attributed the outbreak of crime to the mysterious influence of ley-lines converging on the area. There were many jokes but it did become apparent that the local force was very much on edge. A reporter who had covered the Bamber case and Jeremy's trial soon became aware of the tensions within the Witham squad. 'I think the police got a real fright at the trial,' he said. 'Some of the local officers looked shell-shocked after being cross-examined. Not long after the trial I was reporting on a case where a man had killed himself. I remember turning up at the scene and he was half in a car – only his legs were sticking out.

'The local coppers were just about to pull him out properly when one of the more senior officers from the Bamber case turned up. I have to admit that the journalists started laughing among themselves about what his decision would be on the cause of death – it was bound to be the wrong one. The officer looked worried to death himself and roped off an absolutely huge area, far bigger than he needed. He wouldn't let anyone go within yards of the body until every single thing had been photographed from every angle possible and everything within sight had been dusted for fingerprints. We were there for hours because they refused to move the body even though it was absolutely clear that it was a suicide. The police were so cautious it was unbelievable. They still haven't quite recovered. It's going to take them a long time to put this one behind them.'

13

Aftermath

Jeremy walked from the dock, the journalists called the newsrooms on their mobile phones, the police hurried to their press conference, the spectators pushed their way out of the public gallery and the Bamber relatives sat on in court, not knowing what to do next.

The life sentence ended a nightmarish twelve months for the families which had begun the previous August with five deaths. The Boutflours and the Eatons had suffered the branding of Sheila as a demented murderess; they had seen their own suspicions ignored in favour of a mistaken theory; they had endured months of questioning by police and press and, finally, they had sat through a nineteen-day ordeal which made their family the butt of speculation and accusations.

After a few minutes of silence, court ushers led the relatives into a private room to recover before facing the waiting reporters. They were in terrible confusion – glad

259

that the trial was over but horrified at what Jeremy had done. David Boutflour, whose discovery of the silencer had helped to clinch the case against his cousin, was ashen-faced and said he felt sick. He summed up the feelings of the family: 'I'm very sad. I have feelings of relief and a lot of sadness. No one wins and everybody loses. It can't bring them back.'

There was no blame for Jeremy. Robert Boutflour, the convicted man's uncle, was the only member of the family to even mention the murderer: 'It is not my place to pass comment on Jeremy. That is left to the judge and jury who have heard all the evidence and whose job it has been to see that justice is done,' he said. But Mr Boutflour had plenty of words for the treatment his murdered relatives had received at the hands of the media. He vigorously defended the reputation of Sheila and said that he wanted to clear her name. 'So much has been said and written about her illness, the feeling she had for her children and the drugs she is said to have taken. In fact this represents only the last sad months of her life and entirely overlooks the previous twenty-odd years during which she was an extrovert, fun-loving girl who gave great joy to her parents,' he said. 'She will always be remembered as a tall, beautiful girl who, perhaps because of her unworldliness, found herself unable to cope with the pressures of the artificial world of modelling she had chosen as her career and became a tragic victim of the permissive society.'

Boutflour also tried to dismiss the speculation that had surrounded June Bamber and her religious beliefs. He attacked the tales of June's alleged fanaticism which had cropped up in the trial as well as in the press. 'It has been suggested that June Bamber was some sort of religious eccentric. As anyone who knew her will tell you, this could not be further from the truth,' said Mr Boutflour angrily. 'Her Christian beliefs were not introverted or mystical as might have appeared from some reports: they were practical and outgoing and interpreted by the devotion of her life to helping others less fortunate than herself.'

After their brief interview, the Boutflours and the Eatons drove away and the remaining crowds gradually dispersed. Only an unlucky few were still immersed in the drama. Hidden in an hotel several miles from Chelmsford, Anji Greaves was chewing her nails as she waited for news of the verdict, supported by two girlfriends. She was dressed for a party and had a bag packed ready to accompany Jeremy to London and then on to their holiday, courtesy of a national newspaper. She believed that Jeremy would soon walk through the door and the celebrations would start.

'I planned to give Anji the verdict myself but she had already seen a newsflash on the television,' said the reporter who had arranged the deal with her. 'She was devastated. She was convinced that Bamber was innocent and had even decorated the room with banners. One of them was fifteen foot long and said, "Faith, love, truth, freedom. Welcome home, Jeremy".

'Anji was so upset that she got up and wandered straight out of the hotel without anyone noticing and walked into the road. Luckily, our photographer pulled into the hotel car park and noticed her just as she was about to go under a lorry. It was almost like she was trying to kill herself. Well, he pulled her back, thank God, and I was able to write her story. I suppose I could have done a suicide story, but my superiors would have gone mad if I'd let her die when I was supposed to have been looking after her and we'd paid money for her.'

Anji was distraught. She had supported Jeremy during the long year on remand, visiting him in prison and writing to him constantly. Her persistence had persuaded Kingsley-Napley to take on Jeremy as a client and she had been instrumental in securing a lucrative newspaper deal for her lover. Now her world had collapsed. Yet her staunch belief in his innocence remained strong. 'I feel so much loyalty for Jeremy but I do not know if I can bring myself to go on visiting now. It could be a life sentence for both of us,' she wept. 'I can't believe that someone who blushed like a schoolboy and longed to be hugged all the time could possibly have murdered his family.'

The loyal girlfriend blamed Jeremy's conviction on her former rival, Julie Mugford. 'I was giving him the love in bed she should have been giving him. She was just giving him mouth,' alleged Anji. 'If she had stopped pressurising him, she would have kept him. She would have him now. No one would ever have known,' she concluded, in what appeared to be an acceptance of Jeremy's guilt.

Jeremy's other devoted friend, New Zealander Brett Collins, also struggled to come to terms with the jury's decision. 'I was absolutely shattered when I heard the verdict, so God knows how Jeremy feels. He was always convinced he would walk from that court a free man – there was never any doubt in his mind. All the time he was on remand and during the trial, he could see light at the end of the tunnel. But now there is no more hope. He will be devastated,' he commented immediately after the trial.

Once the news had sunk in, he too began to reassess Jeremy's story. 'I've always believed Jeremy was innocent. And until I hear differently from his lips, I will continue to believe that. But if he told me he killed all those people it would be too much for me to take,' he admitted. 'I think the world of that guy – but how can you support someone who has murdered five people for sheer greed? I hope he hasn't lied to me. If he has, it will break my heart. To me, he's just not the sort who could hurt people. He's warm, generous, and really a big softy.'

Bamber had never confessed his crimes to anyone: even his alleged tale about a hired mercenary was clearly not true and could not be classified as an admittance of guilt. But the doubts which had lingered at the start of the trial had been ruthlessly swept away. The question was no longer did he do it; now everyone was asking why he did it.

Jeremy's status as an adopted child provided fuel for endless speculation about the psychology of a mass murderer. It brought back with a vengeance the old debate over nature or nurture – was Jeremy born 'evil' or did his upbringing make him into a vicious psychopath? The belief that pure evil could exist as a self-contained entity, distinct from the influences of society, made a comeback during the 1980s after several decades in the ideological doldrums. It

263

was a concept in tune with the political and economic climate of Britain in the period, with its emphasis on self-reliance and individual rather than social responsibility. Jeremy Bamber was certainly perceived as pure evil. Despite a good home, caring parents and an expensive education, he had committed an appalling crime.

A strange twist of fate had brought both Jeremy and Sheila into the care of the Bambers. The Bamber children had failed to achieve the bright future which should logically have been theirs. The two babies came from different parents, but both Jeremy and Sheila had created troubled lives for themselves and their parents. Sheila's personality disorders took the form of religious paranoia and self-doubt; Jeremy was defiantly amoral and confident to the point of arrogance. Sheila feared her capacity for evil; Jeremy went one step further – he embraced it.

Both brother and sister had been placed with the Bambers as babies by the Church of England Children's Society and had had no contact with their respective natural parents as they were growing up. But after the trial, the details of the adoptions were published despite strict Press Council guidelines designed to prevent such stories. Sheila, of course, had searched for her mother and had discovered the circumstances of her birth and adoption prior to her death. Jeremy had never expressed any interest in tracing his natural parents and the revelation of their identities came as a complete shock.

The disclosure was horrifying to Jeremy's biological parents. The couple had conceived Jeremy out of wedlock but they had eventually married and were now a highly respected couple on the Queen's staff at Buckingham Palace. They had no idea that the baby boy given up for adoption in 1961 was the notorious Jeremy Bamber until reporters turned up on their doorstep and asked for their comments. Amid rumours that the Queen might sack the couple, they issued a statement in a desperate attempt to fend off the press. The unhappy parents said they had been unaware of any connection between themselves and Jeremy Bamber. 'Indeed, they are not now able to confirm or deny the suggestion that Jeremy Bamber may be their child,' read the statement. 'They greatly regret that this private and personal matter has been thought a proper subject for publicity.'

Sheila's natural mother was devastated by the news of her daughter's death. It was even more painful following, as it did, their brief reunion. They had kept in touch and Sheila had planned to visit her mother in Canada as soon as she was well enough to make the trip.

Jeremy's conviction had settled one potentially troublesome issue. The executors of the Bamber estate confirmed that Jeremy would not profit from his crime. The so-called 'rule of forfeiture' was applied to the £500,000 Bamber inheritance, making it impossible for Jeremy to gain any benefit from the murders. Instead, there was the prospect of many months of complicated legal work to determine exactly how the money would be distributed.

In the event another leading protagonist in the case stood to gain from Jeremy's crime. Julie Mugford, the woman whose evidence formed the greater part of the prosecution case against Jeremy Bamber, sold her 'harrowing inside story' to the highest bidder, the *News of the World*. Julie got £15,000 from the deal which, according to reporters, was already under discussion as the trial began and against the instructions Mr Justice Drake later gave.

The first instalment of the exclusive story appeared on the Sunday following the verdict. Julie was pictured, heavily made up and with her dress hiked up to her thighs, telling readers of her affair with Bamber and of her last meeting with Nicholas and Daniel, the six-year-olds slaughtered by their uncle. 'I adored those children. They were such little characters and so affectionate towards me. I used to feel almost like a second mother to them,' said Julie, whose first job as a primary school teacher had begun only weeks before the start of the trial. 'Four days later, when I learned that the whole family had been massacred, I could hardly bear to think of those children being cut off from life so early. I still cry for them.'

Julie's revelations earned her a great deal of money but also brought repercussions that she had not bargained for. Less than a week after the final instalment of 'Mass Killer's Lover Tells All' hit the news-stands, she was suspended from her teaching job by the Inner London Education Authority. Her employers said she would stay on on full pay until a disciplinary hearing investigated various incidents she had related in court and the contract she had negotiated with the newspaper. During the trial Julie had admitted smoking cannabis, helping Jeremy to steal £1,000 in a burglary and also joining him in passing dud cheques. Her appearance, heavily made up and scantily clad, alongside sexual revelations in the *News of the World* was

266

too much for the education authorities to ignore. 'This is a case where everyone has bent over backwards to help her,' said an ILEA spokesman. 'She is only twenty-two, very young, and the authority has a paternalistic attitude. No one wants to be heavy-handed. The hearing will be an opportunity to air everything.'

Julie's own attitude was defiant: 'A lot of what I have done, many other teachers have done,' she told reporters after the hearing.

Behind the bravado, however, she was aware that many of her friends and colleagues were shocked that she chose to cash in on her association with the mass murderer. They criticised the tone of the articles as sensational and felt that Julie had portrayed herself in a very bad light. 'I think what she did was a terrible mistake,' said one of her friends. 'The articles were dreadful. She looked like a tart. The pictures were disgusting with all that make-up and pulling her dress up. She looked like Myra Hindley. That wasn't the real Julie at all.'

It was six months before Julie returned to work. Her only punishment was to be removed from the south London primary school where she had taught prior to her suspension. She was given a fresh start in a school north of the Thames. 'After what she said in the newspapers and in court we felt she could not go back to where she had been teaching,' said her employers. 'It would have been asking too much of the parents and the staff, even though all these things happened before she became a teacher.'

Despite the vote of confidence she received from the education chiefs, Julie managed only a couple of years' teaching before deciding to quit her job and travel round the world.

Julie was not the only person involved in the case to bare her soul in print. Several of Jeremy's former girlfriends followed her example and sold stories of their passionate nights with Bamber. They were quickly followed by a string of 'kiss-and-tell' penpals. Jeremy replied to many of the letters he received during his long remand and trial and several of the friendships survived and developed.

Soon a steady trickle of young women from all parts of the country made the journey to whatever jail was housing Bamber for the thrill of a brief meeting with the handsome killer. Every detail of the visits were noted down by the shrewd young penpals and then sold for a tidy sum to Sunday newspapers.

A brunette named Sabina Butt, who claimed to hail from a wealthy Saudi Arabian family, was one of the first to enter the fray with the declaration that she and Jeremy planned to have two children, hopefully boys, as soon as he was released. Sabina was convinced of Jeremy's innocence, declaring that he would soon be freed on appeal. Until then she had the comfort of an occasional visit and the 'terribly sexy messages' he sent. 'You look so sexy, horny beyond belief. I don't think I'd be able to control myself in your company,' read one of Bamber's letters. 'Where I miss out is that I can't do to you what I would like to do. I need a bucket of iced water thrown over me.'

Not long after selling her story Sabina found her feelings for Jeremy had disappeared. The newspaper-reading public were told that the love-behind-bars affair was over:

'One day I looked into his eyes and thought I saw a murderer. Suddenly his eyes looked so spooky and I never felt the same way about him,' recalled the disillusioned young woman.

Sabina's revelations inspired yet another of Jeremy's correspondents to take up her pen. 'Bubbly Jayne Beardsley' claimed that it was she, not Sabina, who was the subject of Jeremy's love and lust. 'I love him so much I let him caress me all over,' she said, describing her visits to the killer in Wormwood Scrubs. 'He's got such a good body that I want to rip his clothes off and make love to him. But because we are so closely supervised we have to make do with other things. We wear loose clothing to make sure we can touch each other easily. We get so excited and turned on it's difficult to restrain ourselves,' drooled Jayne.

Like her rival Sabina, she believed Bamber to be innocent of the murders. Jayne, who revealed that Bamber nicknamed her 'my little whippet', declared: 'He's just a lovely, misunderstood young man. He's one of the softest, most gentle men I've ever met. He wouldn't hurt a fly.'

There were other victims of the devastation that Jeremy had wreaked on the Bamber family. Colin Caffell suffered the greatest personal loss from Jeremy's crimes. He had lost his two sons and their much-loved mother. Shortly after the murders Caffell added his own thoughtful tributes to his dead wife and her family.

He now turned his hand from pottery to sculpture, producing several small bronze figures based on his sons and on Sheila – one of them depicting her during pregnancy. In a further attempt to exorcise his sad memories and to counter what he felt had been an unfair portrayal of the woman he knew as 'Bambs', Caffell jotted down his thoughts and feelings until he had compiled a 150,000 word manuscript. 'It was difficult to reconcile my memories of two laughing children and their loving mother with the grossly distorted images that were being presented. Seeing the girl I loved so long become the 'Bambi' of the press could only be seen as a rape of her and our memories of her,' he said.

In an attempt to make some sense of the tragedy, Caffell wrote to former Goon star Michael Bentine after reading a book in which the comedian described how he had coped with death through the help of the spirit world. Bentine arranged for Caffell to meet a medium, and after a couple of sessions, the bereaved father believed he had received a message from Sheila. 'I didn't believe in life after death, but the things she told me convinced me otherwise,' he said. 'The first time she told me Sheila didn't want to be contacted. Then she told me she was totally at peace and was looking forward to the future. I didn't need to believe in spiritualism. I just wanted confirmation that Bambs and the boys were all right. And I was given it.'

Sheila, branded 'the Devil's child' by her mother, had battled for most of her adult life with what she saw as the evil influence of the spirit world. Her own strong belief in spiritualism had influenced many of her girlfriends during her lifetime, and several of them joined 'Bambi' on her weekly visits to clairvoyants. After her death, people who had never dreamed of dabbling in the spiritual world claimed to have felt Sheila's presence around them.

Only hours after Sheila's violent death, Julie Mugford stood in the hospital mortuary seeking to 'commune' with the murdered woman's spirit in an effort to find out what had really happened. Solid, salt-of-the-earth David Boutflour felt that Sheila's spirit had haunted his family, urging them to find the truth about the massacre.

Now it was Colin's turn to be infected by the enthusiasm of his former wife for the world beyond. A year after Jeremy's trial and two years after the death of his family, Caffell claimed to have experienced a premonition of disaster on the eve of the massacre. 'I just went into a blind panic. I went to my girlfriend's and broke down,' he recalled. 'I thought they would think I was crazy ringing up at eleven o'clock to ask if everything was OK. I wonder what would have happened if I had rung?'

After the deaths, Caffell said he became aware of influences on his life that were outside his control. One of the mediums he visited reassured him about the spirits that were affecting his life and began to relay information to him about Sheila and the twins. Caffell welcomed the revelations about his family and believed it gave him an insight into dealing with his own life and work. 'I felt I was being given the evidence to know they were still around and they were still helping me and looking after me,' he maintained. 'I felt I was being helped, especially with the sculptures, which I had never been able to do before. Help had turned up just when I needed it'

Having made peace with his memories of Sheila, Caffell also sought to come to terms with his feelings towards

Jeremy. Not surprisingly, his initial reaction was one of intense anger: 'To destroy so much, simply for greed. I wanted to break every bone in Jeremy's body. I was really disturbed, it made me think very long about human nature,' he recalled.

Over the months, Colin Caffell struggled to retain his own sanity and discovered that a return to normal life could not be possible without an understanding of the crime and of the criminal. He decided to go one step further: he had to try to forgive Jeremy Bamber for the evil he had done. 'If I told myself that I had been condemned to a life sentence of hatred I know that in itself would have killed me. The process of forgiving Jeremy didn't come overnight,' he admitted. 'I had to learn to forgive myself. I felt I had let Sheila down as a husband and once I had forgiven myself for the mistakes I had made, it was a natural progression to forgive Jeremy. I've given up my claim on revenge. I think forgiveness has to be unconditional.'

He began to write to his jailed brother-in-law, declaring that he was not seeking a confession, but simply trying to piece together the life that the brother and sister had led as children.

Caffell also began to help others who had suffered from similar tragedies, joining a group called Parents of Murdered Children and taking part in counselling sessions for the bereaved. He was also featured in a BBC documentary, *As We Forgive Them...?*, in which he described his struggle to come to terms with his feelings towards the murderer of his former wife and children. Nearly five years after the murders the pain is still there, but Colin Caffell has clearly found his feet again. 'Sheila was a product of her childhood and therefore Jeremy must be too,' said Colin. 'I regard him as another victim. You can't condemn children. I do feel at last that I'm at a new beginning and forgiveness has played a large part in that.'

14
Life

'He just walked down the steps, got into the cell, picked up the book he had been reading and carried on reading it without saying a word.'

The officers guarding Jeremy Bamber were amazed. The young man had just received the heaviest sentence ever imposed at Chelmsford Crown Court and he was acting as if he couldn't care less. Upstairs there was pandemonium as reporters phoned through their stories, the spectators shouted the verdict to friends and the clutch of girls who had turned up day after day just to see the handsome young defendant wept loudly. Down below in the holding cell, Jeremy took off his jacket, loosened his tie, unfastened his collar and, putting his feet up, read his book until it was time for the journey to Wormwood Scrubs Prison in west London.

Outside the court Jeremy's solicitor, Paul Terzeon, was cautious rather than optimistic about the possibility of an appeal: 'No decision has been taken but we are looking into the matter. We have twenty-eight days to file any notice of appeal,' he said. 'Any appeal will have to be on a point of law. You cannot appeal simply because you do not like the verdict. There has to be a fault in the summing-up, or a misdirection by the judge on a point of law before you can appeal against the verdict. A decision will probably be taken in about three weeks' time.'

Meanwhile the instigator of all this trouble was ushered from his holding cell and out of the court building to begin his minimum twenty-five years in prison. Surrounded by police officers, Jeremy was marched hurriedly to the prison van. Perversely, he looked more handsome than ever. His tie unknotted, his shirt open at the neck and his smart jacket thrown open, he had the appearance of a dashing young bridegroom relaxing after the wedding. Eager photographers snatched one last shot of him as the prison van swept out of Chelmsford. His face half-obscured by the bars over the van window, all that could really be seen of Jeremy was a pair of huge, staring, expressionless eyes taking in a last long look at the outside world.

It took the Bamber defence team the predicted three weeks to open the long process of appeal. On 20 November 1986 solicitor Paul Terzeon lodged the provisional grounds for the appeal. They based their case on the claim that Mr Justice Drake had misdirected the jury before sending them out to consider their verdict.

Like any other convicted criminal, Bamber had no automatic right to have his case reconsidered. First the papers explaining the reasons for the appeal were compiled

276

by his defence lawyers and sent to a high court judge. The judge would study the papers in private and decide whether there was a case for an appeal hearing to go ahead. Even if the judge felt that there were not strong enough grounds for an appeal and refused the request, Bamber would still be able to put his claim before three high court judges for consideration in open court. Paul Terzeon warned his client – and the press – that it would probably be six months before a judge was available to consider the appeal.

Jeremy was back in prison, but this time it was for real. He had been supremely confident that he would be acquitted, and he had almost walked free. The verdict had been a majority, ten to two. Just one more juror with sufficient doubt and he would have been a free man. But from now on it was going to be an uphill battle to prove his innocence. However, Jeremy was optimistic about the appeal. He felt that a judge rather than a jury would be more likely to regard the evidence against him as flimsy and circumstantial. His preoccupation was with Julie Mugford. Despite police claims that even without Julie's statement they would have arrested Jeremy and secured the conviction against him, he was convinced that if Julie withdrew her evidence the case against him would collapse. If only she could be persuaded to 'tell the truth', as he put it, his release would be a mere formality.

Despite his outward show of confidence in the courtroom, Bamber realised that Julie had given a very effective display in the witness box. His quick mind had begun to plan ahead even before the verdict was announced. He knew Julie's value to the prosecution and realised the trial largely rested on her performance. Moreover, if the verdict went against him, Julie would prove an obstacle to a successful appeal. A story circulated during the trial that Bamber had flirted with the fantasy of getting Julie out of the way.

'It was a death-threat letter about Julie that Bamber got smuggled out of jail during the trial,' said a reporter who claims he was shown the letter. 'What happened was that Bamber got this letter smuggled out to one of his girlfriends, saying that if he got sent down Julie Mugford was going to have to be done away with before his appeal so that she couldn't give evidence at it. I actually got glimpses of the letter but the girl who had it got cold feet and I never got it in my possession.'

But the young lady was not for turning. After the tussles with her education bosses over her Sunday newspaper revelations, Julie kept her head down and resisted any further forays into the limelight. She had been through a traumatic ordeal and had no intention of retracting the statement which had started all the trouble. Despite the predictions of Paul Terzeon the months rolled by without any date being set for the first hearing in the appeal process. Jeremy had no option but to try to adapt to prison life.

D Wing of Wormwood Scrubs houses about 250 prisoners at any one time. Most of these men are serving long sentences and some are imprisoned for life. The west London prison contains the greatest number of maximum-security inmates in England and, for that matter, in Europe. The decision to send Jeremy there was merely a formality. All prisoners newly sentenced to life or long terms are placed in dispersal units for observation and assessment before it is decided to which prison they should be sent. There are eight prisons in England and Wales with dispersal units and Chelmsford, where Jeremy's trial was heard, falls into the catchment area of Wormwood Scrubs.

The process of dispersal can take years to complete. While it is taking place, the prisoners go about their daily routine like anyone else on the wing. Their behaviour and attitude towards the prison system and other inmates are monitored for signs of aggression or psychological disturbance. Once the prison staff feel the assessment is complete a decision will be taken about where the prisoner will be sent next. Lifers and long-term prisoners tend to be moved around the prison system instead of completing the whole of their sentence in one establishment.

Maximum-security prisons have different regimes and troublemakers or inmates with a history of escape attempts are likely to wind up in Albany or Parkhurst, jails notorious for their strict, unyielding discipline. Other prisons are slightly more flexible, although no maximum-security jail could ever be described as soft.

As a D Wing lifer Jeremy was allowed a cell to himself, but his situation was far from luxurious. The Scrubs was built more than a hundred years ago and D Wing was originally designed for women. Consequently the cells were built on a smaller scale than those in other wings of the jail. Jeremy's cell measured eight feet by twelve, with only one small window. But the worst aspect of the wing, common to all Victorian prisons, was the lack of toilet facilities inside the cell.

279

Instead men have to slop out every morning, carrying and emptying out the bucket serves as their toilet. The ritual is humiliating but even worse is the constant and unavoidable stench from the pail. During times when prisoners are locked in their cramped, stinking cells for long periods, often because of staff shortages, the level of tension within an area like D Wing becomes frightening.

Jeremy had not adjusted to prison life during his year on remand and now was unable to accustom himself to his sentence. He was as unpopular in the Scrubs as he had been in Norwich jail. For a start he was a 'nonce' – a child-killer. Although Jeremy's crime did not involve the sexual abuse of his victims – which would have allowed him to be placed on Rule 43, whereby prisoners are segregated from other inmates for his own safety – there were still many fellow prisoners who considered him to be near the bottom of the prison hierarchy which classes child-murderers among the lowest of the low.

In these new repressive surroundings Jeremy still retained many of the traits which had characterised him in his life outside. The inherent laziness which had exasperated his parents was even more pronounced. Jeremy did not work like most of the other prisoners. In a letter to a friend he explained: 'Due to a medical problem I've been excused work. So I spend much of the day chatting, drinking coffee, playing cards and dominoes.'

The 'medical problem' was never explained and Jeremy was certainly fit enough to go to the gym every day and anxious if he missed a work-out. It emerged that

280

documents belonging to Jeremy's medical file were missing and he refused to work pending their discovery. Unlike many inmates Jeremy had money, still accumulating from his family business interests, on the outside and did not have to rely on the pittance paid in prison wages to buy whatever rations he was allowed. He had no wish to go into the prison workshops and as long as he behaved himself it was not worth the bother to force him to comply.

The old Bamber arrogance was still thriving as well. He boasted about 'making a warder look silly', claiming that the action had made him 'a marked man' and describing the retribution dished out to him.

'I was put on punishment for the terrible infringement of having 33p in my possession,' he wrote. 'They fined me 75p. You wouldn't believe how petty prison is. It is worse than junior school.'

Instead of working, Bamber filled his days studying documents for his appeal. He pored over court transcripts, searching for weaknesses in evidence or misdirections by the judge which would convince the authorities to hear his case again. Like so many other prisoners, Jeremy clung to his appeal as the only lifeline that could pull him out of jail.

'I have to hope, I have to hang on to something,' he told Ken Smith, who taught writing classes to inmates at the Scrubs. 'And if the appeal goes down I still have to have something to hope for, perhaps a miracle.'

Despite his brave words, his patience came close to breaking point on several occasions. He wrote to a friend: 'All this waiting grates on my nerves. At this rate I will have served a five-year stretch for nothing.'

Apart from the painstaking analysis of his case, Jeremy's only other diversion was writing reams of letters to friends and strangers who offered themselves as penpals. One of his new girlfriends received enough letters to fill two carrier bags before she sold her story and severed the relationship. Jeremy had always surrounded himself with women and now he could only do the next best thing and surround himself with their letters. 'I love female company more than anything,' he wrote to a friend. 'What wouldn't I give for a cuddle! I miss that terribly. I don't mean sex, but holding hands and friendly hugs.'

The young man who had reportedly loved his pet dog more than his family or girlfriends did manage to find something on which to lavish his affections. One of the few concessions allowed to long-term prisoners is the chance to keep a bird as a pet. The aviary in Wormwood Scrubs is at the west end of D Wing and Jeremy joined many of his companions in paying £10 for his own budgerigar. He named the little blue bird Scooter and brought him into his cell whenever possible.

'Scooter plays with me on my writing table and really brings me a great deal of pleasure. He stops me from cracking up,' he wrote. 'The funniest thing is he scoots about with a paper bag in his beak and dances all over the shop with it.'

It was not the first time Jeremy had named a loved companion Scooter – in the old days in Australia, where he now longed to be, it had been his nickname for Brett Collins.

Unfortunately for Jeremy, the first news about his

282

criminal appeal brought a terrible disappointment. At the end of April 1988, some eighteen months after his conviction, Mr Justice Caulfield considered the case put forward by Bamber's defence and decided that there were not sufficient grounds to allow him to appeal. But this was only the first attempt at getting leave to appeal, and Jeremy's solicitor, Paul Terzeon, still continued to sound optimistic as he outlined the next step he planned to take on behalf of his client. 'He is entitled to go to the full court of appeal to three judges to ask them to consider the question of leave to appeal, and that's what he has done,' stated Terzeon. 'Instead of considering papers the three judges will be asked to hear an oral application by counsel.' He added that Jeremy was concerned about the refusal.

The full hearing was due to begin on 9 June 1988. But Lord Justice Russell, Mr Justice McCullough and Mr Justice Auld were annoyed to find that Bamber's counsel was not ready to start the case and asked instead for an adjournment to allow 'crucial' scientific tests to be carried out. Geoffrey Rivlin QC, acting for Bamber as he had done at the trial, told the judges that his client wanted the effects of hot gases on blood groupings to be tested. He had made the decision after reading a report which was so recent that the defence had not had time to arrange for the tests which Rivlin claimed might 'diminish or destroy' part of the prosecution case. The judges showed their displeasure but after a short recess allowed the adjournment 'with reluctance' and asked the QC to ensure there were no more delays.

Bamber hoped the tests would prove that the blood

found in the rifle silencer could not be accurately classified as belonging to any specific group. It had been demonstrated at the trial that Sheila did not have sufficient reach to shoot herself with the silencer attached to the rifle. It had also been established that the blood inside the silencer came from her wounds. The rationale behind Bamber's tests was that if the blood could not be proved beyond doubt to be Sheila's it could have come from one of the other victims. That left the possibility that Sheila had shot her family with the silencer in place, collecting the drop of blood inside the silencer during the massacre, and then removed the silencer before committing suicide.

The new report which had given Bamber hope claimed that the gases produced when a gun was fired could sometimes reach very high temperatures. It pointed out that proteins in subsidiary blood groups could be altered when exposed to temperatures above 60 degrees centigrade. On this basis, Bamber hoped that the tests he had commissioned would show that the rifle used to slaughter his family could have produced gas so hot that the composition of the speck of blood inside the silencer had been changed and could not be proved to be Sheila's. It was a tortuous argument, but Jeremy was prepared to pay for the tests and see if they supported his theory.

The hearing was resumed nine months later, but little was heard about the scientific tests. Instead, Geoffrey Rivlin QC told Lord Chief Justice Lane, Mr Justice Roch and Mr Justice Henry that Bamber's appeal was based on three main submissions. Firstly, that the summing-up of the trial judge to the jury was weighted heavily against the defendant. Secondly, that the judge repeatedly and unjustly ridiculed Bamber's case using forceful and extravagant language. Thirdly, that the judge produced his own theory about the sequence in which the murders were carried out and that insertion totally undermined the defence case.

'Every man is entitled to a fair trial, no matter how heinous the crime. We regretfully but firmly submit that he did not have a fair trial,' declared Rivlin.

He went on to criticise the handling of Julie Mugford's evidence by the trial judge, Mr Justice Drake. He further claimed that the defence team had not questioned Miss Mugford about her dealings with the press because he had been told by the Crown in good faith that she did not intend to sell her story. But immediately after the case articles had appeared in the popular press.

Jeremy was not in court to hear the fight for his freedom, but his relatives were present. More than three and a half years after the horror of the massacre, Bamber's relations found themselves in a tragic position. They had no option but to hope that Jeremy would stay behind bars because they were convinced that that was where he belonged. As they prayed for his imprisonment, they were aware that this young man was the only surviving member of the family they had lost.

The judgement was unequivocal – Bamber was refused leave to appeal against his conviction. Lord Chief Justice Lane described the case as having 'much of a detective novel' about it and proceeded to dismiss all three grounds for the appeal which had been submitted on Bamber's behalf. Lord Lane rejected the complaint against the summing-up of the trial judge thus: 'A direction to the jury inevitably reflects the sort of case with which the judge is dealing. A strong prosecution case will inevitably result in strong comments,' he declared. 'All in all, we have come to the conclusion there is no proper basis for the criticisms of this summing-up made by Mr Rivlin. There is nothing unfair or unsatisfactory about this conviction.'

Their lordships made one concession when they described as 'unfortunate' certain remarks made by Mr Justice Drake on the matter of the silencer. However Lord Lane added that he did not think the comment impeded the defence case. The defence team departed to relay the crushing news to Jeremy and the young man's relatives left a criminal court for what they hoped would be the last time.

'Justice has finally been done,' commented David Boutflour. 'The incident happened several years ago. We have gone through all the torments of this terrible occasion. It has been brought up many, many times and it has had a destroying effect on a lot of members of the family. We hope it will now be laid to rest.'

Shortly after leave for appeal was rejected, Bamber was moved from Wormwood Scrubs. His time of assessment had come to an end and the prison authorities decided to move him to Full Sutton Prison near York, another maximum-security jail. Packing up the few personal belongings he was allowed to take, including Scooter the budgie, Bamber made the long trip north under heavy guard.

Soon after his arrival at Full Sutton he arranged to take

286

part in yet another legal hearing, this time to finally resolve the tenancy of White House Farm. The repercussions of the White House Farm murders were a legal headache. Even though it had been established that Jeremy would not receive any bequests due to him there was still the question of who would inherit the bulk of the estate. The problem was complicated by the lack of any conclusive evidence about the order in which the family died. No one could state who was the final person to die and whose last will and testament should be implemented to determine the distribution of wealth and property.

The police theory was that Nevill Bamber was shot first, then either the twins or June, and Sheila was the final victim. They believed that the tragic young woman had taken a heavy dose of tranquillisers and was unaware of what was going on around her until she was shot. The pristine state of Sheila's body and nightdress made it clear that, unlike her mother and father, she had made no attempt to defend herself or call for help, but this scenario was speculative rather than proven.

Bamber still claimed he was entitled to the tenancy of the farm and its 300 acres as the son and heir of Nevill Bamber. The main opponents of his bid were the Henry Smith Charity, trustees of the farm, and Bamber's cousin Anne Eaton and her husband Peter, who had acted as caretaker farmers for four years. Immediately after the murders the charity had accepted that the farm would pass to Jeremy if he wanted it. Their offer was withdrawn after Jeremy's arrest. 'He spent a lot of time wandering around the world, but in the last year or so he was getting down to being a farmer,' commented a spokesman for the trustees. 'It seemed as if he were settling down and we hoped it would work out for the future.'

All sides agreed to take the matter to the Agricultural Land Tribunal for a binding ruling and the prison governor allowed the hearing to be held within the jail. The Eatons travelled up from Essex to York, as did the representative of the trustees, but their journeys turned out to have been a waste of time and money. As soon as the hearing got underway Jeremy announced that he was abandoning his claim to the property. His statement gave no indication of whether he had made a spur-of-the-moment decision or whether he had simply enjoyed the spectacle of the relatives he liked to refer to as 'the vultures' having to cross half of England at his insistence.

Either way it was an expensive decision. The tribunal ruled that Bamber would have to pay a 'considerable sum' in costs towards the abortive hearing. Bamber had already financed his own application for appeal, something well out of the reach of most prisoners. Now there was no more capital to fall back on, and he would be reliant on the generosity of friends. The family wealth and land that Bamber had coveted was out of his grasp forever.

The fate of the farm was still undecided, and the trustees let it be known that they were looking for a suitable tenant. 'We realise a farm where these terrible murders happened is not everybody's cup of tea, but we are confident we will relet it,' explained Mr Derek Bright, secretary of the charity.

No prospective new tenants came forward and the Henry

Smith Charity agreed to let Anne and Peter Eaton, who had managed the land ever since the murders, take over White House Farm.

Jeremy Bamber still maintains his innocence, as he has done throughout every stage of the investigation, the trial and his subsequent imprisonment. As the Essex detectives say, Bamber has never 'coughed'. The nearest anyone has come to suggesting a confession from the young farmer was Julie Mugford in her claim that Bamber told her he hired a mercenary to carry out the killings.

Even inside prison Jeremy has made no admissions. He is so adamant in proclaiming his innocence that not even the most determined 'grass' who seeks to win favour by reporting the alleged 'confessions' of other inmates would attempt to claim that Jeremy had admitted his guilt in a moment of weakness. No one would believe it. Even in prison, the most cynical of all societies, some prisoners believe that Jeremy might be innocent. 'He's not that good an actor. He couldn't keep it up,' commented one.

Ken Smith, the writer-in-residence at Wormwood Scrubs, found that Jeremy was one of the few prisoners whose innocence or guilt was a real matter of debate. 'If innocent, how tragic the violent loss of kin and fortune and future, yet he was not crushed by it. And if guilty, how great the effort to maintain innocence, through suspicion, investigation, arrest, interrogation, remand, trial, sentence, and now the continuing rigours of D Wing and all the years ahead. To do all this a man would have to be very determined; he would have to be a very good actor, or a very clever psychopath, or a very innocent man,' wrote Smith in his book on prison life, *Inside Time*.

Just what and who is Jeremy Bamber? Is he the consummate actor, planning his own dramas, setting the scene, remembering every line, playing to a gullible audience? That was certainly the view of the judge and jury at his trial. It was the theory of the police who declared they were duped by the clever young man who cried on cue and staged a tragedy worthy of the Jacobean stage in its blood and gore.

The murder squad detectives who spent time with Jeremy, and who were unable to break him despite all their efforts, felt he was not an actor. They were sure that they were dealing with a psychopath. 'Jeremy has got something missing,' explained one of them. 'I don't think it's the kind of thing that a psychiatrist would pick up on. It's certainly not anything that would get him sent to Broadmoor. It's just that he didn't care about anyone or anything. There was a real gap in him where there should have been feelings. It's not normal.'

This belief was repeated again and again by people who knew Jeremy. 'Something was missing in him,' wrote Ken Smith. Liz Rimington, who knew Jeremy well and even had a brief affair with him, said: 'Jeremy never believed murder was a crime. He believed morality and social conscience were only for the weak. He said morality was like religion, something for people to hang on to,' she recalled. 'I told Jeremy he was a psychopath without conscience. He said, "I know I'm sick, I know I have such evil thoughts, I can't help it."'

290

Julie Mugford claimed she tried to get her lover to show some remorse for his crimes after seeing him dressed in the clothes of the sister he had murdered. She remembered how he had played with his nephews and cuddled them, stroking their hair, only a few days before he shot them in their sleep.

Then there are others who entertain the possibility that Jeremy might not be an actor or a psychopath, but instead might actually be an innocent man. There were, of course, the friends who could not believe Jeremy capable of such an act. Brett Collins described Bamber as 'a big softy' and 'the most gentle of men'. He refused to accept Jeremy's guilt unless his friend admitted the murders himself. Even the Essex police felt that Collins was genuinely convinced Bamber was wrongfully charged.

Then there were the girlfriends. The penpals who wrote and then sold their stories all claimed faith in Bamber: 'I know he's innocent. I'm an ordinary northern girl and wouldn't dream of an affair if I didn't believe it with all my heart. I'm no sicko,' squeaked 'bubbly Jayne Beardsley', who was first convinced of Bamber's innocence during the trial. 'I knew he couldn't have done the killings as he had such a sweet face.'

More thought-provoking testimony came from people who knew what went on behind the handsome exterior of Jeremy Bamber. Suzette Ford, who lived with Jeremy on and off for almost two years, was unconvinced of his guilt. She was shocked by his arrest and during his remand asked Jeremy if he had killed his family. He denied it. Philosophically, she said she had to accept the verdict of the court, but added: 'When I knew him he couldn't bear to hurt the smallest animal. When they had shoots on the farm he would go as a beater rather than have to carry a gun and shoot anything. He was full of life, a fun person, and I find it hard to think he could be so cold as to murder five people. To me he will always be my Jeremy Bear.'

Then there were the two jurors at Jeremy's trial who, despite all the conclusive-sounding proof against him, remained certain that he was not guilty. There are the Essex villagers who persist in believing that Jeremy was innocent and the family were slaughtered by a London hitman or will concede that perhaps the young Bamber went as far as hiring a killer. Few of them think that it was his finger on the trigger that August night.

There is also the dry comment of Bamber's first solicitor, Bruce Bowler, who fought so successfully on behalf of his client. He pondered over Bamber's return to England after his first arrest and release on a burglary charge. 'He went off to France and was arrested when he came back to Dover. He maintained through that period that he was entirely innocent. Why did he come back? It could have been because he was stupid, but he may have come back because he was innocent,' he mused.

Jeremy's behaviour before his arrest could be seen as reckless, arrogant or simply the innocent actions of a man who did not know where to draw the line. Crime reporter Michael Fielder could scarcely believe that someone in Bamber's position, under police scrutiny and in the public eye, would attempt to sell nude photographs of his murdered sister. It was either the height of folly or the depths of bad taste. Anji Greaves described how Bamber and Collins regarded the police investigations as humorous rather than frightening. She claims that, suspecting that Essex detectives had bugged the Morshead Mansions flat where they were staying, the two men treated the whole affair as a joke. 'Jeremy and Brett used to spend half the night grunting and groaning and making out they were having a gay affair just for the listening cops,' she recalled.

The most powerful argument on Jeremy's behalf was never heard in public. The late Detective Chief Inspector Taff Jones was adamant that Bamber was not guilty, even in the face of Julie Mugford's statement and after interviewing the suspect for two days. The DCI stuck to his belief even when the official police theory about the identity of the culprit shifted from Sheila to Jeremy. Those who knew him felt that if his untimely death had not intervened, Taff Jones would never have toed the official police line. 'Up until his very sad death Taff was still convinced Bamber didn't do it. If he'd gone in the witness box in that trial it would have been sensational, because he intended to say what he thought. He was that kind of bloke, he would never lie,' speculated a former colleague.

But if Jeremy did it, exactly how did he do it? The trial established that the murderer probably entered and left by a downstairs window that could be shut from the outside. The prosecution suggested that Jeremy cycled from Goldhanger to White House Farm. But many questions were unanswered. If Jeremy did it, what happened to his clothes, which must have been covered with blood? Even though the police did not suspect him at the time, Jeremy

293

would have run a great risk of a sharp-eyed officer spotting blood on his clothes or his body. Why was he not seen by anyone on his way to or from the farm? Why did he return from France when he knew the police suspected him? Why did he make no effort to stop Julie Mugford going to the police?

'I think Jeremy went to and from the farm along the sea wall,' speculated one of the reporters familiar with Tolleshunt D'Arcy. 'There is a wall running across the fields from near White House Farm which passes within a few hundred yards of Goldhanger. Jeremy could have run or even cycled along the top of that wall. The chances of being seen are remote.

'I think he got in through an outside cellar which has steps running down into the house and then came up in the kitchen of the farmhouse, rather than through a window,' claimed an officer who worked on the case. 'Then I reckon he stripped off before the killings. All he needed to do was to shower after that and he was safe. He may have woken his father up when getting into the house or loading the gun and Nevill came down to investigate. There was a fight and eventually he killed Nevill. Then he shot the twins, shot his mother and then shot Sheila, who had taken a sleeping tablet and wasn't aware of what was going on. June made an attempt to get help and he shot her again. Then it was home, get cleaned up and phone the police.'

The local police officers have had plenty of time to fit together their own version of the puzzle. They believe Bamber may have walked to White House Farm using a farm track that lay at the edge of the fields and was protected from the roads by hedges. In their search of White House Farm they found half a rubber wetsuit. The other half was at Jeremy's cottage in Goldhanger. Jeremy, of course, had tried deep-sea diving as a career earlier in his life and the farmhouse is near to the sea. The police always wondered why they found only one half of the outfit at the farmhouse. As one detective put it, what good is half a wet suit to anyone? The theory grew that Jeremy had donned one part for the killing spree and then showered off in White House Farm before going back to Goldhanger.

June Bamber's bicycle was found at Bamber's cottage the day after the murders and it seems unlikely that she would have lent it to him since she had only recently bought it for her own use.

No one noticed any scratches or bruises on Jeremy's skin. This led the police to conclude that he must have worn some clothing or protection or else he would have been marked during the death-struggle with his father.

As for Bamber's subsequent behaviour the only explanation anyone can offer is that his arrogance was so great that he really did not believe he would be caught. The spending and drinking before his arrest, his disregard of Julie's conscience, his attitude towards questioning all proclaim a young man who felt he was above the laws of normal society.

But Jeremy Bamber still protests his innocence from his top-security confinement. During the researching of this book he sent the author a series of letters, mainly describing his plans for appeal. His first note stated: 'I'm still fighting this ridiculous conviction,' and continued:

'You know already maybe that I did not murder my family, so if we start from that fact we will at least start from a common point.'

Jeremy's overriding obsession is his latest attempt to get leave to appeal. His letters make it clear that he no longer has sufficient money to finance the forensic tests he feels are necessary, nor can he afford to fund an appeal without help from legal aid. He says that he is waiting for the outcome of 'other matters' to provide him with 'sufficient funds' to pay for the tests and to hire a new solicitor. The 'other matters' are a reference to the protracted legal battle over the Bamber estate.

Apart from the farm and the land, Jeremy lived in a cottage bought by his parents, had a stake in forty-eight acres of land they owned and also had 750 shares in the Osea Bay caravan site. There was the London flat bought for Sheila and the twins and family possessions such as valuable antiques, furniture and cars. The ownership and distribution of all these assets have still not yet been resolved by the remaining family relatives. Jeremy is already paying a solicitor to represent him in the negotiations.

The letters which proclaim his innocence are strange documents. Some are printed in laborious capitals while others are in his normal handwriting. All are badly punctuated and sprinkled with drawings of happy or sad faces to illustrate his points. Julie Mugford's testimony is a constant theme as might be expected: 'Julie did say in court that I said a number of incredible things – that I planned to burn my parents' house down with them in it . . . That I paid the local plumber Matthew £2,000 to assassinate my family.'

Bamber's fury was also directed at the forensic evidence produced by the prosecution at his trial. He hopes to be able to undermine the findings produced by the forensic scientists by further tests: 'The outcome of further work . . . will show that due to ignorance, stupidity or malice by the main prosecution forensic scientist, whom I hope to show got his principle [sic] piece of forensic evidence wrong, this misled his fellow scientists (they said in court that if what he says was wrong then they would have to substantially alter their evidence). This in turn misled the police into thinking me a suspect – the rest is history,' he wrote, ending the paragraph with a little drawing of an unhappy face.

Jeremy, who always heads his letters with his surname and prison number, not surprisingly begged there to be no mistake over any reports of a confession: 'I must get you straight on this point,' he wrote. 'At no time have I made a "confession" as to my involvement in the tragic deaths of my family. I wish the media would stop going on about my "confessing". There was never, will never and could never be a confession to something I didn't do!'

After several months of deliberation, Jeremy finally agreed to a meeting with the author, the first time he had ever participated in an interview with a journalist.

Full Sutton is a modern prison set in the middle of fields, about twenty minutes' drive from the town of York. From the outside, the building has the appearance of a modern supermarket rather than a maximum-security jail. The parking bays are filled with rows and rows of cars belonging to the staff and next to the prison are some modern houses built for the warders.

The interview room is comfortably carpeted, with little tables and chairs dotted around. It was deserted and, except for a group of prison officers who sat behind a desk at the far end, it looked exactly like a well-kept junior common room in a college building.

Jeremy walked in, flanked by a warder. He was dressed in a shirt and dark blue dungarees and carried a heap of papers and files. From a distance he appears strikingly good-looking, tall and perfectly proportioned, with thick glossy dark hair and huge dark blue eyes. Close to, he is still attractive, but his features are large and broad rather than finely moulded. When amused, his smile is immensely attractive and charming.

'I was never given any idea that the verdict might go the way it did. Looking back, I think I wouldn't have acted in the way I did. I thought all you had to do was to be innocent. It wasn't until it was too late that I found out that wasn't the case,' he said.

'We should have objected to things that we didn't object to in court, but we hadn't really got all the right preparations. I mean, there were forty-two police statements about White House Farm and I haven't yet seen all of them. So we couldn't question the policemen properly in court. We didn't know what they had done or what we were looking for from them.

'Their forensic evidence was a real shock. We only got their statement of what they were doing [in the way of forensic evidence] on the morning that [the forensic

298

experts] were called. We asked for an adjournment but we didn't get the right experts in to contradict him. We should have done, but we didn't have time. Their evidence was wrong.

'The press were disgusting, the *Sun*, the *News of the World* especially. I tell the guys in here not to believe what they read. But [with a readership of] five and a half million – what can you say? I had a contract with News International for £40,000 – Paul Terzeon arranged it. They just made up stories about me after the trial. Their reporter is an appalling man. He'll pay for it.'

Jeremy has a strong conviction that people who have offended against him will 'pay for it'. It was a phrase that cropped up several times. He really seemed to believe that there would be some kind of vengeance he could wreak on his enemies.

'All these people that I'd never known started saying things about me. People I'd hardly even met. There was all that crap about aeroplanes flying in and dropping drugs. I was a drug baron and all that sort of stuff.

'Then there was all that girlfriend stuff. I'm a normal, healthy heterosexual male, so of course I've had girl-friends, but not the hundreds they made out. I've only really had five or six girlfriends.

'Colin [Caffell] thinks he's going to write a blockbuster. But I make sure I write things to him that he could never publish, things that aren't good for him.'

Bamber spoke in a contemptuous manner about his former brother-in-law. But he regretted his comments about Colin Caffell almost immediately and was at pains to try to remove the rather unpleasant impression created by his criticism of the man who had lost both his children and a beloved ex-wife:

'I really like Colin, he's a very straightforward guy. He isn't at all devious. It was terrible for him to have his sons killed, he's suffered very badly, but he's not quite what he's made out to be. I mean his relationship with Sheila wasn't really how he's always tried to portray it. I wouldn't like to say he's making things up, but he's going for things that aren't right and he knows they aren't right.'

Jeremy's real bitterness is reserved for his relatives – 'the vultures' – and Julie Mugford. He believes they have enjoyed the financial rewards that have come to them through his imprisonment.

In retrospect, Jeremy believes that he could have escaped jail if his attitude had been less cavalier and he had taken more thought with some of the decisions he made at the time, such as his legal representation.

'I'm sorry I went with Napley and Co. Not because they were no good, but I'm sorry I left Bruce Bowler [his original solicitor] because he was in it from the start. Napley and his lot didn't know properly about the arrest and the way they held me illegally. They shouldn't have held me on a burglary charge – it wasn't a burglary anyway. But the way they held me was wrong. Zander will give his opinion on that [Professor Michael Zander, a leading professor of law, has pronounced on this for Bamber].'

He also regrets his very public penpal relationships, which were at first a source of amusement and carried a certain cachet inside the prison.

'I like to write to girls and tease and flirt a bit. I didn't realise that they would go off and sell their stories. One or two of the girls have got thousands for just a couple of letters I sent them. I do write silly things sometimes – you know I'm a normal guy, I like to flirt a bit. Now I'm only writing to people who can do me any good, apart from my friends. Loads of journalists have written to me and they all want my side of the story. I should be able to get a lot of money for it.'

Jeremy was well aware that the police had been divided over his guilt. He was devastated when DCI Taff Jones died before the case came to trial.

'It was such bad luck that Taff Jones died because he would have destroyed the police case. He knew I was innocent.

'The police changed their version of what happened that morning three times. They would go and ask people about me – what I was like, that sort of thing. They would say to people, "He's killed two little boys, he's a monster. What did you think of him?"'

Jeremy has now been moved once again, this time to a jail near Hull. His chances of gaining leave to appeal have looked brighter since his case caught the attention of an organisation called Justice For All.

His new move to appeal again rests on the analysis of the blood found inside the silencer. Independent tests question whether it can be safely concluded that the blood found on the sound moderator was definitely Sheila's. His submission also questions the conduct of the tests carried out at the

Huntington laboratories where the rifle and the silencer were sent for examination.

Bamber has the support of several members of the legal profession and has relied largely on the Justice For All organisation for the financing of the new research and the cost of the proposed appeal.

The trial judge recommended that Bamber serve a minimum of twenty-five years for the five murders, and at the time of the trial the slaughter put Bamber in an infamous 'top ten' of mass murderers alongside the Yorkshire Ripper and homosexual killer Dennis Nilsen.

Jeremy Bamber will be at least fifty years old by the time he leaves prison. There can be little comfort for a young man who despised religion and felt that morality was for the weak to help him through the long years ahead. His one source of strength is his insistence that he did not do it and that one day the miracle he has talked about will happen and he will be set free.

In the graveyard of the church of St Nicholas, Tolleshunt D'Arcy, is a small, plain, white headstone which reads: 'In Loving Memory of R. Nevill and June Bamber, both aged sixty-one years. Tragically taken from us, 7 August 1985. Forever with the Lord.'

In the vast expanse of Highgate Cemetery, London, is another grave. This one contains the remains of three more people, a mother and her twin six-year-old boys.

These five people were proven innocent.

Index

Note: Abbreviations used in this index are JB for Jeremy Bamber; CC for Colin Caffell; SC for Sheila Caffell; JM for Julie Mugford.

Bright, Derek 288
Bruce-Lockhart, Logie 38
Buckingham Palace 265
Bunyard, Chief Constable
    Robert 116, 183, 249–50
    252–3
Butt, Sabina 268–9
Byford, Sir Lawrence 250, 253

Caffell, Colin: with Sheila
    36–7, 42–5; wedding 43;
    divorce 50–51; after divorce
    53, 59–60, 69–70, 72, 74, 81,
    83, 91; after the murders
    91–2, 96–7; and funerals
    109–10, 113; after JB's
    conviction 269–73; JB
    speaks of 299–300
Caffell, Daniel and Nicholas:
    birth 43–4; childhood 2, 53,
    59–60, 64, 68–70, 72–4, 80,
    81, 83, 96; deaths 6, 100,
    198–9; funeral 109, 113;
    recalled 266, 269–70
Caffell, Sheila Jean ('Bambi';
    formerly Bamber): adopted
    21–2, 264; childhood 22–4,
    26–7, 29–30, 31–2;
    adolescence 32–6, 42;
    secretarial college 32, 36;
    abortion 35–6; relations with
    parents 23–4, 26–7, 32–5,
    59–60, 63–4, 78, 80, 82, 229,
    230–31; with Colin 36–7,
    42–5; wedding 43; as model
    36–7, 42–3, 44, 60–62, 64–8,
    70, 74–9; miscarriage 42; as
    mother 43–4, 53, 72–4, 80,

96, 97; mental illness 2–3,
    34–5, 44, 52–3, 79–83,
    228–32, 264; divorce 50–51;
    London life alone 50–51,
    59–80; natural mother 51–2,
    264, 265; nude photographs
    76–9, 165–9; death and state
    of her body 7, 10, 107–8, 175,
    198, 205, 218, 232, 287;
    suspected of the killings 13,
    88–9, 90, 91–2, 95–6, 100,
    101, 109, 176, 185, 199–200,
    220–21, 231–3, 237; funeral
    109–12, 113; spoken of by
    Jeremy 2–4, 9, 11, 13, 224–5;
    described by neighbours
    203; by relatives 208, 231,
    260; posthumous spiritual
    contact 270–71
Caroline (model) 67, 68, 69,
    71–2
Cartledge, Detective
    Superintendent Maynard
    247–8
Caulfield, Mr Justice 283
Chelmsford, Essex 16, 195–6,
    256; magistrates' court
    152–3, 159–62; Nag's Head
    pub 166–7
Chelmsford Crown Court
    191–2, 195–218, 219–42,
    275–6
Chelmsford Police Station 239,
    244–5; on day of the murders
    1–2, 224, 227; JM
    interviewed 120–21, 123,
    133–9, 142; JB arrested and
    questioned 146–61, 169–70

Paddington Recreation
Ground 60, 61
Parents of Murdered Children
272
police *see* Chelmsford Police
Station; Essex police;
Witham
Police 253
Police and Criminal Evidence
bill 155–6
Police Complaints Authority
255–6
prisons: dispersal 278–80; *see
also* Full Sutton; Hull;
Norwich; Wormwood
Scrubs

Rimington, Liz 124, 132–3,
135, 140–42, 290
Rivlin, Geoffrey, QC 191–2;
defends JB in court 205, 207,
212–13, 214–17, 219–22, 225,
231, 233, 234–5, 237; and
JB's appeal 283, 284–6
Roch, Mr Justice 284
Royal Agricultural College,
Gloucestershire 17
Russell, Lord Justice 283

School Dinners restaurant
75–6
Scooter (budgerigar) 282
silencer, gun 200, 233–4; found
104–105, 175, 205–6; in
police hands 105, 108, 176,
206; blood-spot in 200, 218,
233–4, 283–4, 301–2
Simpson, Assistant Chief

Constable Peter 135–8, 170,
245; speaks to press 157,
158–9, 162–3, 163–4, 178–9,
184
Sloppy Joe's restaurant,
Colchester 53–4
Smith, Ken 281, 289–90
Sonja (model) 52, 62, 63–4, 76,
82, 92
Sotheby's 93–4, 114
Speakman, June *see* Bamber
Speakman, Leslie 18
spiritualism 270–71
St Andrew's Hospital,
Northampton 53, 81
St James's Church, West
Hampstead 113
St John's Wood 60–80, 82, 92
St Tropez 169
Stone, Deputy Chief
Constable Ronald 245–7,
248, 249, 252
Stone, Tim 153
Stringfellow's nightclub 57
Sun newspaper 160–61, 165–8,
193, 299
Swiss Cottage, college 32, 36

Terzeon, Paul 186, 187–8,
275–7, 283, 299
Tiptree, Essex 19
Tolleshunt D'Arcy, Essex 2,
18–21, 85–6, 93, 109, 115–16,
158–9, 163, 294; Red Lion
pub 26, 85; sea wall 294; St
Nicholas church 20–21, 85,
109–11, 302; *see also* White
House Farm

309